Presented to

_____

By

_____

On the Occasion of

_____

Date

_____

TEACH ME TO PRAY

Daily Devotional Insights from Andrew Murray

BARBOUR
PUBLISHING

Compiled by Daniel P. Anderson, Douglas Ed Cox, and Edward A. Elliott Sr., with Carol Rebell as style editor.

ISBN 1-59310-375-1

Cover image © PhotoDisc

Published by Barbour Publishing, Inc., P.O. Box 719, Uhrichsville, Ohio 44683, www.barbourbooks.com

Our mission is to publish and distribute inspirational products offering exceptional value and biblical encouragement to the masses.

Member of the
Evangelical Christian
Publishers Association

Printed in the United States of America.
5 4 3 2

Andrew Murray

Though he lived most of his life in the nineteenth century, Andrew Murray has much to say to Christians of the twenty-first century. His extensive writings encourage a fully committed, deeply personal relationship with Jesus Christ.

Murray was born in Cape Town, South Africa, in 1828. His homeland would later benefit from his missionary efforts: evangelistic tours and his leadership of the South Africa General Mission. He received honorary doctorates from the universities of Aberdeen (where he received part of his education) and the Cape of Good Hope for his contributions to spreading the gospel of Christ.

In addition to his missionary work, Murray spent much time writing on the "deeper Christian life." The titles of many of his works hint at his passion for total consecration to Christ: *Absolute Surrender, The Inner Life, The Secret of Adoration,* and *Your Will Be Done.* Some 240 works were published in his name.

Throughout his long life, Murray also ministered as a pastor in several cities, spoke at both the Northfield and Keswick Conventions, served as Moderator of the Cape Synod of the Dutch Reformed Church, and became president of the YMCA. He died in 1917.

Foreword

A deeper spiritual life cannot grow without deeper daily devotion to God's Word and to prayer.

No one knew this better than Andrew Murray. One of the best-loved and most widely read writers on the deeper Christian life, this South African pastor, preacher, and missions speaker prayed for—and witnessed—remarkable spiritual revival on three continents, and every day experienced the need for personal renewal.

If you share that hunger for God's presence, this daily devotional will satisfy you with an astonishing banquet of riches. Here, thoughtfully chosen from the best of Murray's 240 books and carefully updated in today's language, are his treasured insights on prayer along with simple tools that will help you use them to draw closer to God.

Every day for a full year you'll read a selection from Murray's classic devotional writing—*Absolute Surrender, The Ministry of Intercession, The Prayer Life, The Secret of Power from On High,* and many others. A daily Scripture selection deepens your insight, while a brief prayer focuses your devotions and a prayer prompt inspires application to every area of your life.

"Time alone with the Lord Jesus each day is indispensable," insisted Andrew Murray. As you begin to satisfy your hunger for God with this inspiring devotional, you won't want to miss a single moment.

"Be careful for nothing;
but in every thing by prayer and supplication
with thanksgiving let your requests be made known unto God.
And the peace of God,
which passeth all understanding,
shall keep your hearts and minds through Christ Jesus."

PHILLIPIANS 4:6–7 KJV

Wait upon God

He [Daniel] prayed three times a day,
just as he had always done,
giving thanks to his God.
DANIEL 6:10

The more I think of and pray about the religious situation in our country, the deeper my conviction becomes that Christians do not realize that the aim of conversion is to bring them into daily fellowship with the Father in heaven.

For the believer, taking time each day with God's Word and in prayer is indispensable. Each day we need to wait upon God for His presence and His love to be revealed.

It is not enough at conversion to accept forgiveness of sins or even to surrender to God. That is only a beginning. We must understand that we have no power on our own to maintain our spiritual life. We need to receive daily new grace from heaven through fellowship with the Lord Jesus. This cannot be obtained by a hasty prayer or a superficial reading of a few verses from God's Word. We must take time to come into God's presence, to feel our weakness and our need, and to wait on God through His Holy Spirit to renew our fellowship with Him. Then we may expect to be kept by the power of Christ throughout the day.

It is my aim to help Christians to see the absolute necessity of spending time with the Lord Jesus. Without this, the joy and power of God's Holy Spirit in daily life cannot be experienced.

From Day to Day

*Though our bodies are dying, our spirits
are being renewed every day.*

2 CORINTHIANS 4:16

All Christians, young or old, must learn the absolute necessity of fellowship with Jesus each day. This lesson is not always taught at the beginning of the Christian life. The grace we have received of the forgiveness of sins and of joy in the Holy Spirit can only be preserved by daily renewal in fellowship with Jesus Christ Himself.

Many Christians backslide because this truth is not clearly taught. Some are unable to stand against temptation or their old nature. Though they strive to do their best to fight against sin and to serve God, they have no strength. They have never really grasped the secret that the Lord Jesus will continue His work in the believer every day from heaven. But there is one condition: Time alone with the Lord Jesus each day is the indispensable condition of growth and power.

Read Matthew 11:25–30. Listen to Christ's word: "Come to Me. . .and I will give you rest. Let me teach you. . .and you will find rest for your souls." Let the Lord teach you just how gentle and humble He is. Bow before Him; tell Him that you need Him and His love; He will let His love rest on you. This applies not only to young Christians but to all who love the Lord.

Fellowship with God

I have loved you even as the Father has loved me.
Remain in my love.
JOHN 15:9

The three Persons in the Godhead are the Father, the Son, and the Holy Spirit—each one is different from the others. God desires to reveal Himself as a person. Each one of us is an individual distinct from others and standing in certain relationships to others. God will reveal Himself to us as a person, and we are called to enter into fellowship with Him.

God greatly desires this relationship with us, but sin has come between us and our God. Even in Christians who know God, there is often great ignorance and even indifference to this personal relationship of love to God.

People believe that at conversion their sins are forgiven, that God accepts them so that they may go to heaven, and that they should try to do God's will. But they do not realize that, even as a father and his child on earth enjoy being together, so they must have this intimate fellowship with God each day.

Our relationship to Christ rests on His deep, tender love to us. We are not capable on our own to render Him this love, but the Holy Spirit will do the work in us. Meditate quietly on this thought: "And because they love me, my Father will love them, and I will love them" (John 14:21). Take time to experience this personal fellowship.

Jesus

You are to name him Jesus,
for he will save his people from their sins.
MATTHEW 1:21

The Lord Jesus was a person on this earth. He had His own individual name. His mother, His disciples, all His friends called Him by this name—Jesus. But they probably thought little of what that name meant. Nor do the majority of Christians know what a treasure is contained in that name—Jesus—"He shall save His people from their sins."

Many think about His death on the cross and His resurrection, but do they realize that He is a living person in heaven who thinks of us each day? He wants us to bring Him our love and worship.

When we first ask Jesus Christ to save us from our sins, we know very little about how this is done. The living Christ reveals Himself to us, and through the power of His love, our desire to sin is taken away. Through personal fellowship with Him, Jesus saves us from our sins. First we must come to Jesus confessing all the sin in our hearts. We must know Him as the almighty personal Savior in whom God's holiness dwells. As we fellowship together in the expression of mutual love, by the work of His Holy Spirit in our hearts, His love will expel and conquer all the sin.

Alone with God

When you pray, go away by yourself,
shut the door behind you,
and pray to your Father secretly.
MATTHEW 6:6

Have you ever thought what a wonderful privilege it is to have the liberty of asking God to meet with you and to hear what you have to say? We should use such a privilege gladly and faithfully.

"When you pray," says Jesus, "go away by yourself, shut the door behind you, and pray to your Father secretly." This means two things. 1) Shut the world out; withdraw from all the thoughts and concerns of the day. 2) Shut yourself in alone with God to pray in secret. Let this be your chief object in prayer, to realize the presence of your heavenly Father. Let your goal be: "Alone with God."

Being alone in His presence and praying to the Father in secret is only the beginning. Come to Him in the full assurance that He knows how you long for His help and guidance. He will listen to you.

Then follows the great promise of verse 6: "Then your Father, who knows all secrets, will reward you." Your Father will see to it that your prayer is not in vain. Prayer in secret will be followed by the secret working of God in my heart.

The Importance of Faith

Don't be afraid. Just trust me.
MARK 5:36

This is a lesson of the greatest importance. When praying alone in the presence of God, we must trust implicitly in the love of God and in the power of the Lord Jesus. Take time to ask yourself this question: Is my heart full of a steadfast faith in God's love? If this is not the case, focus on this before you begin to pray. Faith does not come of itself. Consider quietly how impossible it is for God to lie. He is ready with infinite love to give you His blessing. Take some text of Scripture in which God's power, faithfulness, and love are revealed. Apply the words and say: "Yes, Lord, I will pray with firm faith in You."

It is a mistake to limit the word "faith" to the forgiveness of sins and to our acceptance as children of God. Faith includes far more. We must have faith in all that God is willing to do for us. We must have faith according to our special needs. Jesus Christ gives grace for each new day, and our faith must reach out according to the needs of the day.

When you enter into the Father's presence and before you begin to pray, ask yourself: "Do I really believe that God is here with me and that the Lord Jesus will help me to pray?" Jesus often taught His disciples how indispensable faith was to true prayer. He will teach us as well.

Obey the Word of God

*People need more than bread for their life;
they must feed on every word of God.*
MATTHEW 4:4

Bread is indispensable to life. We all understand this. However strong a person may be, if he takes no nourishment he will grow weaker and eventually die. Even so with the Word of God.

Bread must be eaten. I may know all about bread. I may give it to others. I may have bread in my house and on my table in great abundance, but that will not help me. I must eat the bread. If through illness I am unable to eat it, I shall die. Likewise, mere knowledge of God's Word and even preaching it to others will not help me. It is not enough to think about it. I must feed on God's Word and take it into my heart and life.

Bread must be eaten daily, and the same is true of God's Word. The psalmist says: "They delight in doing everything the Lord wants; day and night they think about his law" (Psalm 1:2). "Oh, how I love your Law! I think about it all day long" (Psalm 119:97). To secure a strong and powerful spiritual life, spending time in God's Word every day is indispensable. When on earth the Lord Jesus learned, loved, and obeyed the word of the Father. If you seek fellowship with Him, you will find Him in His Word.

The Word and Prayer

Restore my life again, just as you promised.
PSALM 119:107

Prayer and the Word of God are inseparable and should always go together. In His Word God speaks to me, and in prayer I speak to God. If there is to be true communication, God and I must both take part. If I simply pray without using God's Word, I am apt to use my own words and thoughts. Taking God's thoughts from His Word and presenting them before Him really gives prayer its power. God's Word is indispensable for all true prayer!

Through the Word the Holy Spirit shows me who God is. The Word also teaches me how sinful I am. It reveals to me all the wonders that God will do for me and the strength He will give me to do His will. The Word teaches me how to pray—with a strong desire, a firm faith, and constant perseverance. The Word teaches me not only who I am but who I may become. Above all it reminds me that Christ is the great intercessor and allows me to pray in His name.

Learn to renew your strength each day in God's Word and to pray according to His will.

Obedience

*If you obey me and do whatever I command you
. . .I will be your God.*
JEREMIAH 11:4

God gave this command to Israel when He gave them the law, but Israel had no power to keep the law. So God gave a "new covenant" to enable His people to live a life of obedience. We read in Jeremiah 32:40: "I will make an everlasting covenant with them. . .I will put a desire in their hearts to worship me, and they will never leave me." Ezekiel 36:27 says: "I will put my Spirit in you so you will obey my laws and do whatever I command." These wonderful promises gave the assurance that obedience would be their desire.

Listen to what Jesus says about obedience in John 14:21, 23: "Those who obey my commandments are the ones who love me. And because they love me, my Father will love them, and I will love them. . . . And we will come to them and live with them."

No father can train his children unless they are obedient. No teacher can teach a child who continues to disobey him. No general can lead his soldiers to victory without prompt obedience. Ask God to imprint this lesson on your heart: The life of faith is a life of obedience. As Christ lived in obedience to the Father, so we need to live in loving obedience to God.

Do you think it's impossible for you to be obedient? It may be impossible to you, but not to God. He has promised to "put my Spirit in you so you will obey my laws." Pray and meditate on these words.

Confession of Sin

*If we confess our sins to him, he is faithful
and just to forgive us and to cleanse us
from every wrong.*
1 JOHN 1:9

Too often the confession of sin is superficial and neglected. Few Christians realize how absolutely necessary confession is. An honest confession of sin gives power to live a life of victory over sin. We need to confess with a sincere heart every sin that may be a hindrance in our Christian lives.

Listen to what David says, "I confessed all my sins to you and stopped trying to hide them. I said to myself, 'I will confess my rebellion to the Lord.' And you forgave me! All my guilt is gone. For you are my hiding place; you protect me from trouble. You surround me with songs of victory" (Psalm 32:5, 7). David speaks of a time when he was unwilling to confess his sin. "When I refused to confess my sin, I was weak and miserable" (verse 3). But when he had confessed his sin, a wonderful change came.

Confession means not only that I confess my sin with shame and repentance, but that I turn it over to God, trusting Him to take it away. Such confession implies that I am unable to get rid of my guilt unless, by an act of faith, I trust God to deliver me. This deliverance means that I know my sins are forgiven and that Christ undertakes to cleanse me from the sin and keep me from its power.

The First Love

But I have this complaint against you.
You don't love me or each other as you did at first!
REVELATION 2:4

In Revelation 2:2–3, eight signs are mentioned showing the zeal of the church at Ephesus, but there was one bad sign. The Lord said: "Turn back to me again and work as you did at first. If you don't, I will come and remove your lampstand from its place among the churches" (verse 5). What was this sin? "You don't love me or each other as you did at first!" (verse 4).

We find the same sin in the church today. There is enthusiasm for the truth, there is continuous hard work, but what the Lord values most is missing: tender, fervent love for Him.

A Christian may be a good example in all he does, yet the tender love for Jesus is missing. There is no personal, daily fellowship with Christ. All the many activities with which people satisfy themselves are nothing in the eyes of the Master.

Dear friend, this book speaks of the fellowship of love with Christ and spending time in His presence. Everything depends on this. Christ came from heaven to love us just as the Father loved Him. He suffered to win our hearts for this love. His love can be satisfied with nothing less than deep personal love.

Christ considers this of prime importance. Let us do so, too. Even though we are doing many good things "for the Lord," we must not leave "our first love."

The Holy Spirit

He will bring me glory by revealing to you
whatever he receives from me.
JOHN 16:14

The last night that He was with His disciples, Jesus promised to send the Holy Spirit as a Comforter. Although His bodily presence was removed, they would realize His presence in them and with them in a wonderful way. The Holy Spirit of God would reveal Christ in their hearts so that they would experience His presence with them continually. The Spirit would glorify Christ and would reveal to them the glorified Christ in love and power.

Do not fail to understand, to believe, and to experience this wonderful truth. Doing the Lord's work is not a duty performed in one's own strength. No, that is impossible; it the Holy Spirit alone who will teach us to love Him sincerely.

God must have entire possession of us. He claims our whole heart and life. He will give us the strength to have fellowship with Christ, to keep His commandments, and to abide in His love. Once we have grasped this truth, we will begin to feel our deep dependence on the Holy Spirit and ask the Father to send Him in power into our hearts.

Christ's Love to Us

*I have loved you even as the Father
has loved me. Remain in my love.*
JOHN 15:9

In relationships between friends and relatives, everything depends on their love to each other. What value is wealth if love is lacking between husband and wife, or parents and children? What value is knowledge and enthusiasm in God's work without the knowledge and experience of Christ's love? (See 1 Corinthians 13:1–3.) Christians need to know by experience how much Christ loves them, and to learn how they may abide and continue in that love.

Christ says: "As the Father has loved Me,"—that is a divine, everlasting, wonderful love! "I also have loved you." The same love with which He had loved the Father He now gives us. He really desires that this everlasting love should rest upon us. What a blessing! Christ wants us to live in the power of the love of God that He also experienced.

In your fellowship with Christ in private or in public, you are surrounded by God's love. Jesus longs to fill you with His love.

Read from time to time what God's Word says about the love of Christ. Meditate on the words and let them sink into your heart. Sooner or later you will begin to realize: The greatest happiness of your life is that you are loved by the Lord Jesus and can live in fellowship with Him every day.

Our Love to Christ

You love him even though you have never seen him.
Though you do not see him, you trust him.
1 PETER 1:8

People who had never seen Christ still truly loved Him and believed on Him. Their hearts were filled with unspeakable joy. Such is the life of a Christian who really loves the Lord.

The chief attribute of the Father and of the Son is love to each other and love to man. This should be the chief characteristic of the true Christian. Life becomes a well of living water, flowing out as love to the Lord Jesus.

This love is not merely a happy feeling. It is an active principle. It takes pleasure in doing the will of the Lord. It is joy to keep His commandments. As the love of Christ was shown to us by His death on the cross, our love must be exhibited in unselfish, self-sacrificing lives. Please understand this: In the Christian life, love to Christ is everything!

Great love results in great faith—faith in His love to us, faith in the powerful revelation of His love in our hearts, faith that He will work all His good pleasure in us. The wings of faith and love will lift us up to heaven and we shall be filled with joy beyond words. The joy of the Christian is an indispensable witness to the world of the power of Christ to change hearts and to fill them with love and gladness.

Take time daily in His presence to drink in His love.

Love to Christians

So now I am giving you a new commandment:
Love each other.
JOHN 13:34

Jesus told His disciples that as the Father had loved Him, even so He loved them. And now, following His example, we must love one another with the same love. "Your love for one another will prove to the world that you are my disciples" (John 13:35). He had prayed: "My prayer for all of them is that they will be one, just as you and I are one, Father—that just as you are in me and I am in you, so they will be in us, and the world will believe you sent me" (John 17:21). If we exhibit the love that was in God towards Christ, and in Christ to us, the world will be obliged to confess that our Christianity is genuine.

This is what actually happened. The Greeks and Romans, Jews and heathen, hated each other. Between all the nations of the world there was hardly a thought of love. The very idea of self-sacrifice was a strange one. When unbelievers saw that Christians from different nations, under the powerful working of the Holy Spirit, loved one another even to the point of self-sacrifice in times of need—they were amazed. They said: "Behold, how these people love one another!"

Often Christ's love is not evident among Christians. Ask God to enable you to love your fellow believers as Christ loves you.

Love to Sinners

*You can be sure that the one who brings that
person back will save that sinner from death.*
JAMES 5:20

What a wonderful thought—that I may save a sinner from ever-lasting death. This can happen if I bring that person back to the truth. This is the calling of every Christian.

When Christ and His love took possession of our hearts, He gave us this love that we might bring others to Him. This is how Christ's kingdom is extended. Everyone who has the love of Christ is constrained to tell others. In the early Christian Church people went out and shared the love of Christ. Secular writers have told us that the rapid spread of Christianity in the first century was because each convert tried to bring the good news to others.

What a change has come over the Church! Many Christians never try to bring others to Christ. May the time soon come when Christians will feel constrained to share the love of Christ.

In a revival in Korea the converts were filled with such a burning love for Christ that they felt bound to tell others of His love. It was even taken as a test of membership that each one should have brought another to the Lord before being admitted to the church.

The Spirit of Love

For we know how dearly God loves us,
because he has given us the Holy Spirit
to fill our hearts with his love.
ROMANS 5:5

Is it impossible for a Christian to live this life of love? Often we make little progress in this spirit of love because of our unbelief and lack of faith in God's promises.

We need continually to remind ourselves that it is not in our own strength that we can reach the love of Christ. The love of God is shed abroad in our hearts daily by the Spirit of God. It is only as we are wholly surrendered to the Spirit that we will be able to live according to God's will. When the inner life of love is renewed from day to day, we shall love others.

You can pray with Paul: "When I think of the wisdom and scope of God's plan, I fall to my knees and pray to the Father. . . that from his glorious, unlimited resources he will give you mighty inner strength through his Holy Spirit. And I pray that Christ will be more and more at home in your hearts as you trust in him. May your roots go down deep into the soil of God's marvelous love. And may you have the power to under-stand, as all God's people should, how wide, how long, how high, and how deep his love really is" (Ephesians 3:14–18). You may know this love on one condition: you must be strengthened by the Spirit so that Christ may dwell in your heart.

Take this message from God's Word. Unless you are on your knees you cannot live in this love. A life of prayer will make a life of love to Christ, other Christians, and those without Christ a reality in your experience.

Persevering Prayer

Keep on praying.
1 THESSALONIANS 5:17

One of the greatest drawbacks to the life of prayer is that the answer does not come as quickly as we expect. We are discouraged and think: "Perhaps I do not pray right." So we do not persevere. Jesus often talked about this. There may be a reason for the delay and the waiting may bring a blessing. Our desire must grow deeper and stronger, and we must ask with our whole heart. God puts us into the practicing school of persevering prayer so that our weak faith may be strengthened.

Above all God wants to draw us into closer fellowship with Him. When our prayers are not answered we learn that the fellowship and love of God are more to us than the answers of our requests, and then we continue in prayer.

Do not be not impatient or discouraged if the answer does not come. "Always be prayerful." "Keep on praying." You will find real blessing in doing so. Ask whether your prayer is really in accordance with the will of God and the Word of God. Ask if it is in the right spirit and in the name of Christ. You will learn that the delay in the answer is one of the most precious ways God gives you His grace.

Those who have persevered before God are those who have had the greatest power in prayer.

The Prayer Meeting

They all met together continually for prayer. . . .
And everyone present was filled with the Holy Spirit.
ACTS 1:14; 2:4 (SEE ALSO MATTHEW 18:19–20)

In a genuine prayer meeting God's children meet together, not as in church to listen to one speaker, but to lift up their hearts unitedly to God. Christians are drawn closer to each other. Those who are weak are strengthened and encouraged by the testimony of the older and more experienced members, and young Christians have the opportunity of telling of the joy of the Lord. As a result, God's blessing is poured out at home and abroad.

But there are also dangers to be considered. Some may attend and be edified but never learn to pray themselves. Others go for the religious fervor, and have a form of godliness, but do not know the hidden life of prayer. Unless there is much prayer alone in the presence of God, attendance at a prayer meeting may be a mere ritual.

A "living prayer" meeting will have great influence when its roots are nourished by the life of prayer alone in God's presence. Prayer should include God's people all over the world. As on the Day of Pentecost, there must be waiting on God for the filling of the Holy Spirit.

Remember, you do not live for yourself alone but are part of the Body of Christ. As the roots of the tree hidden deep in the earth and the branches that spread out to heaven are one, so the hidden prayer life is inseparably bound up with united prayer.

Intercession

*Pray at all times and on every occasion
in the power of the Holy Spirit.*
EPHESIANS 6:18

Will God really make the pouring out of blessing on others dependent on our prayers? Yes, He makes us His fellow workers. He has taken us into partnership in His work. If we fail to do our part, others will suffer and His work will suffer.

God has appointed intercession as one of the means by which others will be saved and Christians built up in the faith. People all over the world will receive life and blessing through our prayers. Should we not expect God's children to endeavor with all our strength to pray for God's blessing on the world?

Begin to use intercession as a means of grace for yourself and for others. Pray for your neighbors. Pray for sinners that they may come to Christ. Pray for your minister and for missionaries. Pray for your country and for government leaders. If you live a life completely for God, you will realize that the time spent in prayer is an offering pleasing to God.

Yes, "pray at all times. . .and be persistent in your prayers for all Christians everywhere." In so doing you will learn the lesson that intercession is the chief means of bringing others to Christ and bringing glory to God.

Prayer and Fasting

Jesus told them. . .
"But this kind of demon won't leave
unless you have prayed and fasted."
MATTHEW 17:21

Jesus teaches us that a life of faith requires both prayer and fasting. Prayer grasps the power of heaven, fasting loosens the hold on earthly pleasure.

Jesus Himself fasted to get strength to resist the devil. He taught His disciples that fasting should be in secret, and the Father would reward it openly. Abstinence from food, or moderation in taking it, helps to focus on communication with God.

Let's remember that abstinence, moderation, and self-denial are a help to the spiritual life. After having eaten a hearty meal, one does not feel much desire to pray. To willingly sacrifice our own pleasure or enjoyment will help to focus our minds more fully on God and His priorities. The very practice needed in overcoming our own desires will give us strength to take hold of God in prayer.

Our lack of discipline in prayer comes from our fleshly desire of comfort and ease. "Those who belong to Christ Jesus have nailed the passions and desires of their sinful nature to his cross and crucified them there" (Galatians 5:24). Prayer is not easy work. For the real practice of prayer—taking hold of God and having communion and fellowship with Him—it is necessary that our selfish desires be sacrificed.

Isn't it worth the trouble to deny ourselves daily in order to meet the holy God and receive His blessings?

The Spirit of Prayer

*For the Spirit pleads for us believers
in harmony with God's own will.*
ROMANS 8:27

Prayer is not our work. It is God's work in us by His almighty power. As we pray our attitude should be one of silent expectation that the Holy Spirit will help in our weakness and pray for us with groanings that cannot be expressed.

What a thought! When I feel how imperfect my prayer is, when I have no strength of my own, I may bow in silence before God in the confidence that His Holy Spirit will teach me to pray. The Spirit is the Spirit of prayer. It is not my work, but God's work in me. The Spirit will make perfect the work even in my weakness.

We see an example of this in the story of Jacob. The same One who wrestled with him and seemed to withhold the blessing was in reality strengthening him to continue and to prevail in prayer. Prayer is the work of the Triune God: the Father, who gives the desire and will provide all we need; the Son, who through His intercession teaches us to pray in His name; and the Holy Spirit, who in secret will strengthen our weak desires.

The Spirit of truth will glorify Christ in us, and the Spirit of love will shed this love abroad in our hearts. And we have the Spirit of prayer, through whom our life may be one of continual prayer. Thank God that the Holy Spirit has been given to teach us to pray.

Wholly for Christ

Christ died for everyone. . .
so that those who receive his new life
will no longer live to please themselves.
2 CORINTHIANS 5:14–15

Paul describes here a threefold life. First, the life of the Christian who lives according to his old nature: for himself alone. The second, the life of the true Christian: he lives wholly for Christ. Third, the life of Christ in heaven: He lives wholly for us.

We need to be convinced of the foolishness of living only for ourselves. At conversion we focus more on our own salvation and less on the claim that Christ has on us. Many Christians continue to live for themselves, content with doing little for the Master. Happiness comes to the believer who realizes the privilege of consecrating one's life entirely to God.

The great hindrance to such a life is the unbelief which says it is impossible. But when the truth takes hold—Christ in heaven lives for me and will impart His life to me—then we know that He will enable us to live wholly for Him.

May this be your earnest desire, your prayer, and your firm expectation: Christ has not only died for me but lives in heaven to keep me, His purchased possession. Christ will keep you as a member of His Body, to work and live for Him. Pray for grace to live completely for God, whether in sharing with unbelievers or in serving His people. Take time to be united with Christ in prayer that you can say with all your heart: I live wholly for Him.

The Cross of Christ

I have been crucified with Christ.
GALATIANS 2:19

The cross of Christ is His greatest glory. Because He humbled Himself by dying on the cross in our place, therefore God has highly exalted Him. The cross was the power that conquered Satan and sin.

As Christians we share with Christ in the cross. Christ lives in us through the Holy Spirit, and we live as one who has died with Christ. As we realize the power of Christ's crucifixion, we live as one who has died to the world and to sin. Christ, the crucified One, lives in us.

Jesus said to His disciples: "If any of you wants to be my follower. . .you must put aside your selfish ambition, shoulder your cross, and follow me" (Mark 8:34). They had seen men carrying a cross. They knew that it meant a painful death. All His life Christ bore His cross—the death sentence that He should die for the world. As Christians we must bear the cross, acknowledging that we are worthy of death, believing that we are crucified with Christ, and that the crucified One lives in us. "Our old sinful selves were crucified with Christ" (Romans 6:6). "Those who belong to Christ Jesus have nailed the passions and desires of their sinful nature to his cross and crucified them there" (Galatians 5:24). When we have accepted this life of the cross, we will be able to say: "God forbid that I should boast about anything except the cross of our Lord Jesus Christ" (Galatians 6:14).

Allow the Holy Spirit to teach you more about this deep spiritual truth.

The World

When you love the world,
you show that you do not have
the love of the Father in you.
1 JOHN 2:15

John teaches us what he means by the world in 1 John 2:16. He says: "For the world offers only the lust for physical pleasure, the lust for everything we see, and pride in our possessions. These are not from the Father. They are from this evil world."

Because all mankind has fallen through sin, we have come under the power of the world and are deceived by the god of this world. The world with its pleasures surrounds the Christian each day with temptations.

This was the case with Eve in the Garden of Eden. We find in Genesis the three characteristics John mentions: 1) The lust of the flesh—"The woman saw the tree that it was good for food." 2) The lust of the eyes—"It was pleasant to the eyes." 3) The pride of life—"A tree to be desired to make one wise" (Genesis 3:6). Our life in the world is full of danger—so much to occupy our eyes and our hearts, so much worldly wisdom and knowledge.

So John tells us: "Stop loving this evil world and all that it offers you, for when you love the world, you show that you do not have the love of the Father in you." Just as the Lord called His disciples, He calls us to leave all and follow Him.

Put on Christ

> *For as many of you as have been baptized*
> *into Christ have put on Christ.*
> GALATIANS 3:27 KJV

The word that is here translated "put on" is the same that is used in regard to putting on clothes. We have put on "the new man," and we have the new nature as a garment that is worn so all can see who we are. The Christian is known as one who has put on Christ and exhibits Him in his whole life and character.

Paul says to "put on the Lord Jesus," not only at conversion, but from day to day. As you put on your clothes each day, so the Christian must daily put on the Lord Jesus. In that way you reflect the image of Jesus, the new person formed in His likeness.

Put on Christ! This must be done by spending time alone in His presence. As my clothes protect me from wind and sun, even so Christ will be my protection and my joy. As I fellowship with Him in prayer, He strengthens me.

Take time to meditate on this wonderful truth. As your clothing is a necessity, let it be equally indispensable for you to "put on" Jesus Christ, to spend time with Him, and walk with Him all the day. Take the time and the trouble to do this. Your reward will be great.

The Strength of the Christian

*A final word: Be strong with
the Lord's mighty power.*
EPHESIANS 6:10

Since we as Christians have no strength of our own, where may we get it? Notice the answer: Be strong with the Lord's mighty power.

Paul had spoken of this power in the earlier part of Ephesians (1:17–20). He had prayed to God to give them the Spirit that they might know the greatness of His power which He displayed when He raised Christ from the dead. This is the literal truth: the greatness of His power which raised Christ from the dead works in every believer. We hardly believe it and much less experience it. That is why Paul prays that God would teach us to believe in His almighty power.

In Ephesians 3:16–17, Paul asks the Father to strengthen them by His Spirit, that Christ might dwell in their hearts. And then in verse 20: "Now glory be to God! By his mighty power, at work within us, he is able to accomplish infinitely more than we would ever dare to ask or hope."

Read over these Scriptures again and pray for God's Spirit to make these words real to you. Believe in the divine power working in you. Pray that the Holy Spirit may reveal it to you. Appropriate the promise that God will show His power in your heart, supplying all your needs. It is clear that much time is needed with the Father and the Son, if you would experience the power of God within you.

The Whole Heart

I have tried my best
[with my whole heart—KJV]
to find you.
PSALM 119:10

Notice how often the psalmist speaks of the "all the heart" or the "whole heart": "search for him with all their hearts" (verse 2); "I will put it into practice with all my heart" (verse 34); "I obey your commandments with all my heart" (verse 69); "I pray with all my heart" (verse 145). In seeking God, in observing His law, in crying for His help—each time it is with his whole heart.

When we want to be successful in business, we put our whole heart into it. Isn't this even more necessary in the service of a holy God? He is worthy. The whole heart is needed in the service of God when we worship Him.

We often forget this. In prayer, in reading His word, in seeking to do His will, we fail to say continually: "I have tried my best—with my whole heart—to find You." Let us learn to say: "I desire to seek God and to serve Him with my whole heart."

Meditate and pray about this. Spend time before God until you know that you really mean what you say and you have the assurance that God will hear your prayer. Then each morning as you approach God in prayer you can honestly say, "I seek You with my whole heart." You gradually will feel the need of waiting in holy stillness upon God so that He may take possession of your whole heart. You will learn to love Him with your whole heart and your whole mind.

A Blessed Reality

*God alone made it possible for you
to be in Christ Jesus.*
1 CORINTHIANS 1:30

During His last day with His disciples, the Lord Jesus made several references to being "in Christ Jesus." "When I am raised to life again, you will know that I am in my Father, and you are in me, and I am in you" (John 14:20). Following that in 15:5: "Those who remain in me, and I in them, will produce much fruit." "If you stay joined to me and my words remain in you, you may ask any request you like, and it will be granted!" (15:7). We cannot apply these promises unless we first prayerfully accept the words "in Christ."

Paul expressed the same thought in Romans 6:4: "We. . . were buried with Christ." "You should consider yourselves dead to sin and able to live for the glory of God through Christ Jesus" (Romans 6:11). "There is no condemnation for those who belong to Christ Jesus" (Romans 8:1). And in Ephesians 1:3: "How we praise God. . .who has blessed us with every spiritual blessing in the heavenly realms because we belong to Christ." Colossians 2:9: "For in Christ the fullness of God lives in a human body." Colossians 2:6: "Just as you accepted Christ Jesus as your Lord, you must continue to live in obedience to him." Colossians 4:12: "asking God to make you strong and perfect, fully confident of the whole will of God."

By faith take hold of the truth that "God establishes us in Christ" and then follow the leading of the Spirit in prayer.

Christ in Me

Examine yourselves to see if your faith
is really genuine.
2 CORINTHIANS 13:5

Christ is in me. What a difference it would make if we could take time every morning to focus on the thought: Christ is in me.

Christ made it clear to His disciples. The Spirit would teach them: "When I am raised to life again, you will know that I am in my Father, and you are in me, and I am in you" (John 14:20). Through the power of God we who believe were crucified with Christ and raised again with Him. As a result Christ is in us! Through faith in God's Word, the Christian accepts it.

Paul expresses this thought in the prayer of Ephesians 3:16: "I pray that from his glorious, unlimited resources he will give you mighty inner strength through his Holy Spirit." Notice that it is not the ordinary gift of grace, but a special revelation of the riches of His love that Christ may dwell in your heart by faith. Have you been able to grasp that?

Paul said: "I fall to my knees and pray to the Father" (Ephesians 3:14). That is the only way to obtain the blessing. Take time in prayer in His presence to realize: "Christ dwells in me." Even in the midst of your daily schedule, look upon your heart as the dwelling place of the Son of God. Then Christ's words: "Those who remain in me, and I in them, will produce much fruit" (John 15:5) will become your daily experience.

Christ Is All

Christ is all that matters,
and he lives in all of us.
COLOSSIANS 3:11

Christ is all—in the eternal counsel of God, in the redemption on the cross, as King on the throne in heaven and on earth. In the salvation of sinners, in the building up of Christ's Body, in the care for individuals—Christ is all. Every hour and every day this knowledge provides comfort and strength to the child of God.

You feel too weak, too unworthy, too untrustworthy. But if you will only accept the Lord Jesus in childlike faith, you have a guide who will supply all your need. Believe the word of our Savior in Matthew 28:20: "And be sure of this: I am with you always," and you will experience His presence each day.

However cold and dull your feelings may be, however sinful you are, meet the Lord Jesus in secret and He will reveal Himself to you. Tell Him how miserable you really are, and then trust Him to help and sustain you.

Each day as you spend time in His presence, let this thought be with you: Christ is all. Make it your goal: Christ is all—to teach me to pray, to strengthen my faith, to give me the assurance of His love, to give me direct access to the Father, to make me strong for the schedule of the day.

The Love of God

God is love, and all who live in love live in God,
and God lives in them.

1 JOHN 4:16

The love of God—what an unfathomable mystery! Jesus said: "Only God is good" (Matthew 19:17). The glory of God in heaven is that He wills to do all that is good. That includes the two meanings of the word: good—all that is right and perfect; good—all that makes happy.

The God who wills nothing but good is a God of love. He does not demand His own way. He does not live for Himself but pours out His love on all living creatures. All created things share in this love so that they may be satisfied with that which is good.

A characteristic of love is that it "does not demand its own way" (1 Corinthians 13:5). It finds happiness in giving to others. It sacrifices itself wholly for others. God offered Himself to mankind in love in the person of His Son, and the Son offered Himself upon the cross to bring that love to men and women. The everlasting love with which the Father loved the Son is the same love with which the Son loves us.

The love of God to His Son, the love of the Son to us, the love with which we love the Son, the love with which we love each other and try to love all men—all is the same eternal, incomprehensible, almighty love of God. Love is the power of the Godhead in the Father, Son, and Holy Spirit.

The Love of Christ

Whatever we do,
it is because Christ's love controls us.
2 CORINTHIANS 5:14

God sent His Son into the world to let us know His everlasting love, even as it was known in heaven. Even the angels in heaven are filled with praise and worship because of God's love. God's desire is that on this sinful earth His love would take possession of the hearts of men and women.

In order to reveal His love and win our hearts to Himself, God sent Christ, the Son of His love, to earth. The Lord Jesus Christ became man and, even though He was God, humbly made Himself nothing. In His dealings with the poor, the unbelieving, and the rebellious—and through His miracles—He poured out His love into the hearts of sinful men.

God gave the greatest proof of love that the world has ever seen. On the cross He took our sins upon Himself. He bore the suffering and the scorn of His enemies so that friend and foe alike might know God's eternal love.

Then, after He had ascended to heaven, He gave the Holy Spirit to shed abroad this love in our hearts. Impelled by the love of Christ, the disciples in turn offered their lives to make this love known to others.

Think about this. God longs to have our hearts filled with His love so that He can use us as channels for this love to flow out to others. Let us be satisfied with nothing less and sacrifice everything to secure a place for this love in the hearts of men and women.

The Love of the Spirit

He has given us the Holy Spirit
to fill our hearts with his love.
ROMANS 5:5

As God's children, we must confess that we know very little of fervent, childlike love for our heavenly Father. Why is this? Perhaps we have not learned the lesson that there must be a constant renewal of faith in what God is able to do. We try to stir up love towards God in our hearts. Yet, in our own strength, we cannot awaken the slightest love to God.

Child of God, believe that the love of God will work as the power in your heart that enables you to love God and to love others. Cease to expect love in yourself. Believe in the power of God's love resting on you and teaching you to love God with His own love.

Learn the lesson of our text: "He has given us the Holy Spirit to fill our hearts with his love." The Spirit will enable us to love God, our friends, and even our enemies. Be assured of two things. First, in your own strength you cannot love God or your fellow Christians. And second, the Holy Spirit is within you every day and every hour, seeking to fill you with the Spirit of love. Each morning as you commit yourself into the keeping of the Holy Spirit, let this prayer arise:

Lord, grant me the assurance that You will pour forth the love of Christ into my own heart, and then let it stream forth to all around me! Amen.

The Power of Love

Overwhelming victory is ours through Christ,
who loved us.
ROMANS 8:37

In days of uncertainty, strong racial feelings, and unrest, we need to experience the love of God. Let us anchor our hope in the truth, "God is love." God's power, by which He rules the world, is the power of undying love. He works through the hearts and wills of men and women who are wholly yielded to Him. He waits for us to open our hearts to Him in love. Then, full of courage, we become witnesses for Him.

This is how Christ's kingdom is manifested and His reign of love on earth begun. Christ died in order to establish this kingdom. The only means He used to gain influence was by showing a serving, suffering love. He saw the possibility of redemption in even the worst of people, knowing that their hearts could never resist the steady influence of love. It was in the fervor of that love that Jesus' disciples were able to do the impossible.

The spirit of hatred and bitterness can never be overcome by argument or reproaches. Some think things can never be different but, if we really believe in the omnipotence of God's love, we may trust His power. Our faith in love as the greatest power in the world should prepare us for a life in communion with God in prayer and for a life of service.

The Sign of a True Church

Your love for one another will prove to the world that you are my disciples.
JOHN 13:35

We are taught in most of our creeds that the true church is to be found where God's Word is faithfully and accurately preached and the sacraments are dispensed as instituted by Christ. Christ Himself takes a much broader view. To Him the distinguishing mark of His followers is not merely what the Church teaches—but how we live our lives showing love to each other.

Jesus' death on the cross was love at its highest. We owe everything to this love. Love is the power that moved Christ to die for us. In love, God highly exalted Him as Lord and Christ. Love is the power that broke our hearts, and love is the power that heals them. Love is the power through which Christ dwells and works in us. Love can change my nature and enable me to surrender to God. It gives me strength to live a holy, joyous life, full of blessing to others. Every Christian should show the love of God.

Many Christians are sure it is impossible to lead such a life, and they do not even greatly desire it. They do not understand that we may and can love with God's own love.

If we fully believe that the Holy Spirit, dwelling within us, will maintain this heavenly love from hour to hour, we will be able to understand the words of Christ: "Anything is possible if a person believes" (Mark 9:23). Then we will be able to love God with all our hearts, to love family and friends, and even our enemies.

Race-Hatred

Once we, too, were foolish and disobedient.
We were misled by others and became slaves
to many wicked desires and evil pleasures.
TITUS 3:3

Our text paints a dark picture of the state of human nature! What causes such a sad condition? The answer is "Adam's fall." Think how Cain, the first child born of the man God created, shed the blood of his brother Abel. The first child born on earth came under the power of the devil, who "was a murderer from the beginning" (John 8:44). "Now the Lord observed the extent of the people's wickedness, and he saw that all their thoughts were consistently and totally evil" (Genesis 6:5). No wonder He destroyed mankind by a flood.

Humanity's love of their own people, implanted in their hearts by nature, soon changed to hatred of other peoples. Love of country became the source of race-hatred and bloodshed. Note how God has placed the races side by side to see if our Christianity will enable us to overcome race-hatred. Will we, in the power of Christ's love, prove that "In this new life, it doesn't matter if you are a Jew or a Gentile, circumcised or uncircumcised, barbaric, uncivilized, slave, or free. Christ is all that matters, and he lives in all of us" (Colossians 3:11)?

What an opportunity there is for the Church to prove the power of God's love to change race-hatred into brotherly love! God has abundant power to make this happen. As Christians we need to pray for ourselves and for each other that we would obey the Word of God and live in the power of Christ's love.

Love Your Enemies

You have heard that the law of Moses says,
"Love your neighbor" and hate your enemy.
MATTHEW 5:43

Religious teachers in Christ's day judged that they had a right to say this [Matthew 5:43] because of Leviticus 19:17–18: "Do not nurse hatred in your heart for any of your relatives. Confront your neighbors directly so you will not be held guilty for their crimes. Never seek revenge or bear a grudge against anyone, but love your neighbor as yourself." They argued that it was only their own people whom they may not hate; it was all right to hate their enemies. But our Lord said: "Love your enemies! Pray for those who persecute you!" (Matthew 5:44).

How often we as Christians follow the example of those religious leaders! The new commandment to love requires much grace, costs time, and needs much earnest prayer.

When I was a minister in Cape Town I met a German deaconess. She had a class for several Kaffirs who were preparing to join the church. One evening she spoke about loving our enemies. She asked one man if his people had enemies. "Oh yes!" "Who are they?" "The Fingoes." She asked if he could love a Fingo. His answer was decided. "I can't love Fingo." She told him that in that case he could not go to the Communion. He seemed very downcast. He was not received into the church with the others but continued to attend the class. Then one evening he appeared with a bright face and said, "I now love Fingo." He had prayed about it; God heard his prayer and enabled him to love his enemy.

There is only one way we can love our enemies: by the love of Christ, sought and found in prayer.

As God Forgives

And forgive us our sins—
just as we forgive those who
have sinned against us.
LUKE 11:4

The forgiveness of sins is the one great gift that sets the sinner free. Forgiveness gives us boldness toward God and is the source of our salvation. The forgiveness of sins gives us a reason to be thankful every day of our lives.

As we walk with God in the assurance of sins forgiven, He desires that we should live as those who have been freely forgiven. We can only prove our sincerity by forgiving those who have offended us as willingly as God has forgiven us.

In the Lord's Prayer we are taught to pray: "Forgive us our sins—just as we forgive those who have sinned against us." Then at the end: "But if you refuse to forgive others, your Father will not forgive your sins" (Matthew 6:15). In Matthew 18:21 we have the question of Peter: "Lord, how often should I forgive someone who sins against me?" Our Lord answered, "Seventy times seven!"

Then follows the parable of the servant whose lord forgave him his debt but who would not show compassion on his fellow servant. His lord asked: "Shouldn't you have mercy on your fellow servant, just as I had mercy on you?" So the servant was sent to prison. The Lord warns us: "That's what my heavenly Father will do to you if you refuse to forgive your brothers and sisters in your heart" (Matthew 18:33, 35).

The Two Leaders

I urge you, first of all, to pray for all people.
As you make your requests,
plead for God's mercy upon them,
and give thanks.
1 TIMOTHY 2:1

At the time of the unveiling of the Women's Monument at Bloemfontein, South Africa, I spoke a few words about the suffering, praying, all-conquering love of these women. They prayed that God would help them love their enemies and keep them from hatred. I expressed the hope that the feeling of peace and unity might continue and this prayerful love be ours. I said that there were some who feared disunion, not only between the two races in the country, but between those who were of the same race. Not long after we heard that there had been a breach between the leaders of the two parties.

I felt impelled to write an article on the question: "For whom do you pray?" Someone answered: "I pray for the man at the head of my party who, under God's guidance, has now become the leader of all South Africa." And another, "I pray especially for the man who has brought the interests of my people into the foreground." Would it not be sad if we came into God's presence divided into two camps praying one against the other? We must pray both for our leaders and for all who are in authority. As leaders of the people, their influence for good or evil is inexpressible. Their hearts are in God's hands, and He can turn them wherever He wills. Let us pray to God in all sincerity for our leaders, that God will grant what is good for the whole land.

Love and Prayer

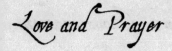

Be earnest and disciplined in your prayers.
Most important of all,
continue to show deep love for each other.
1 PETER 4:7–8

Earnest prayer and fervent love are closely linked. If we pray only for ourselves, we will not find it easy to be in the right attitude toward God. But when our hearts are filled with love for others, we will continue to pray for them, even for those with whom we do not agree.

Prayer holds an important place in the life of love; they are inseparably connected. If you want your love to increase, forget yourself and pray for God's children. If you want to increase in prayerfulness, spend time loving those around you, helping to bear their burdens.

There is a great need for earnest, powerful intercessors! God desires His children to present themselves each day before the throne of grace to pray down the power of the Spirit upon all believers. Unity is strength. Spiritual unity will help us to live unselfishly, wholly for God and others. Let us apply Peter's words to our lives—"earnest in prayer. . .showing deep love for each other."

As we meditate on love to those around us, we will be drawn into fellowship with God. This will come, not by reading or thinking, but by spending time with the Father and with the Lord Jesus through the Holy Spirit. Love leads to prayer—to believing prayer is given the love of God.

The First Commandment

The LORD your God will cleanse your heart. . .
so that you will love him with all your heart and soul.

DEUTERONOMY 30:6

God greatly desires our love. It is the nature of all love to want to be acceptable and to be accepted. God longs to have the love of our whole heart.

How can we love God with all our heart and soul? In the same way that we receive salvation—through faith alone. Paul says, "I live my life in this earthly body by trusting in the Son of God, who loved me and gave himself for me" (Galatians 2:20). When we take time to wait upon God and remember how God sought to win our love through the gift of His Son, we shall realize that God has a strong longing for our love.

Our hearts are blind. It is easy to forget that God longs for the love of His child. Once we believe it, we will feel constrained to wait before God and ask Him to let His light shine into our hearts. As the sun gives us its light, God is a thousand times more willing to give us the light of His love.

As we wait silently before God, we become strong in the assurance of faith. God, who longs for our love, is almighty and will fill us with His love by the Holy Spirit.

Take time each day to love God and believe Him with firmer faith. God will work within us, granting the desire to love Him with our whole heart. He will enable us to prove our love by keeping His commandments.

Pray for Love

And may the Lord make your love grow and overflow
to each other and to everyone else,
just as our love overflows toward you.
1 THESSALONIANS 3:12

Paul gives us a powerful prayer in this text: that the Lord would make them abound in love toward each other, so that their hearts would be without blame. Without love, true holiness was impossible. Let us use this prayer often.

In 2 Thessalonians 3:5 we read: "May the Lord bring you into an ever deeper understanding of the love of God." That is what the Lord Jesus will do for us. As the Apostle makes love the chief thing, let us do the same.

"I want you to know how much I have agonized for you. . . . My goal is that [you] will be encouraged and knit together by strong ties of love. I want [you] to have full confidence because [you] have complete understanding of God's secret plan, which is Christ himself" (Colossians 2:1–2). Paul considers love indispensable for growth in the knowledge of God. God's love can only be experienced when Christians are knit together in love and live for others, not only for themselves.

Take time to meditate on these prayers of Paul. As the sun freely gives its light to the grass that it may grow, so God is more willing to give His love to us. As you pray and ponder these words, you will gain a strong assurance of what God is able to do for you. He will make you to abound in love and strengthen you to live before Him in holiness and love for others.

A Song of Love

These are three things that will endure—
faith, hope, and love.
—and the greatest of these is love.
1 CORINTHIANS 13:13

Today is wholly devoted to the praise of love. The first three verses of 1 Corinthians 13 speak of the absolute necessity of love as the chief thing in our religion. "If I could speak in any language in heaven or on earth. . .if I had the gift of prophecy. . .if I had the gift of faith so that I could speak to a mountain and make it move. . .if I gave everything I have to the poor and even sacrificed my body. . .but if I didn't love others" then, three times repeated, "I would only be making meaningless noise like a loud gong or a clanging cymbal. . .what good would I be? . . .I would be of no value whatsoever." If I have not love, I am of no value.

There are fifteen things said about love, but one sentence sums up its whole nature: "It does not demand its own way" (verse 5). And again: "Love will last forever" (verse 8). Prophecies, unknown languages, and knowledge shall vanish away. Even faith and hope shall be changed into sight. But love lasts forever.

"Love does not demand its own way." Think and pray about this. "Love will last forever." Consider all that means. "The greatest of these is love." Let this love rule in your life.

God is love. "God is love, and all who live in love live in God, and God lives in them" (1 John 4:16). Let your heart be filled with love so that, by God's almighty power, you may be a witness to the transforming power of love. Then you will be a blessing to all around you.

Like Christ

I have given you an example to follow.
Do as I have done to you.
JOHN 13:15

The love of Christ is the basis not only of our salvation but also of our daily life and conduct. Jesus clearly says: "Do as I have done to you." The love of Christ is my only hope of salvation. Walking in that love is the way to enjoy that salvation.

"We should please others. If we do what helps them, we will build them up in the Lord. So accept each other just as Christ has accepted you; then God will be glorified" (Romans 15:2, 7). God will work within us to "accept each other just as Christ has accepted [us]."

"Follow God's example in everything you do, because you are his dear children. Live a life filled with love for others, following the example of Christ, who loved you and gave himself as a sacrifice to take away your sins" (Ephesians 5:1–2). Paul reminds us that love is everything. Christ loved us so much He died on the cross so we could be God's dear children. It follows that we should walk in love. Those who keep close to Christ will walk in love.

"Since God chose you to be the holy people whom he loves, you must clothe yourselves with tenderhearted mercy. . . .You must make allowance for each other's faults and forgive the person who offends you. Remember, the Lord forgave you, so you must forgive others. And the most important piece of clothing you must wear is love. Love is what binds us all together in perfect harmony" (Colossians 3:12–14). As we walk in fellowship with Him, we are given strength to be like Him!

The Power of God's Word

The very words I have spoken to you
are spirit and life.
JOHN 6:63

Frequently the question is asked: Why do God's children often fail to realize the great value and absolute necessity of loving each other? One answer is unbelief. Without faith there can be no thought of the power of love within us. True faith acknowledges God's loving care for us and His power to work wonders in our hearts.

It is necessary to be deeply convinced of our total inability to produce this love on our own. We must have a burning desire to receive this heavenly love into our hearts—a love that is holy and can conquer sin and unbelief. When we gain an insight into what God's Word is—a living power in our hearts—we will be filled with the love of God by the Holy Spirit, living and working within us.

Are we ready to acknowledge our deep sinfulness and yield our hearts unreservedly for this love to take possession of us? Are we ready to take time in God's presence in the confidence that His Word will work in us as a seed of new life? If so, then we will love Jesus and each other with a love like God's love for us.

The Love That Suffers

Live a life filled with love for others,
following the example of Christ,
who loved you and gave himself as
a sacrifice to take away your sins.
EPHESIANS 5:2

It is strange that love, which is the source of the greatest happiness, should also be the cause of the most intense suffering. Suffering always follows when love seeks to save the object of its love. It is only by suffering that love can gain its end and so attain the highest happiness.

Even the almighty power of God's love could not achieve its purpose without suffering. By suffering, Christ bore the sins of the whole world. Love in the midst of suffering manifested the greatest glory and attained its end perfectly.

Love worthy of the name manifests itself in a life of continual self-sacrifice. Love gives strength to endure, whatever the circumstances. Loving others may mean tears, heartache, and much persevering in prayer; but love overcomes all obstacles.

Do you long to know the love of Christ in all its fullness? Then yield yourself to Him. Think of yourself as a channel through which the highest love can reach its aim. Begin to suffer with and intercede for those around you. Eventually you will realize what this life of love is: to live wholly for the welfare and happiness of others.

The Lack of Prayer

And yet the reason you don't have what
you want is that you don't ask God for it.

JAMES 4:2

Recently I attended several conventions at which prayer was often the subject of conversation. A businessman said that the spirit of intercession is what the Church of our day needs. Everywhere people confessed, "We pray too little!" Yet there seemed to be a fear that, because of pressure from work and the force of habit, it was almost impossible to hope for change. Such thinking can only hinder our own joy and our power in God's service.

Dr. Whyte of Edinburgh said that, as a young minister, he thought any time left over from pastoral visitation ought to be spent with his books. He wanted to feed his people with the very best he could prepare. But now he had learned that prayer was more important than study. He felt as if it were almost too late to regain what he had lost and urged us to pray more. What a solemn confession and warning: We pray too little!

Is the call of God for our time and attention more important than our work? If God is waiting to meet us and to give us power from heaven for His work, it is short-sighted to put other work in His place. If there is to be a significant experience of God's presence, there must be more definite and persevering prayer.

Time for Prayer

Yet no one calls on your name or pleads
with you for mercy.
ISAIAH 64:7

At a ministerial meeting the superintendent of a large district said: "I rise in the morning and have half an hour with God. I am occupied all day with numerous engagements. Not many minutes elapse without my breathing a prayer for guidance. After work I speak to God of the day's work. But I know little of the intense prayer of which Scripture speaks."

There are earnest Christians who have just enough prayer to maintain their spiritual position but not enough to grow spiritually. Seeking to fight off temptation is a defensive attitude rather than an assertive one which reaches for higher attainment. The scriptural teaching to cry out day and night in prayer must, to some degree, become our experience if we are to be intercessors.

A man said to me, "I see the importance of much prayer, and yet my life hardly allows time for it. Am I to give up? How can I accomplish what I desire?"

I admitted that the difficulty was universal and quoted a Dutch proverb: "What is heaviest must weigh heaviest." The most important must have the first place. The law of God is unchangeable. In our communication with heaven, we only get as we give. Unless we are willing to pay the price—to sacrifice time and attention and seemingly necessary tasks for the sake of the heavenly gifts—we cannot expect much power from heaven in our work.

Finding the Root Cause

And God will generously provide all you need.
Then you will always have everything you need
and plenty left over to share with others.

2 CORINTHIANS 9:8

I met a clergyman who used the expression "the distraction of business." It was one of the greatest difficulties he had to deal with. Every day he had to visit four different offices in his town. In addition, his predecessor left him the responsibility of several committees where he was expected to do all the work. Everything conspired to keep him from prayer.

Various difficulties make a full prayer life almost impossible. But thank God the things which are impossible with men are possible with God! God's call to prayer need not be a burden nor a cause of guilt. He means for it to be a joy. Through prayer He can give us strength for all we do and bring down His power to work through us in the lives of others.

Let us confess the sin that shames us and then confront it in the name of our Redeemer. The same light that shows us our sin and condemns us for it will show us the way out of it. Deficiency in our Christian life is the root cause of unfaithfulness in prayer. God will use this discovery to bring us both the power to pray that we long for and also the joy of a new and healthy life, of which prayer is the spontaneous expression.

Health for the Soul

He was amazed to see that no one intervened
to help the oppressed.
ISAIAH 59:16

How can our lack of prayer be transformed into a blessing? How can it be changed into the path where evil may be conquered? How can our relationship with the Father become one of continual prayer?

We must begin by going back to God's Word to study the place God intends for prayer to have in the life of His child. A fresh understanding of what prayer is and what our prayers can be will free us from our wrong attitudes concerning the absolute necessity of continual prayer.

We need insight into how reasonable this divine appointment is. We need to be convinced of how it fits in with God's love and our happiness. Then we will be freed from the false impression of prayer being an arbitrary demand. We will yield to it and rejoice in it as the only way for the blessing of heaven to come to earth. It will no longer be a task and burden of self-effort and strain. As simple as breathing is in the physical life, so will praying be in the Christian life that is led by the Spirit.

Our failure in the prayer life is a result of our failure in the Spirit life. Any thought of praying more and of praying effectively will be in vain unless we are brought into closer intimacy with our Lord. His life of prayer on earth and of intercession in heaven is breathed into us in the measure that our surrender and our faith allow.

Ministration of the Spirit and Prayer

If you sinful people know how to
give good gifts to your children,
how much more will your heavenly Father
give the Holy Spirit to those who ask him.
LUKE 11:13

Jesus said: "Keep on asking, and you will be given what you ask for." God's giving is inseparably connected with our asking. He applied this principle especially to the Holy Spirit. As surely as a father gives bread to his child, so God gives the Holy Spirit to those who ask. The whole ministration of the Spirit is ruled by the one great law: God must give, we must ask. When the Holy Spirit was poured out at Pentecost, it was in answer to prayer.

Along with our confession of the lack of prayer, we also need an understanding of the place prayer occupies in God's plan of redemption. Nowhere is this clearer than in the first half of the Acts. The outpouring of the Holy Spirit at the birth of the Church is the true measure of the presence of the Spirit.

The Spirit came in answer to prayer. "They met together continually for prayer." Then there follows, "On the day of Pentecost, seven weeks after Jesus' resurrection, the believers were meeting together in one place. And everyone present was filled with the Holy Spirit. . . . Those who believed. . .were. . . added to the church—about three thousand in all" (Acts 1:14; 2:1, 4; 2:41).

The Holy Spirit had been promised by Christ. He sat down on His throne and received the Spirit from the Father. But one more thing was needed: the ten days of united, continued supplication of the disciples.

Spiritual Roots

After this prayer,
the building where they were meeting shook,
and they were all filled with the Holy Spirit.
ACTS 4:31

Definite, determined prayer is what we need. Peter and John had been threatened with punishment. When they returned to their friends, they lifted up their voices to God with one accord. When they prayed, "the building where they were meeting shook. . . . They preached God's message with boldness."

It is as if the story of Pentecost is repeated (the prayer, the filling with the Spirit, the speaking God's Word with boldness), in order to imprint permanently on the Church that it is prayer that lies at the root of the spiritual life and power of the Church. The degree with which God gives His Spirit is determined by our asking.

Later people complained about the neglect of the Grecian Jews in the distribution of alms. The apostles proposed the appointment of deacons to serve the tables. "Then we can spend our time in prayer and preaching and teaching the word" (Acts 6:4). There is nothing in honest business that prevents fellowship with God. Least of all should ministering to the poor hinder the spiritual life. And yet the apostles felt it would hinder their ministry of prayer and the Word.

What does this teach? Maintenance of the spirit of prayer is possible in many kinds of work, but it is not enough for those who are the leaders of the Church. They need to communicate with the King and keep the heavenly world in clear focus for the maintenance of their own spiritual life and also for those around them.

A Higher Gift

*Your prayers and gifts to the poor have
not gone unnoticed by God!*
ACTS 10:4

At Samaria Philip had preached with great blessing and many believed. But the Holy Spirit had not yet fallen on them. The apostles sent Peter and John to pray for them that they might receive the Holy Spirit.

The power for such prayer was a higher gift than preaching. It was the work of men who had been in closest contact with the Lord. Of all the gifts of the early Church, there is none more needed than the gift of prayer. This power is given to those who say, "We will give ourselves to prayer."

The outpouring of the Holy Spirit in the house of Cornelius provides another testimony to the interdependence of prayer and the Spirit. Peter went up to pray on the housetop. He saw heaven opened and there came a vision that revealed the cleansing of the Gentiles. Then came the message of the men from Cornelius, a man who "prayed regularly" and had heard from an angel, "Your prayers. . .have not gone unnoticed by God." Then the voice of the Spirit was heard saying, "Go with them" (Acts 10:20).

It is a praying Peter to whom the will of God is revealed and who is brought into contact with a praying and prepared company of hearers. In answer to all this prayer comes blessing beyond all expectation and the Holy Spirit is poured out upon the Gentiles.

Stone Walls Give Way

But while Peter was in prison,
the church prayed very earnestly for him.
ACTS 12:5

When we pray consistently we will receive an entrance into God's will of which we would otherwise know nothing. We will receive blessing above all we ask or think. The teaching and power of the Holy Spirit are unalterably linked to prayer.

The power that the Church's prayer has is shown not only as the apostles pray but also as the Christian community does. In Acts 12 Peter is in prison awaiting execution. The death of James had aroused the Church to a sense of great danger; the thought of losing Peter, too, wakened all their energies. They went to prayer.

Prayer was effective; Peter was delivered. When he came to the house of Mary he found "many were gathered for prayer" (Acts 12:12). Double chains, soldiers, and the iron gate—all gave way before the power from heaven that prayer brought to his rescue. The power of the Roman Empire was nothing in the presence of the power that the Church wielded in prayer.

Those Christians stood in close and living relationship with their Lord. They knew well that the words "I have been given complete authority" and "Be sure of this: I am with you always" were absolutely true. They had faith in His promise to hear them whatever they asked. They prayed in the assurance that the powers of heaven not only could work on earth but also that they would work at the Church's request on its behalf.

Linking with the King

So after more fasting and prayer,
the men laid their hands
on them and sent them on their way.

ACTS 13:3

Acts names five men at Antioch who had dedicated themselves to ministering to the Lord with prayer and fasting. The Holy Spirit met them and gave them insight into God's plans. He called them to be fellow workers with Himself. There was a work to which He called Barnabas and Saul. The five men's part would be to send Barnabus and Saul with renewed fasting and prayer and to let them go, sent forth by the Holy Spirit.

God in heaven would not send His chosen servants without the cooperation of His Church. People on earth were to have a partnership in the work of God. Prayer prepared them for this. The Holy Spirit gave authority to praying Christians to do His work and use His name. It was through prayer the Holy Spirit was given. Prayer is still the only secret of true Church extension—prayer that is guided from heaven to find and send forth God-called and God-empowered men and women.

In answer to prayer the Holy Spirit will indicate the people He has selected. In response to prayer that sets them apart under His guidance, He will give the honor of knowing that they are people sent forth by the Holy Spirit. Prayer links the King on the throne with the Church at His footstool. The Church, the human link, receives its divine strength from the power of the Holy Spirit who comes in answer to prayer.

A Living Connection

Jesus Christ is the same
yesterday, today, and forever.
HEBREWS 13:8

In the history of the Church two great truths stand out. Where there is much prayer, there will be much of the Spirit; where there is much of the Spirit, there will be ever-increasing prayer. When the Spirit is given in answer to prayer, it stimulates more prayer to prepare for a fuller revelation and communication of His divine power and grace. If prayer was the power by which the early Church flourished and triumphed, is it not the one need of the Church today?

Perhaps these should be considered axioms in our ministries:

1. Heaven is still as full of stores of spiritual blessing as it was then.
2. God still delights to give the Holy Spirit to those who ask Him.
3. Our life and work are still as dependent on the direct impartation of divine power as they were in Pentecostal times.
4. Prayer is still the appointed means for drawing down these heavenly blessings in power on ourselves and those around us.
5. God still seeks for men and women who will, with all their other work of ministering, specially give themselves to persevering prayer.

A Model of Intercession

They will pray to the Lord day and night
for the fulfillment of his promises.
Take no rest, all you who pray.
ISAIAH 62:6

"Then, teaching them more about prayer, he [Jesus] used this illustration: 'Suppose you went to a friend's house at midnight, wanting to borrow three loaves of bread. You would say to him, "A friend of mine has just arrived for a visit, and I have nothing for him to eat." He would call out from his bedroom, "Don't bother me. The door is locked for the night, and we are all in bed. I can't help you this time." But I tell you this—though he won't do it as a friend, if you keep knocking long enough, he will get up and give you what you want so his reputation won't be damaged' " (Luke 11:5–8).

Prayer is the one power on earth that commands the power of heaven. The early days of the Church are a great object lesson of what prayer can do. Prayer can pull down the treasures of heaven into earth.

Prayer is both indispensable and irresistible. Unknown blessing is stored up for us in heaven; that power will make us a blessing to men and enable us to do any work or face any danger. It is the one secret of success. It can defy all the power of the world and prepare men to conquer that world for Christ.

In all this prayer there was little thought of personal need or happiness. Rather there was desire to witness for Christ and bring Him and His salvation to others. It was the thought of God's kingdom and glory that possessed these disciples. We, too, must enlarge our hearts for the work in intercession.

The Urgent Need

If you keep knocking long enough,
he will get up and give you what you want
so his reputation won't be damaged.
LUKE 11:8

By intercession our faith, love, and perseverance will be aroused. How may we become more successful in prayer? In the parable of the friend at midnight, Jesus teaches us that intercession for the needy calls forth our power of prevailing prayer. Intercession is the most perfect form of prayer; it is the prayer Christ ever lives to pray on His throne.

Intercession has its origin in urgent need. The friend came at midnight. He was hungry and could not buy bread. If we are to learn to pray as we should, we must open our eyes and hearts to the needs around us.

We hear of the billions of unreached people living in midnight darkness, perishing for lack of the bread of life. We hear of millions of nominal Christians, the majority almost as ignorant and indifferent as the heathen. We see millions in the Church, not indifferent, and yet knowing little of the power of a life fed by bread from heaven. If we believe what we profess, that God certainly will help in answer to prayer, this ought to make intercessors of us. It should motivate us to give our lives to prayer for those around us.

Let's face the need—Christless souls perishing of hunger, while there is bread enough and to spare! Our own neighbors and friends, people entrusted to us, die without hope! Christians around us live fruitless lives! Prayer is needed.

Willing Love

A friend of mine has just arrived for a visit,
and I have nothing for him to eat.
LUKE 11:6

The friend took his weary, hungry friend into his house and into his heart, too. He did not excuse himself by saying he had no bread. At midnight he went out to seek food for him. He sacrificed his night's rest and his comfort to find the needed bread. "Love does not demand its own way" (1 Corinthians 13:5). It is the very nature of love to forget itself for the sake of others. It takes their needs and makes them its own. It finds real joy in living and dying for others as Christ did.

The love of a mother for her prodigal son makes her pray for him. When we have true love for others we will have the spirit of intercession. It is possible to do much faithful and earnest work for others without true love for them. Just as a lawyer or a physician, out of a love of their profession and a high sense of faithfulness to duty, may become deeply involved with the needs of clients or patients without any special love for them, so servants of Christ may give themselves to their work with devotion and self-sacrificing enthusiasm without any strong, Christlike love. It is this lack of love that causes a lack of prayer. Love will compel us to prayer as that love and diligence are combined with the tender compassion of Christ.

The Sense of Inadequacy

"Don't bother me.
The door is locked for the night,
and we are all in bed. I can't help you this time."
LUKE 11:7

We often speak of the power of love. In one sense this is true, and yet the truth has limitations. The strongest love may be utterly inadequate. A mother might be willing to give her life for her dying child but still not be able to save it. The host at midnight was most willing to give his friend bread, but he had none. It was this sense of inadequacy that sent him begging, "A friend of mine has just arrived. . .and I have nothing for him to eat." This sense of inadequacy gives strength to the life of intercession.

"I have nothing for him to eat." As we are aware of our inadequacies, intercession becomes the only hope and refuge. I may have knowledge, a loving heart, and be ready to give myself for those under my charge, but I cannot give them the bread of heaven. With all my love and zeal, still "I have nothing to set before them."

Blessed are you if you have made "I have nothing" the motto of your ministry. You think of the judgment day and the danger of those without Christ and recognize a supernatural power is needed to save people from sin. You feel utterly insufficient—all you can do is to meet their natural need. "I have nothing" motivates you to pray. Intercession appears to you as the only thing in which your love can take refuge.

Faith in Prayer

Suppose you went to a friend's house at midnight wanting to borrow three loaves of bread.
LUKE 11:5

What the man in Luke 11 has not, another can supply. He has a rich friend nearby who will be both able and willing to give the bread. He is sure that if he only asks, he will receive. This faith makes him leave his home at midnight. If he himself has not the bread to give, he can ask another.

We need this simple, confident faith that God will give. Where that faith really exists, there will surely be no possibility of our not praying. In God's Word we have everything that can motivate and strengthen such faith in us. The heaven our natural eye sees is one great ocean of sunshine, with its light and heat giving beauty and fruitfulness to earth. In the same manner, Scripture shows us God's true heaven, which is filled with all spiritual blessings—divine light and love and life, heavenly joy and peace and power—all shining down upon us. It reveals to us our God waiting, even delighting, to bestow these blessings in answer to prayer.

Many promises and testimonies in Scripture call and urge us to believe that prayer will be heard. What we cannot possibly do ourselves for those whom we want to help can be done and received by prayer. Surely there is no question as to our believing that prayer will be heard.

Persistency That Prevails

"Don't bother me.
The door is locked for the night,
and we are all in bed.
I can't help you this time."
LUKE 11:7

The faith of the host in Luke 11 met a sudden and unexpected obstacle—the rich friend refuses to hear: "I can't help you this time." The loving heart had not counted on this disappointment and cannot accept it. The asker presses his threefold plea: Here is my needy friend; you have abundance; I am your friend. Then he refuses to accept a denial. The love that opened his house at midnight and then left it to seek help must conquer.

Here is the central lesson of the parable: in our intercession we may find that there is difficulty and delay in the answer. It may be as if God says, "I can't help you this time." It is not easy to hold fast our confidence that He will hear and then to continue to persevere in full assurance that we shall have what we ask. Even so, this is what God desires from us. He highly prizes our confidence in Him, which is essentially the highest honor the creature can render the Creator. He will therefore do anything to train us in the exercise of this trust in Him. Blessed the man who is not staggered by God's delay or silence or apparent refusal, but is strong in faith giving glory to God. Such faith perseveres, importunately if need be, and cannot fail to inherit the blessing.

Certainty of a Rich Reward

> *But I tell you this—though he won't do it as a friend,*
> *if you keep knocking long enough,*
> *he will get up and give you what you want*
> *so his reputation won't be damaged.*
>
> LUKE 11:8

Oh, that we might believe in the certainty of an abundant answer! Would that all who find it difficult to pray much would focus on the reward and in faith trust the divine assurance that their prayer cannot be in vain.

If we will only believe in God and His faithfulness, intercession will become the very first thing we do when we seek blessing for others. It will be the very last thing for which we cannot find time. It will become a thing of joy and hope because we recognize that we are sowing seed that will bring forth fruit a hundredfold. Disappointment is impossible: "But I tell you this—though he won't do it as a friend, if you keep knocking long enough, he will get up and give you what you want so his reputation won't be damaged" (Luke 11:8).

Time spent in prayer will yield more than time given to work. Only prayer gives work its worth and its success. Prayer opens the way for God Himself to do His work in and through us. Let our primary ministry as God's messengers be intercession; in it we secure the presence and power of God.

"Suppose you went to a friend's house at midnight, wanting to borrow three loaves of bread" (Luke 11:5). This friend is none other than our God. In the darkness of midnight, in the greatest need, when we have to say of those we care for "I have nothing for him to eat," let us remember that we have a rich Friend in heaven.

Start Now

Commission Joshua and encourage him.
DEUTERONOMY 3:28

Let us confess before God our lack of prayer. Lack of prayer is the proof of the lack of faith. It is the symptom of a life that is not spiritual—that is still under the power of self and the flesh and the world. Let us by faith in the Lord Jesus give ourselves to be intercessors. May every sight of those needing help, every stirring of the spirit of compassion, every sense of our own inadequacy to bless, every difficulty in the way of our getting an answer, all combine to urge us to do this one thing: with perseverance cry to God who alone can and will help.

If we indeed feel that we have failed in a life of intercession until now, let us do our utmost to train a young generation of Christians to profit by our mistake and avoid it. Moses could not enter the land of Canaan, but there was one thing he could do. He could at God's bidding "Commission Joshua and encourage him" (Deuteronomy 3:28). If it is too late for us to make good our failure, let us at least encourage those who come after us to enter into the good land, the blessed life of unceasing prayer.

Because of His Persistence

If you keep knocking long enough,
he will get up and give you what you want
so his reputation won't be damaged.

LUKE 11:8

"One day Jesus told his disciples a story to illustrate their need for constant prayer and to show them that they must never give up. Then the Lord said, 'Learn a lesson from this evil judge. Even he rendered a just decision in the end, so don't you think God will surely give justice to his chosen people who plead with him day and night? Will he keep putting them off? I tell you, he will grant justice to them quickly!' " (Luke 18:1, 6–8).

Our Lord Jesus thought it so important for us to know the need of perseverance in prayer that He gave two parables to teach us. This aspect of prayer contains prayer's greatest difficulty and its highest power. In prayer we must expect difficulties which can be conquered only by determined perseverance.

In the first parable Jesus tells us that our Father is more willing to give good things to those who ask than any earthly father is to give his child bread. In the second He assures us that God longs to grant justice to His elect.

Urgent prayer is not needed because God must be made willing. The need lies in ourselves. He uses the unwilling friend and the unjust judge to teach that perseverance can overcome every obstacle.

The difficulty is in our incapacity to receive the blessing. Because of our lack of spiritual preparedness, there is a difficulty with God, too. His wisdom, His righteousness, even His love, dare not give us what would do us harm if we received it too soon or too easily.

A Strengthening Prayer Life

Listen to me! You can pray for anything,
and if you believe, you will have it.
MARK 11:24

The consequence of sin that makes it impossible for God to give at once is a barrier on God's side as well as ours. The attempt to break through the power of sin is what makes the striving and the conflict of prayer such a reality.

Throughout history people have prayed with a sense that there were difficulties in the heavenly world to overcome. They pleaded with God for the removal of the unknown obstacles. In that persevering supplication they were brought into a state of brokenness, of entire resignation to Him, and of faith. Then the hindrances in themselves and in heaven were both overcome. As God prevails over us, we prevail with God.

God has made us so that the more clearly we see the reasonableness of a demand, the more heartily we will surrender to it. One cause of our neglecting prayer is that there appears to be something arbitrary in the call to such continued prayer. This apparent difficulty is a divine necessity and is the source of unspeakable blessing.

Try to understand how the call to perseverance and the difficulty that it throws in our way is one of our greatest privileges. In the very difficulty and delay will the true blessedness of the heavenly life be found. There we learn how little we delight in fellowship with God and how little we have of living faith in Him. There we learn to trust Him fully and without reservation. There we truly come to know Him.

> *He prayed more fervently,*
> *and he was in such agony of spirit that*
> *his sweat fell to the ground*
> *like great drops of blood.*
> LUKE 22:44

Have you ever noticed how much difficulties play a part in our life? They call forth our power as nothing else can. They strengthen character.

All nature has been so arranged by God that nothing is found without work and effort. Education is developing and disciplining the mind by new difficulties which the student must overcome. The moment a lesson has become easy, the student is advanced to one that is more difficult. It is in confronting and mastering difficulties that our highest accomplishments are found.

It is the same in our relationship with God. Imagine what the result would be if the child of God had only to kneel down, ask, get, and go away. Loss to the spiritual life would result. Through difficulties we discover how little we have of God's Holy Spirit. There we learn our own weakness and yield to the Holy Spirit to pray in us. There we take our place in Christ Jesus and abide in Him as our only plea with the Father. There our own will and strength are crucified. There we rise in Christ to newness of life. Praise God for the need and the difficulty of persistent prayer as one of His choice means of grace.

Think what Jesus owed to the difficulties in His path. He persevered in prayer in Gethsemane and the prince of this world with all his temptation was overcome.

Persistence in Prayer

You can pray for anything,
and if you believe,
you will have it.
MARK 11:24

Persistence has various elements—the main ones are persever-
ance, determination, and intensity. It begins with the refusal to
readily accept denial. This develops into a determination to per-
severe, to spare no time or trouble, until an answer comes. This
grows in intensity until the whole being is given to God in sup-
plication. Boldness comes to lay hold of God's strength. At one
time it is quiet; at another, bold. At one point it waits in patience,
but at another, it claims at once what it desires. In whatever dif-
ferent shape, persistence always means and knows that God
hears prayer; I must be heard.

Think of Abraham as he pleads for Sodom. Time after time
he renews his prayer until he has to say, "Please don't be angry,
my Lord" (Genesis 18:30). He does not cease until he has
learned how far he can go, has entered into God's mind, and has
rested in God's will. For his sake Lot was saved. "God had lis-
tened to Abraham's request and kept Lot safe" (Genesis 19:29).

Think of Jacob when he feared to meet Esau. The angel of
the Lord met him and wrestled with him. When the angel saw
that he did not prevail, he said, "Let me go." Jacob said, "I will
not let you go" (Genesis 32:26). So the angel blessed him
there. That boldness pleased God so much that a new name
was given to Jacob: Israel, he who strives with God, "because
you have struggled with both God and men and have won"
(Genesis 32:28).

Pray and Prevail

The earnest prayer of a righteous person
has great power and wonderful results.
JAMES 5:16

When Israel had made the golden calf, Moses returned to the Lord and said, "Alas, these people have committed a terrible sin. . . . But now, please forgive their sin—and if not, then blot me out of the record you are keeping" (Exodus 32:31–32). That was persistence. Moses would rather have died than not have his people forgiven.

When God had heard him and said He would send His angel with the people, Moses came again. He would not be content until, in answer to his prayer, God himself should go with them. God had said, "I will indeed do what you have asked" (Exodus 33:17). After that in answer to Moses' prayer, "Let me see your glorious presence" (Exodus 33:18), God made His goodness pass before him. Then Moses at once began pleading, "O Lord, then please go with us" (Exodus 34:9). "Moses was up on the mountain with the Lord forty days and forty nights" (Exodus 34:28).

Moses was persistent with God and prevailed. He proves that the person who truly lives near to God shares in the same power of intercession which there is in Jesus.

James teaches us to pray for each other. "The earnest prayer of a righteous person has great power and wonderful results." Praise God! He still waits for us to seek Him. Faith in a prayer-hearing God will make a prayer-loving Christian.

The Mark of a Praying Christian

*The earnest prayer of a righteous person
has great power and wonderful results.*
JAMES 5:16

Remember the marks of the true intercessor: a sense of the need of those without Christ, a Christlike love, an awareness of personal inadequacy, faith in the power of prayer, courage to persevere in spite of refusal, and the assurance of an abundant reward. These are the qualities that change a Christian into an intercessor.

These are the elements that mark the Christian life with beauty and health. They fit a person for being a blessing in the world. These are the attitudes that call forth the heroic virtues of the life of faith.

Nothing shows more nobility of character than the spirit of enterprise and daring which battles major difficulties and conquers. So should we who are Christians be able to face the difficulties that we meet in prayer. As we "work" and "strive" in prayer, the renewed will asserts its royal right to claim what it will in the name of Christ.

We should fight our way through to the place where we can find liberty for the captive and salvation for the perishing. The blessings which the world needs must be called down from heaven in persevering, believing prayer.

Our work is often insignificant due to our little prayer. Let us change our method and make unceasing prayer be the proof that we look to God for everything and that we believe that He hears us.

The Life That Can Pray

I chose you.
I appointed you to go and produce fruit that will last,
so that the Father will give you
whatever you ask for, using my name.
JOHN 15:16

Our power in prayer depends upon our life. When our life is right, we will know how to pray in a way pleasing to God, and our prayer will be answered. "If you stay joined to me," our Lord says, "you may ask any request you like, and it will be granted" (John 15:7). According to James it is the prayer of a righteous man that "has great power and wonderful results" (James 5:16).

In the parable of the vine Jesus taught that the healthy, vigorous Christian may ask what he or she wishes and will receive it. He says, "If you stay joined to me and my words remain in you, you may ask any request you like, and it will be granted." Again He says, "You didn't choose me. I chose you. I appointed you to go and produce fruit that will last, so that the Father will give you whatever you ask for, using my name" (John 15:16).

What life must one lead to bear fruit? What must a person be in order to pray with results? What must one do to receive what he or she asks? The answer is simple. Live as a branch depending on the vine for strength. The source of power in prayer is the vine. If we are branches, abiding in Christ, the vine, He will supply the power. If we trust the vine, then we can ask what we wish and it will be granted.

Bearing Fruit

*The earnest prayer of a righteous person
has great power and wonderful results.*
JAMES 5:16

A branch is a growth of the vine, produced to bear fruit. It has only one purpose: that through it the vine may bear and ripen its fruit. As the vine lives to produce the sap that makes the grape, so the branch receives that sap and bears the grape. Its work is to serve the vine so that, through the branch, the vine may do its work.

The believer, the branch of Christ the heavenly Vine, is to live exclusively so Christ may bear fruit through him. A true Christian is to be devoted to the work of bearing fruit to the glory of God.

With our life abiding in Him, and His words abiding and ruling in our heart, there will be grace to pray as we should and faith to receive whatever we ask.

The promises of our Lord's farewell discourse appear to us too large to be taken literally. We rationalize them to meet our human ideas of what we think they ought to be. We separate them from the life of devotion to Christ's service for which they were given.

God's covenant is: give all and take all. One who is willing to be nothing but a branch of Christ, the Vine, will receive liberty to claim Christ's riches in all their fullness and the wisdom and humility to use them properly.

Ask and It Will Be Done

> *Dear friends, if our conscience is clear,*
> *we can come to God with bold confidence.*
> 1 JOHN 3:21

Think for a moment of the men of prayer in Scripture and see in them lives that could pray in power. Abraham was an intercessor. What gave him such boldness? He knew that God had called him away from his home and people to walk with Him so that all nations might be blessed in him. He knew that he had obeyed and forsaken all for God. Implicit obedience, to the very sacrifice of his son, was the law of his life. He did what God asked, so he dared to trust God to do what he asked.

Moses was an intercessor. He too had forsaken all for God and lived at God's disposal. Often it is written of him that he did what the Lord commanded. No wonder he was very bold. His heart was right with God. He knew God would hear him.

We only pray the way we live. God longs to prove himself the faithful God and mighty helper of His people. He waits to answer praying hearts wholly turned from the world and to Himself.

The branch that abides in Christ, the heavenly Vine, will bear fruit in the salvation of others. Such people may dare ask what they will—and it shall be done.

Pruning for Prayer

*He prunes the branches that do bear fruit
so they will produce even more.*
JOHN 15:2

The more aware we become of our inability to pray in power,
the more we are helped to press on toward the secret of power
in prayer. Jesus said, "I am the true vine, and my Father is the
gardener" (John 15:1). We not only have Jesus Himself. We
have the Father, as the husbandman, watching over our growth
and fruit-bearing. It is not left to our faith. God himself will see
to it that the branch is what it should be. He will enable us to
bring forth just the fruit we were appointed to bear. "He prunes
the branches that do bear fruit so they will produce even more."
The Father seeks more fruit. More fruit is what the Father Him-
self will provide.

Of all fruit-bearing plants there is none that produces so
much wild wood as the vine. Every year it must be pruned. It is
like this for the Christian. The branch that desires to abide in
Christ and bring forth fruit must yield itself to divine cleansing.

The gardener cuts away true, honest wood that the branch
has produced. It must be pruned because it draws away the
strength of the vine and hinders the flow of the juice to the
grape. The luxuriant growth of wood must be cast away so that
abundant life may be seen in the cluster.

There are things in you that sap away your interest and
strength. They must be pruned. Pruning results in a life that
can pray.

Is Prayerlessness Sin?

I will not remain with you any longer
unless you destroy the things among you
that were set apart for destruction.
JOSHUA 7:12

If we are to deal effectively with the lack of prayer, we must ask, "Is it sin?" Jesus is Savior from sin. When we experience sin, we can know the power that saves from sin. The life that can pray effectively is one that knows deliverance from the power of sin. But is prayerlessness sin?

Experiencing the presence of God is the great privilege of God's people and their power against the enemy. Throughout Scripture the central promise is that God is with us. The whole-hearted person lives consciously in God's presence.

Defeat and failure are due to the loss of God's presence. This was true at Ai. God brought His people into Canaan with the promise of victory. With the defeat at Ai, Joshua knew that the cause must be the withdrawal of God's power. God had not fought for them.

In the Christian life defeat is a sign of the loss of God's presence. If we apply this to our failure in prayer, we see that it is because we are not in full fellowship with God.

The loss of God's presence is due to sin. Just as pain is nature's warning of a physical problem, defeat is God's voice telling us there is something wrong. He has given himself wholly to His people. He delights in being with them. He never withdraws himself unless they compel Him to do so by sin.

Revealed Sin

As for me, I will certainly not sin against the LORD
by ending my prayers for you.
And I will continue to teach you what is good and right.
1 SAMUEL 12:23

We may think we know what sin is keeping us from prayer, but only God can truly reveal it. For example, after the defeat at Ai, He spoke to Joshua. "Israel has sinned and broken my covenant." Israel had sinned. God himself revealed it.

God must reveal to us that the lack of prayer is a greater sin than we have thought. It means we have little taste for fellowship with God. Our faith rests more on our own work than on the power of God. We are not ready to sacrifice ease for time with God.

When the pressure of work becomes the excuse for not finding time in His presence, there is no sense of absolute dependence upon God. There is no full surrender to Christ.

If we would yield to God's Spirit, all our excuses would fall away and we would admit that we had sinned. Samuel once said, "As for me, I will certainly not sin against the LORD by ending my prayers for you. And I will continue to teach you what is good and right" (1 Samuel 12:23). Ceasing from prayer is sin against God.

When God discloses sin it must be confessed and cast out. If we have reason to think prayerlessness is the sin that is in "our camp," let us begin with personal and united confession. With God's help let us put away and destroy the sin. Then we can know His presence and power.

God's Presence Restored

Restore to me again the joy of your salvation.
PSALM 51:12

When sin is cast out, God's presence is restored. This truth is so simple. God's presence restored means victory secured. Then, if there is defeat, we are responsible for it. Sin somewhere is causing it. We need to discover the sin and repent. The moment the sin is put away, we may confidently expect God's presence.

God never speaks to His people of sin except with the purpose of saving them from it. The same light that shows the sin will show the way out of it. The same power that condemns will give the power to rise up and conquer.

God is speaking to us about this sin: "He was amazed to see that no one intervened to help the oppressed" (Isaiah 59:16). The God who says this will work the change in His children when they seek His face. He will make the shame of sin confessed a door of hope. Let us simply confess that we have sinned; we dare not sin any longer.

In the matter of prayer God does not demand impossibilities. He does not give us an impracticable ideal. He does not ask us to pray without giving the grace to enable us to do so. Believe Him. He will give the grace to do what He asks.

The Secret of Effective Prayer

You can pray for anything,
and if you believe, you will have it.
MARK 11:24

The more we enter into the mind of our Lord and think about prayer as He thinks, the more His words will grow in us. They will produce in us their fruit—a life corresponding to the truth they contain. Christ, the living Word of God, gives in His words a power which brings into existence what they say. This power accomplishes in us what He asks. It equips us for what He demands. View His teaching on prayer as a promise of what He, by His Holy Spirit, is going to build into your character.

The Lord gives us the five essential elements of prayer.

— the heart's desire
— the expression of that desire in prayer
— the faith that carries the prayer to God
— the acceptance of God's answer
— the experience of the desired blessing.

Each Christian can say, "I want to ask and receive in faith the power to pray just in the way and just as much as my God expects of me." During the next few days let us meditate on our Lord's words in the confidence that He will teach us how to pray for this blessing.

Desire

> *You can pray for anything,*
> *and if you believe, you will have it.*
> MARK 11:24

Desire is the power that moves our whole world and directs the course of each person. Desire is the soul of prayer. The cause of insufficient prayer is often the lack of desire. Some may doubt this. They are sure they have earnestly desired what they ask. But if they judge whether their desire has been as wholehearted as God would have it, they may see that it was the lack of desire that caused the failure.

What is true of God is true of each of His blessings. "If you look for me in earnest, you will find me when you seek me" (Jeremiah 29:13).

We may have a strong desire for spiritual blessings. But alongside them are other desires occupying a large place in our interests. The spiritual desires are not all-absorbing. We are puzzled that our prayer is not heard. It is because God wants the whole heart. If there are desires which occupy more of our heart than He Himself, the desires that we are praying for cannot be granted.

We desire the gift of intercession, grace and power to pray as we should. Our hearts must give up other desires; we must give ourselves wholly to this one. By focusing on the blessedness of this grace, by believing with certainty that God will give it to us, desire may be strengthened. The first step will have been taken toward the possession of the desired blessing.

Express Your Desires

You can pray for anything,
and if you believe, you will have it.
MARK 11:24

The desire of the heart must become the expression of the lips. The Lord Jesus more than once asked those who cried out to Him what they wanted. He wanted them to say what they desired. To declare it brought them into contact with Him and wakened their expectation. To pray is to enter into God's presence, to have distinct dealing with Him, to commit our need to Him and to leave it there. In so doing we become fully conscious of what we are seeking.

There are some who often carry strong desires in their heart but don't bring them to God in a clear expression of repeated prayer. There are others who go to the Word and its promises to strengthen their faith but do not pointedly ask God to fulfill them. Therefore their heart does not gain the assurance that the matter has been put into God's hands. Still others come in prayer with so many requests and desires that it is difficult for them to say what they really expect God to do.

If you want God to give you this gift of faithfulness in prayer and power to pray as you should, begin to pray about it. Declare to yourself and to God.

Faith

> *You can pray for anything,*
> *and if you believe,*
> *you will have it.*
> MARK 11:24

It is only by faith that we receive Jesus Christ or live the Christian life. Faith also is the power of prayer. If we are to have our prayer for the grace of prayer answered, we must begin to pray in faith as never before.

Faith is the opposite of sight. They are contrary to each other. "We live by believing and not by seeing" (2 Corinthians 5:7). If heart and prayer are to be full of faith, we must withdraw from the visible. The person that seeks to enjoy life, who gives first place to the duties of daily life, is inconsistent with a strong faith.

"We don't look at the troubles we can see right now." The negative action needs to be emphasized if the positive "rather, we look forward to what we have not yet seen" (2 Corinthians 4:18) is to become natural to us. In praying, faith depends upon our living in the invisible world.

The reason for our lack of faith is our lack of knowledge of God and communion with Him. Jesus said to have faith in God when He spoke of removing mountains. When a soul knows God and allows the light of God to illuminate his life, unbelief will become impossible. All the mysteries connected with answers to prayer—however little we may be able to solve them intellectually—will be swallowed up in the assurance that this God is our God. He does answer prayer. He will delight to give the grace to pray that I am asking for.

Accept the Answer

You can pray for anything,
and if you believe,
you will have it.
MARK 11:24

Faith must accept the answer given by God in heaven before it is found on earth. This is the essence of believing prayer. Spiritual things can only be spiritually grasped. The spiritual blessing of God's answer to your prayer must be accepted in your spirit before you see it physically. Faith does this.

A person who not only seeks an answer, but first seeks after the God who gives the answer, receives the power to know that he has obtained what he has asked. If he knows that he has asked according to God's will, he believes that he has received.

There is nothing so heart-searching as this faith, "if you believe, you will have it." As we strive to believe, and find we cannot, we are compelled to discover what hinders us. Blessed are those who, with their eyes on God alone, refuse to rest till they have believed what our Lord bids. Here is the place where faith prevails, and prevailing prayer is born out of human weakness. Here enters the real need for persevering prayer that will not rest or go away or give up till it knows it is heard and believes that it has received.

Experience the Blessing

*You can pray for anything,
and if you believe,
you will have it.*
MARK 11:24

Receiving from God in faith the answer with perfect assurance that it has been given, is not necessarily the possession of the gift we have asked for. At times there may be a long interval before we have it physically. In other cases we may enjoy at once what we have received. When the interval is long we have need of faith and patience. We need faith to rejoice in the assurance of the answer bestowed and to begin to act upon that answer though for the present there is no visible proof of its presence.

We can apply this principle to our prayer for the power to be faithful intercessors. Hold fast to the divine assurance that as surely as we believe, we receive. Rejoice in the certainty of an answered prayer. The more we praise God for it, the sooner will the experience come. We may begin at once to pray for others in the confidence that grace will be given us to pray with more perseverance and more faith than we have done before.

If we do not find an immediate increase in our desire to pray, this must not discourage us. We have accepted a spiritual gift by faith; in that faith we are to pray, doubting nothing. We may count upon the Holy Spirit to pray in us, even though it is with groanings which cannot find expression. In due time we shall become conscious of His presence and power.

The Spirit's Presence

And be sure of this:
I am with you always,
even to the end of the age.
MATTHEW 28:20

When the Lord chose His twelve disciples, it was "to be his regular companions" and that He might "send them out to preach" (Mark 3:14). A life in fellowship with Him was to be their preparation for fulfilling the Great Commission.

When Christ spoke of His leaving them to go to the Father, their hearts were filled with great sorrow. The presence of Christ had become indispensable to them; they could not think of living without Him. To comfort them, Christ gave them the promise of the Holy Spirit, which would be a heavenly presence far more intimate than they had ever known.

Unbroken fellowship with Him was the power the disciples would need to preach and to testify of Him. When Christ gave them the Great Commission to go into all the world and preach the gospel to every creature, He added the words: "And be sure of this: I am with you always, even to the end of the age."

This principle forever holds true for all His servants. Without the experience of His presence always abiding with us, our daily walk will have no power. The secret of our strength is in the Spirit of Jesus Christ being with us every moment, inspiring and directing and strengthening us. As you pray, be deeply convinced of Christ's words: "And be sure of this: I am with you always."

The Omnipotence of Christ

I have been given complete authority
in heaven and on earth.
MATTHEW 28:18

Before Christ gave His disciples their Great Commission, He first revealed Himself in His resurrected power as a partner with God Himself. It was the faith of this that enabled the disciples to undertake their mission with boldness.

Just think of what the disciples had learned of the power of Christ Jesus when He was here on earth. Yet that was little compared with the greater works that He would do in and through them. Christ provided the power to work even in the feeblest of His servants with the strength of the almighty God.

We too are to count literally upon the daily experience of being "strong with the Lord's mighty power" (Ephesians 6:10). But remember, this power is never meant to be experienced as if it were our own. It is only as Jesus Christ as a living person dwells and works within our own heart and life that there can be power in our prayer and personal testimony. It was when Christ had said to Paul, "My power works best in your weakness" that he could say what he had never learned to say before: "When I am weak, then am I strong" (2 Corinthians 12:9–10). It is the disciple of Christ who truly understands that all power has been entrusted to Christ and that we must receive that power from Him hour by hour.

The Omnipresence of Christ

I will be with you.
EXODUS 3:12

When Christ said to His disciples, "I have been given complete authority in heaven and on earth," the promise immediately followed, "I am with you always" (Matthew 28:18, 20). The Omnipotent One is truly the Omnipresent One. The writer of Psalm 139 speaks of God's omnipresence as something beyond his comprehension: "Such knowledge is too wonderful for me, too great for me to know!" (verse 6).

The revelation of God's omnipresence in the man Christ Jesus makes the mystery still deeper. The fact that we can experience this presence every moment is inexpressibly wonderful. And yet many of us find it difficult to understand all that Christ's presence implies and how, through prayer, it can become the practical experience of our daily life.

When Christ says "always," He means to give us the assurance that there should never be a moment in which that presence cannot be our experience. Yet, it does not depend upon what we can effect, but upon what He undertakes to do.

The omnipotent Christ is indeed the omnipresent Christ. His promise to us is: "I am with you always." Let your faith in Christ, the Omnipresent One, be in the quiet confidence that He will be with you every day and every moment. Meet Him in prayer, and let His presence be your strength for service.

Christ the Savior of the World

He is indeed the Savior of the world.
JOHN 4:42

Omnipotence and omnipresence are what are called natural attributes of God. They have their true worth only when linked to and inspired by His moral attributes, holiness, and love. What lies at the root of these attributes is His divine glory as the Savior of the world and Redeemer of all men. It was because He humbled Himself and became obedient unto death that God so highly exalted Him. His share in the attributes of God was owing to the work He had done in His perfect obedience to the will of God. His finished redemption made salvation possible for humanity.

It is only when His servants demonstrate that they obey Him in all His commands that they can expect the fullness of His power and His presence to be with them. It is only when they are living witnesses to Christ's redemptive power to save and to keep from sin that they can experience His abiding presence. Then they will have the power to train others to the life of obedience that He asks.

The abiding presence of our Savior is promised to all who have accepted Him in the fullness of His redeeming power. What a privilege to meet in prayer with the One who has redeemed us. Our lives and words should proclaim to the world what a wonderful Savior He is.

Christ Crucified

God forbid that I should boast about anything
except the cross of our Lord Jesus Christ.
GALATIANS 6:14

Christ's highest glory is His Cross. It was in this that He glorified the Father and the Father glorified Him. In the fifth chapter of Revelation, Christ receives the worship of the ransomed and the angels and all creation. And it is as the Crucified One that His servants have learned to say: "God forbid that I should boast about anything except the cross of our Lord Jesus Christ." Is it not reasonable that Christ's highest glory should be our only glory, too?

It is the crucified Jesus who promises, "I am with you always" (Matthew 28:20). One reason why we may find it so difficult to expect and enjoy His abiding presence is because we do not glory in the cross. We have been crucified with Christ; our "old sinful selves were crucified with Christ" (Romans 6:6). This means we are crucified to the world and are free from its power. Consequently, we are to deny ourselves—to have the mind that was in Christ. He emptied Himself and took the form of a servant. He humbled Himself and became obedient even to the death of the Cross.

As we pray, it is the crucified Christ who comes to walk with us and in whose power we are to live the life that can say: "Christ crucified lives in me."

Christ Glorified

*For the Lamb who stands in front of
the throne will be their Shepherd.*
REVELATION 7:17

"And be sure of this: I am with you always" (Matthew 28:20).
Who is it that speaks these words? We must take time to know
Him well if we are to understand what we can expect from Him
as He offers to be with us every day. Who is He? None other
than the Lamb who had been slain in the midst of the throne!
The Lamb in His deepest humiliation is enthroned in the glory
of God. This is He who invites me to the closest fellowship
with Himself.

It takes time in adoring worship and prayer to come under
the full impression that Christ, before whom all heaven bows, is
the one who offers to be my companion. He desires to lead me
like a shepherd and to make me one of those who follows Him
wherever He goes.

Read Revelation 5 until your heart is possessed by the
thought that all heaven falls prostrate before Christ, and the eld-
ers cast their crowns before the throne. The Lamb reigns amid
the praises and the love of His ransomed ones and the praises of
all creation. And if this is He who comes to me in my daily life
and offers to walk with me, I cannot expect Him to abide with
me unless my heart bows in surrender to a life of prayer, praise,
and service.

The Great Question

Jesus asked them,
"Do you believe I can make you see?"
"Yes, Lord," they told him, "we do."
MATTHEW 9:28

"Jesus told her. . .'Those who believe in me, even though they die like everyone else, will live again. . . . Do you believe this?' 'Yes, Lord,'" she told Him. From what we have seen and heard of Christ Jesus, our heart is ready to say with Martha: "I have always believed you are the Messiah, the Son of God, the one who has come into the world from God" (John 11:25–27). But when it comes to believing Christ's promise to us of His abiding presence, we do not find it so easy to say, "I believe." Yet it is this faith that Christ desires to work within us.

We must understand clearly what the conditions are on which Christ offers to reveal to us the secret of His abiding presence. God will not force His blessings on us against our will. He seeks in every possible way to stir our desire and to help us to realize that He is able and willing to make His promises true. The resurrection of Christ from the dead is His great, all-prevailing evidence.

Now the great question is whether we are willing to take Him at His word and rest in the promise: "I am with you always." Christ's question to us is: "Do you believe?" Let us not rest until we have bowed before Him in prayer and said: "Yes, Lord, I do believe."

Christ Revealing Himself

> *Those who obey my commandments are*
> *the ones who love me. And because they love me,*
> *my Father will love them, and I will love them.*
>
> JOHN 14:21

Christ had promised the disciples that the Holy Spirit would come to reveal His presence with them. When the Spirit came, Christ showed Himself to them in a new, spiritual way. They would know Him far more intimately than they ever had while He was on earth.

The condition of this revelation of Himself is based on one word—love: "Those who obey my commandments are the ones who love me. And because they love me, my Father will love them, and I will love them." This is the meeting of Divine and human love. The love with which Christ had loved them had taken possession of their hearts, and they would demonstrate that love by full and absolute obedience. The Father would see this, and Christ would respond to their loving hearts by revealing Himself to them.

But Christ doesn't just promise to reveal Himself to us. He also promises to dwell in the heart that loves Him. "My Father will love them, and we will come to them and live with them" (John 14:23). It is within the heart that is fully surrendered, showing itself in love and obedience, that the Father and the Son will take up residence.

Christ's promise remains the same today: "And be sure of this: I am with you always." Oh, that everyone would believe and prayerfully claim the blessed promise: "I will reveal myself to each one of them."

Mary: The Morning Watch

"Mary," Jesus said.
She turned toward him
and exclaimed, "Teacher!"
JOHN 20:16

Here we have the first manifestation of the risen Savior—to Mary Magdalene, the woman who loved Jesus so much.

Think of what the morning watch meant to Mary. Is it not a proof of the intense longing of a love that would not rest until it had found the Lord? It meant a separation from all else in her longing to find Christ. It meant the struggle of fear against a faith that refused to let go its hold of Christ's wonderful promise: "Those who obey my commandments are the ones who love me. . .and I will love them. And I will reveal myself to each one of them" (John 14:21).

That first morning watch, waiting in prayer for the risen Lord to reveal Himself, has been a joy to thousands of souls! With a burning love and strong hope, they wait for Jesus to manifest Himself as the Lord of Glory. There they learn to dwell in the keeping of His abiding presence.

There is nothing that can prove a greater attraction to our Lord than the love that sacrifices everything and rests satisfied with nothing less than Himself. It is to such a love that Christ reveals Himself. He loved us and gave Himself for us. It is to our love that He speaks the word: "And be sure of this: I am with you always" (Matthew 28:20). It is love that accepts, rejoices, and lives in that word.

Emmaus: The Evening Prayer

> As they sat down to eat. . .
> Suddenly, their eyes were opened,
> and they recognized him.
>
> LUKE 24:31

Mary teaches us what the morning watch can mean for the revelation of Jesus to the soul. Emmaus reminds us of the place that the evening prayer has in preparing for the full manifestation of Christ in the soul.

When Jesus Himself approached the two disciples as they traveled, they did not recognize Him. But as the Lord spoke with them, their hearts began to burn within them. Yet they never thought that it might be Christ Himself. How often does Jesus come near with the purpose of manifesting Himself to us, and yet we don't see Him?

When Jesus told the two disciples He must continue on His journey, their plea to spend the night caused Him to stay. We, too, should reserve time toward the end of the day when our whole heart prays with the urgency that constrains Him.

So what was it that led our Lord to reveal Himself to these two men? Nothing less than this: their intense devotion to their Lord. There may be much ignorance and unbelief, but if there is a burning desire that longs for Christ, He will make Himself known to us. In such intense devotion and constraining prayer, the Lord will open our eyes and we will know Him and enjoy the secret of His abiding presence.

The Disciples: Their Divine Mission

Suddenly, Jesus was standing there among them!
"Peace be with you," he said.
JOHN 20:19

The disciples had received Mary's message of Christ's resurrection. Late in the evening the men from Emmaus told how He had been made known to them. Now their hearts were prepared for when Jesus stood in their midst and said, "Peace be unto you" and showed them His hands and His feet. "They were filled with joy when they saw their Lord! He spoke to them again and said, 'Peace be with you. As the Father has sent me, so I send you'" (John 20:20–21).

With Mary, He revealed Himself to her fervent love that could not rest without Him. With the men at Emmaus, it was their constraining prayer that received the revelation. Here He meets the willing servants whom He had trained for His service. He changes their fear into boldness to carry out the work the Father had entrusted to them.

For this divine work they needed nothing less than Divine power. He breathed upon them the resurrection life and fulfilled the promise He gave: "For I will live again, and you will, too" (John 14:19).

The word is spoken to us, too: "As the Father has sent me, so I send you. . . . Receive the Holy Spirit" (John 20:21–22). If our hearts are set on nothing less than the presence of the living Lord, we can be confident that it will be given to us. Jesus never sends His servants out without the promise of His abiding presence and His almighty power.

Thomas: The Blessedness of Believing

Blessed are those who haven't seen me and believe anyway.

JOHN 20:29

Christ revealed Himself and allowed Thomas to touch His hands and His side. No wonder Thomas could find no words but those of holy adoration: "My Lord and my God." And yet Christ said: "You believe because you have seen me. Blessed are those who haven't seen me and believe anyway."

True, living faith gives a far deeper and more intimate sense of Christ's divine nearness than even the joy that filled the heart of Thomas. Thomas had proved his intense devotion to Christ when he said, "Let's go, too—and die with Jesus" (John 11:16). To such a love, even when it was struggling with unbelief, Jesus Christ revealed Himself.

We, too, can experience the presence and power of Christ in a far deeper reality than Thomas did. To those who have not seen Jesus and yet believe, He has promised that He will reveal Himself and that the Father and He will come and dwell in them.

Yet, we, are often inclined to think of this full life of faith as something beyond our reach. Such a thought robs us of the power to believe. Take prayerful hold of Christ's word: "Blessed are those who haven't seen me and believe anyway." This blessing only comes by the faith that receives the love and the presence of the living Lord.

Peter: The Greatness of Love

He said, "Lord, you know everything.
You know I love you."
Jesus said, "Then feed my sheep."
JOHN 21:17

In Christ's appearances after His death, it was to the intense devotion of the prepared heart that He revealed Himself. Now in the manifestation of Himself to Peter, it is again love that is the keynote.

We can easily understand why Christ asked the question three times, "Do you love me?" It was to remind Peter of the terrible self-confidence in which he had said: "No, not even if I have to die with you! I will never deny you!" (Matthew 26:35). Peter was clearly in need of prayerful soul-searching so he could be sure that his love was true. He needed to understand that true love was the one thing needed for the full restoration to his place in the heart of Jesus.

God is love. Christ is the Son of His love. "I have loved you even as the Father has loved me" (John 15:9). Jesus asked that His disciples prove their love to Him by keeping His commandments and loving each other.

To everyone who longs to have Jesus reveal Himself, the essential requirement is love. Peter teaches us that such love it is not in the power of man to offer. If the self-confident Peter could be changed so dramatically, we must believe that Christ will work that change in us, too. He will then reveal Himself to that loving heart in all the fullness of His precious word: "And be sure of this: I am with you always" (Matthew 28:20).

John: Life from the Dead

> Don't be afraid!
> I am the First and the Last.
> I am the living one who died.
> Look, I am alive forever and ever!
> REVELATION 1:17–18

Sixty or more years after the Resurrection, Christ revealed Himself to the beloved disciple. John immediately fell as dead at His feet. We learn from this that man's sinful nature cannot see the vision of the divine glory and live. It needs the death of the natural life in order for the life of God to enter in.

Christ then laid His hand on John and said, "Don't be afraid! . . .I am the living one who died. Look, I am alive forever and ever!" He reminded John that He, too, had passed through death so He could rise to the life and the glory of God. For the Master Himself and for every disciple, there is only one way to the glory of God—death to sin and self.

This lesson is a necessary one. Fellowship with Jesus—and the experience of His living power—is not possible without the sacrifice of all that there is in us of the world and its sin. The disciples experienced this reality when Christ made this great charge to them: deny self, bear the cross, and follow Me.

Let us accept this lesson—through death to life. Since Christ's death now works in us, we must yield ourselves in prayer to His power and let Him live in and through us.

Paul: Christ Revealed in Him

For it pleased God in his kindness
to choose me and call me. . . .
Then he revealed his Son to me.
GALATIANS 1:15–16

Paul tells us that it pleased God to reveal His Son in him. He gives his testimony to the result of that revelation: "Christ lives in me" (Galatians 2:20). The chief mark of that life is that he is crucified with Christ. This enables him to say, "I no longer live." In Christ Paul had found the death of self. Just as the cross is the chief characteristic of Christ, so the life of Christ in Paul made him inseparably one with his crucified Lord. So completely was this the case that he could say: "God forbid that I should boast about anything except the cross of our Lord Jesus Christ. Because of that cross, my interest in this world died long ago" (Galatians 6:14).

So if Christ actually lived in Paul so that he no longer lived, what became of his responsibility? His answer was clear: "I live my life in this earthly body by trusting in the Son of God, who loved me and gave himself for me" (Galatians 2:20). Paul's life was a life of faith in Christ who had loved him and had given Himself completely for him. Consequently, Christ had undertaken at all times to be the life of His willing disciple.

The indwelling Christ was the secret of his life of faith, his power in prayer, the one aim of all his life and work. Let us believe in the abiding presence of Christ as the sure gift to each one who trusts Him fully.

Why Could We Not?

But this kind of demon won't leave unless
you have prayed and fasted.
MATTHEW 17:21

The disciples had often cast out demons. But here they had been powerless. They asked the Lord what the reason might be. His answer is very simple: "You didn't have enough faith."

How is it that we cannot live that life of unbroken fellowship with Christ which the Scripture promises? Simply because of our unbelief. We do not realize that faith must accept and expect that God will, by His almighty power, fulfill every promise He has made. We do not live in that utter helplessness and dependence on God alone which is the very essence of faith. We are not strong in the faith, fully persuaded that what God has promised He is able and willing to perform.

But what is the reason why this faith is so often lacking? "But this kind of demon won't leave unless you have prayed and fasted." To have a strong faith in God requires a life in close touch with Him by persistent prayer. We cannot call up faith at our bidding; it needs close communion with God through prayer. It needs the denial of self—the sacrifice of a worldly heart. Just as we need God to give us faith and power, He, too, needs our whole being to be utterly given up to Him. Prayer and fasting are essential to this.

The Power of Obedience

And the one who sent me is with me—
he has not deserted me.
For I always do those things that are pleasing to him.
JOHN 8:29

In these words Christ tells us what His life with the Father was. At the same time He reveals the law of all communion with God—simple obedience.

In John 14 He says three times: "If you love me, obey my commandments" (vs. 15, 21, 23); also in chapter 15: "When you obey me, you remain in my love, just as I obey my Father and remain in his love. You are my friends if you obey me" (vs. 10, 14).

Obedience is the proof and the exercise of the love of God in our hearts. It comes from love and leads to love. It assures us that we are abiding in the love of Christ. It seals our claim to be called the friends of Christ. So it is not only a proof of love but of faith, too. It assures us that we "will receive whatever we request because we obey him and do the things that please him" (1 John 3:22).

Obedience enables us to abide in His love and gives us the full experience of His unbroken presence. It is to the obedient that the word comes: "And be sure of this: I am with you always" (Matthew 28:20) and to whom all the fullness of its meaning will be revealed.

The Power of Intercession

*Then we can spend our time in prayer
and preaching and teaching the word.*
ACTS 6:4

In his travels throughout Asia, Dr. Mott was moved by the need for united prayer in the missionary endeavor. He writes: "There is no better way to serve the deepest interest of the Church than by multiplying the number of real intercessors and by focusing their prayers on those situations which demand the almighty working of the Spirit of God. Far more important than any service we can give to missions is that of helping to release the superhuman energy of prayer. Immeasurably more important than any other work is the linking of all we do to the fountain of divine life and energy. The Christian world not only has a right to expect mission leaders to set forth the facts and methods of the work, but also a larger discovery of superhuman resources and spiritual power."

And where is there a greater need of focusing the united intercession of Christians than on the great army of missionaries? They tell of their need for the presence and the power of God's Spirit in their life and work. They long for the experience of the abiding presence and power of Christ every day. They need it; they have a right to it. Shouldn't we become a part of that great army that pleads with God for the power which is so absolutely necessary for effective work?

The Power of Time

My times are in thy hand.
PSALM 31:15 KJV

"My time is in Your hand. It belongs to You. You alone have a right to command it. I yield it wholly and gladly to Your disposal." What mighty power time can exert if wholly given up to God!

Time is lord of all things. The history of the world is proof of how, slowly but surely, time has made man what he is today. All around us we see the proofs, such as the growth of a child to manhood. It is under the law of time and its inconceivable power that we spend our lives.

This is especially true in communion with God—all on the one condition: that we have sufficient time with God. Yet we often confess the weakness of our spiritual life and the inadequate results of our work. This is due to the failure to take time for daily communion with God.

What can be the cause of this sad confession? Nothing less than a lack of faith in the God-given assurance that time spent alone with Him will indeed bring into our lives the power to do His work.

Through prayer, submit your timetable to the inspection of Christ and His Holy Spirit. A new life will be yours if you fully believe and put into daily practice the word: "My time is in Your hand."

The Power of Faith

Anything is possible if a person believes.
MARK 9:23

Scripture teaches us that there is not one truth on which Christ insisted more frequently than the absolute necessity of faith and its unlimited possibilities. Experience has taught us that there is nothing in which we fall so short as the simple and absolute trust in God to literally fulfill in us all He has promised. A life in Christ's abiding presence must of necessity be a life of unceasing faith.

What are the marks of true faith? First of all, faith counts upon God to do all He has promised. It seeks nothing less than to claim every promise that God has made, in its largest and fullest meaning. It trusts the power of an almighty God to work wonders in the heart in which He dwells and rests in the hope of what He will do.

In the pursuit of the power which such a life of faith can give, our soul must take God at His word and claim the fulfillment of His promises. We must then look to Him, even in utter darkness, to perform what He has spoken.

The life of faith to which the abiding presence will be granted must have complete mastery of our whole being. This faith will be able to claim and experience the words of the Master: "And be sure of this: I am with you always" (Matthew 28:20).

John's Missionary

*We are telling you about what we ourselves
have actually seen and heard,
so that you may have fellowship with us.*
1 JOHN 1:3

This is the calling of the preacher of the gospel. His message is nothing less than to proclaim that Christ has opened the way for us simple men to have living fellowship with the holy God. He is to preach this as a witness to the life that he himself experiences. In the power of that testimony, he is to prove its reality and show how sinful man on earth can indeed live in fellowship with the Father and the Son.

The message suggests to us that the very first duty of the minister is to maintain close communion with God. He must be conscious of the fact that his life and conversation are the proof that his preaching is true, so that his words will appeal with power to the heart.

It is this living testimony that will encourage and compel us to surrender ourselves to Christ. It is this intimate fellowship with Christ that is the secret of daily service and prayer. It has the power to inspire whole-hearted devotion to His service. It is in this intimate and abiding fellowship with Christ that the promise "I am with you always" (Matthew 28:20) finds its meaning.

This is what all Christians need—an abiding fellowship with God that will divinely influence the workers and the converts with whom they come in contact.

Paul's Missionary Message

*For this is the secret: Christ lives in you,
and this is your assurance that
you will share in his glory.*
COLOSSIANS 1:27

In Paul's mind, the very substance of his gospel was the indwelling Christ. He spoke of the "riches of the glory of this mystery— Christ in you, the assurance of glory." Though he had preached this gospel for so many years as a missionary, he still asked for prayer that he might make that secret known.

The complaint is often made in regard to our churches that, after a time, there appears to be no further growth and very little of the joy and power for bearing witness to Christ Jesus. The question comes whether the church at home is living in the experience of this indwelling Christ, so that the sons and daughters whom she sends out also know the secret. The answer is in Paul's missionary message which culminates in the words: "Christ in you. . .your assurance that you will share in his glory."

Paul deeply felt the need for prayer to enable him to give this message faithfully. Is there not a call to all those who pray for our missionaries, and to our missionaries themselves, to obtain the power that leads Christians into the enjoyment of their rightful heritage? May the church at home also share in the blessing of this truth.

The Missionary's Life

You yourselves are our witnesses—
and so is God—
that we were pure and honest and faultless
toward all of you believers.
1 THESSALONIANS 2:10

Paul more than once appeals to what his converts had seen of his own life. So he says: "We can say with confidence and a clear conscience that we have been honest and sincere in all our dealings. We have depended on God's grace, not on our own earthly wisdom. That is how we have acted toward everyone, and especially toward you" (2 Corinthians 1:12). Christ had taught His disciples as much by His life as by His teaching. Paul also sought to be a living witness to the truth of all that he had preached about Christ.

Paul appeals to the example of his own life throughout his writings. In Philippians 4:9 Paul writes: "Keep putting into practice all you learned from me and heard from me and saw me doing, and the God of peace will be with you." In 1 Timothy 1:14–16: "Oh, how kind and gracious the Lord was! He filled me completely with faith and the love of Christ Jesus. . . . Then others will realize that they, too, can believe in him and receive eternal life."

Let us believe that when Paul said, "I myself no longer live, but Christ lives in me" (Galatians 2:20), he spoke of an actual abiding of Christ in him. Christ was working in him to do all that was well-pleasing to the Father. While in prayer, do not rest until you can say, "The Christ of Paul is my Christ. His empowerment is mine, too."

The Holy Spirit

*He [the Holy Spirit] will bring me
glory by revealing to you
whatever he receives from me.*
JOHN 16:14

When our Lord spoke the words to the disciples in Matthew 28:20 "And be sure of this: I am with you always," they did not at first understand or experience their full meaning. At Pentecost they were filled with the Holy Spirit. It was then that the Spirit brought down into their hearts the new life of Christ's abiding presence.

All our attempts to claim to live that life of continuous communion with Christ will be in vain unless we yield ourselves completely to the power and indwelling of the Holy Spirit. For the Spirit of God to show us what He can enable us to be, He demands complete possession of our whole being.

Christ meant the promise of His abiding presence to be accepted as absolute, divine truth. "And God has given us his Spirit as proof that we live in him and he in us" (1 John 4:13). But this truth can only be experienced when the Spirit of God is known and believed in and obeyed.

We need to understand that the Holy Spirit came as God to make known the Son in us. He claims absolute subjection and is willing to take possession of our whole being and will enable us to fulfill all that Christ asks of us.

Filled with the Spirit

Let the Holy Spirit fill and control you.
Then you will sing psalms and hymns
and spiritual songs among yourselves,
making music to the Lord in your hearts.
EPHESIANS 5:18–19

If we had the expression "filled with the Spirit" only in regard to the story of Pentecost, we might naturally think that it was something special and not meant for ordinary life. But our text teaches us that it is meant for every Christian and for everyday life.

To realize this more fully, think of what the Holy Spirit was in Christ Jesus and under what conditions He was, as man, filled with the Spirit. He received the Spirit when He was praying and yielded Himself as a sacrifice to God by going down into the sinner's baptism. Full of the Holy Spirit, He was led to the forty days' fasting, sacrificing the needs of the body to be free for fellowship with the Father and for victory over Satan. He even refused, when He was famished, to listen to the temptation of Satan to use His power to make bread to supply His hunger. And so He was led by the Spirit all through life until He, by the Spirit, offered Himself without blemish unto God.

In Christ, the Spirit meant prayer, obedience, and sacrifice. It is only as we are led by the Spirit that we can abide in Christ Jesus, conquer the flesh and the world, and live the life with God in prayer and service.

The Christ Life

Christ lives in me.
GALATIANS 2:20

Christ's life was more than His teaching, more than His work, even more than His death. It was His life in the sight of God and man that gave value to what He said and did and suffered. It is this life that He gives to His people and enables them to live it out before men.

It was the life in the new brotherhood of the Holy Spirit that made both Jews and Greeks feel that there was some superhuman power about Christ's disciples. They gave living proof of the truth that God's love had come down and taken possession of them.

Everything depends upon the life with God in Christ being right. It is the simplicity and intensity of our life in Christ Jesus, and of His life in us, that sustains us in our daily walk. It makes us conquerors over self and everything that could hinder the Christ life. Through prayer, it gives us the victory over the powers of evil.

The life in Christ must be everything to us because Christ Himself lives in us. When Jesus spoke the words "And be sure of this: I am with you always" (Matthew 28:20), He meant nothing less than this: "All day and every day, I am with you. I am the secret of your life, your joy, and your strength."

The Christlike Life

*Your attitude should be the same
that Christ Jesus had.*
PHILIPPIANS 2:5

What was the attitude that was in Christ Jesus? "Though he was God, he did not demand and cling to his rights as God. He made himself nothing; he took the humble position of a slave and appeared in human form. And in human form he obediently humbled himself even further by dying a criminal's death on a cross" (Philippians 2:6–8). Self-emptying and self-sacrifice, obedience to God's will, and love to men, even unto the death of the Cross—this was the character of Christ for which God so highly exalted Him. It is the character of Christ that we are to imitate. He was made in the likeness of men, so we could be conformed into the likeness of God.

Self-effacement and self-sacrifice that God's will might be done and that man might be saved—this was the attitude of Christ. He lived only to please God and to bless men.

Don't say that this is an impossibility. What is impossible with men is possible with God. We are called to work out this salvation of a Christlike character with fear and trembling; for "God is working in you, giving you the desire to obey him and the power to do what pleases him" (Philippians 2:13). As we pray, let this be our one aim: to have the attitude that was in Christ Jesus.

Christ, the Nearness of God

Draw close to God,
and God will draw close to you.
JAMES 4:8

It has been said that the holiness of God is the union of God's infinite distance from sinful man with God's infinite nearness in His redeeming grace. Faith must always seek to realize both the distance and the nearness.

In Christ, God has come very near to man. Now the command comes: If you want God to come still nearer, you must draw near to Him. The promised nearness of Christ Jesus expressed in the promise, "And be sure of this: I am with you always" (Matthew 28:20), can only be experienced as we draw near to Him.

This means that at the beginning of each new day, we must yield ourselves to His holy presence. It means a voluntary, intentional, and whole-hearted turning away from the world to wait on God to make Himself known to our souls. It means making time to allow Him to reveal Himself. It is impossible to expect the abiding presence of Christ with us through the day without the daily exercise of strong desire and childlike trust in His word.

As you pray, let these words come to you with new meaning each morning: "Draw close to God, and God will draw close to you." Wait patiently and He will speak in divine power: "I am with you always."

Jesus knew that his hour had come
to leave this world and return to his Father.
He now showed the disciples
the full extent of his love.
JOHN 13:1

These are the opening words of the talk that Jesus had with His disciples in the last hours before He went to Gethsemane (John 13 to 17). They are the revelation of that divine love which was manifested in His death on the Cross.

He begins with the new commandment: "to love each other in the same way that I love you" (John 15:12). The new life in Christ Jesus is to be the unfolding of God's love in Christ. He continues: "I have loved you even as the Father has loved me. Remain in my love. When you obey me, you remain in my love, just as I obey my Father and remain in his love. . . . I command you to love each other in the same way that I love you. And here is how to measure it—the greatest love is shown when people lay down their lives for their friends" (John 15:9–13).

Can words make it plainer that the love with which the Father loved the Son is to be in us? If by prayer we are to claim His daily presence, it can only be as a relationship of infinite tender love between Him and us. This love must be rooted in the faith of God's love to Christ coming into our hearts and showing itself in obedience to His commandments and in love to one another.

The Trial and Triumph of Faith

Anything is possible if a person believes.
MARK 9:23

What a glorious promise: "Anything is possible if a person believes." Yet it is the greatness of this promise that constitutes the trial of faith. At first we do not really believe its truth. But when we have grasped it, then comes the real trial in the thought: such a faith is utterly beyond my reach. But what constitutes the trial of faith soon becomes its triumph.

When the father of the child heard Christ say "Anything is possible if a person believes," he felt that this would only cast him into deeper despair. How could his faith be able to work the miracle? Yet we read that the father believed that Jesus not only had the power to heal his child but also the power to inspire him with the needed faith. The impression Christ generated upon him produced the second miracle: that he could have such great faith. And with tears he cried, "I do believe, but help me not to doubt!" The very greatness of faith's trial was the greatness of faith's triumph.

Through our trials we can experience the abiding presence of Him who speaks to us now: "I am with you always." Let us wait upon God in prayer until we can say in faith, "I do believe."

Exceeding Abundantly

By his mighty power at work within us,
he is able to accomplish infinitely more than
we would ever dare to ask or hope.
EPHESIANS 3:20

In the great prayer which Paul had just written, he had apparently reached the highest expression possible of the life to which God's mighty power could bring the believer. But Paul is not content. In this doxology he rises still higher and lifts us up to give glory to God as "able to accomplish infinitely more than we would ever dare to ask or hope." Pause for a moment to consider what "infinitely more" means.

Think of the words, "he has given us all of his rich and wonderful promises" (2 Peter 1:4). Think of "the incredible greatness of his power for us who believe him. This is the same mighty power that raised Christ from the dead" (Ephesians 1:19–20). With these words Paul hopes to lift our hearts to believe that God is able to do "infinitely more than we would ever dare to ask or hope." The power of God that works in us is nothing less than the exceeding power that raised Christ from the dead. This should cause us to think that there is something that God will do in us that is beyond all our imagination.

As we worship Him in prayer, let us believe that the Almighty God, who is working in our hearts, is able and willing to fulfill every one of His exceeding great and precious promises.

The Dispensation of the Spirit

How much more will your heavenly Father
give the Holy Spirit to those who ask him.
LUKE 11:13

As he was meditating on prayer, the writer of a little book on prayer says: "I felt deeply that in this time of the working of the Holy Spirit, all we do in God's service is of little value unless it is inspired by the power of the Holy Spirit." This reminded me of the well known text, "How much more will your heavenly Father give the Holy Spirit to those who ask him."

A priority for each of us every day should be asking the Father for the gift of the Holy Spirit to meet our daily needs. Without this we cannot please God nor can we be of any real help to others. Our prayer that our lives fulfill God's purpose must have its origin in God Himself, the highest source of power. Water cannot rise higher than its source. If the Holy Spirit prays through us as human channels, our prayers will rise again to God who is their source. The prayers will be answered by God working in us. The Christian life of each one of us depends chiefly on the quality of our prayers and not on the quantity.

What material for deep meditation, for earnest prayer!

The Fruit of the Spirit

But when the Holy Spirit controls our lives,
he will produce this kind of fruit in us: love, joy, peace. . . .
GALATIANS 5:22

The first two lessons on prayer are: We must ask the Father to give us the Spirit anew every morning, and then ask the Spirit to teach us and help us. Here is a third lesson—commit to memory today's text.

Christians often think that they only need to ask God to teach them to pray and that He will do it at once. This is not always the case. What the Spirit does is strengthen our spiritual lives so we are able to pray better. When we ask Him to teach us, it is important that we first of all surrender ourselves to the working of the Spirit. This surrender consists in naming before Him the fruit of the Spirit, with the earnest prayer to be filled with this fruit.

Think of the first three—love, joy, peace—the three chief characteristics of a strong faith life. Love: to God, to believers, and to all men. Joy: the proof of the provision for every need of courage and faith for all the work we have to do. Peace: the blessed state of undisturbed rest and security in which God can keep our hearts and minds.

In His last talk with the disciples, Christ used these words: "remain in his love. . .so that you will be filled with my joy" (John 15:10–11). "I am leaving you with a gift—peace of mind and heart" (John 14:27).

Led by the Spirit

For all who are led by the Spirit of God
are children of God.
ROMANS 8:14

Let us think about four other fruits of the Spirit: patience, kindness, goodness, gentleness. These all denote attributes of God. They will reach maturity in us as we pray for the working of the Holy Spirit.

Patience—In the Old Testament God's patience was praised. All Scripture bears witness to the patience God had for sinful man. "No, he is being patient for your sake. He does not want anyone to perish, so he is giving more time for everyone to repent" (2 Peter 3:9). This attribute of the Spirit will enable us to exercise divine patience with all sin and wrong so that sinners may be saved.

Kindness—We read wonderful things in the Psalms about God's kindness. "For his unfailing love toward those who fear him is as great as the height of the heavens above the earth" (Psalm 103:11). God can enable us to show this same mercy toward those around us.

Goodness—"Only God is truly good" (Luke 18:19). All goodness comes from God, and He gives to His children as each heart asks and desires. This goodness is manifested in sympathy and love to all in need.

Gentleness—It was chiefly in God's Son that the divine gentleness was shown. Jesus says: "Let me teach you, because I am humble and gentle" (Matthew 11:29). The Holy Spirit longs to impart gentleness to our hearts.

These four attributes of God may be brought to maturity in our hearts by the Holy Spirit so that we may be like Jesus.

The Spirit of Faithfulness

*We have the same kind of faith
the psalmist had when he said,
"I believed in God, and so I speak."*

2 CORINTHIANS 4:13

Have you memorized Galatians 5:22–23 yet? If not, it is important to do so. It will strengthen your desire to have the fruit of the Spirit in you. Your expectation of God's blessing will be increased. Let us consider the last two fruits of the Spirit—faithfulness and self-control.

When the disciples asked the Lord: "Why couldn't we cast out that demon?" His reply was: "This kind of demon won't leave unless you have prayed and fasted" (Matthew 17:19, 21). They lacked faithfulness. Even if they had prayed, they had not the enthusiasm and self-sacrifice needed for prevailing prayer. Here we see faith and self-control working together.

Faithfulness is a fruit of the Spirit. Such faithfulness believes God's Word, clings to Him, and waits in perfect trust that His power will accomplish all that He has promised.

Self-control enables us to use restraint, carefulness, and unselfishness in our desires and in all our relationships. Our goal should be: "We are instructed to turn from godless living and sinful pleasures. We should live in this evil world with self-control, right conduct, and devotion to God" (Titus 2:12). We should show self-control in all our dealings with the world and its temptations, seek to be righteous in doing God's will, and live in close communion with God Himself.

Memorize this text. Let the Holy Spirit lead you each day to the Father so that the fruit of the Spirit will be seen in all your actions.

Worship God in the Spirit

We put no confidence in human effort.
Instead, we boast about what Christ Jesus has done for us.
PHILIPPIANS 3:3

Today let us worship God in the Spirit. We have come to the Father asking for the Holy Spirit. We have requested the guidance of the Holy Spirit. Now we begin to pray.

First we pray to God the Father, thanking Him for His blessings. We acknowledge our entire dependence on Him and express our trust in His love and care for us. We wait before Him until we have the assurance of His presence.

Then we direct our prayer to the Lord Jesus and ask for grace to abide in Him always, for without Him we can do nothing. We look to Him as our Lord, our preserver, our life, and give ourselves into His keeping.

Finally, we pray to the Holy Spirit. Ask Him to strengthen us so that what we have asked of the Father and the Son may happen. He is the dispenser of the power and gifts of the Father and of the Lord Jesus.

"We who worship God in the Spirit are the only ones who are truly circumcised. We put no confidence in human effort. Instead, we boast about what Christ Jesus has done for us." We have no power in ourselves to do good. We count on the Lord Jesus through the Holy Spirit to work in us. Take time to meditate on these things, asking God to grant His fruit in your life.

Intercession

Pray for each other.
JAMES 5:16

There is value in intercession. It is an indispensable part of prayer. It strengthens our love and faith in what God can do, and it brings blessing and salvation to others. Prayer should be mainly for others, not for ourselves alone. Begin by praying for those near and dear to us, those with whom we live, that we may be of help to them and not a hindrance.

Pray for your friends and all with whom you come into contact. Pray for all Christians, especially for ministers and those in responsible positions.

Pray for those who do not yet know the Lord as their Savior. Make a list of the names of those God has laid upon your heart and pray for their conversion. Christ needs you to bring to Him in prayer the souls of those around you. Pray, too, for all poor and neglected ones. Pray for mission work. Use a mission calendar with daily subjects of prayer.

Do you think this will take too much time? Just think what an inconceivable blessing it is to help others through your prayers. Look to the Holy Spirit for further guidance. If morning is not the best time for you, schedule another time later in the day. Cultivate the attitude: "I am saved to serve."

Time

*Couldn't you stay awake and
watch with me even one hour?*
MATTHEW 26:40

Every minute spent in prayer is valuable. If ten minutes is all the
time you can give, see what you can do in that time. Most peo-
ple can spare more time. If you will only persevere from day to
day, time will come of its own accord.

Is it possible that Christians can say that they cannot afford to
spend a quarter or half an hour alone with God and His Word?
When a friend comes to see us or we have to attend an impor-
tant meeting or there is anything to our advantage or pleasure,
we find time easily enough.

But God has a right to us and longs for us to spend time with
Him, and we find no time for fellowship with Him. Even God's
own servants are so occupied with their own work that they find
little time for that which is all-important—waiting on God to
receive power from on high.

Dear child of God, let us never say "I have no time for God."
Let the Holy Spirit teach us that the most important and prof-
itable time of the whole day is the time we spend alone with
God. Communion with God through His Word and prayer is as
indispensable to us as the food we eat and the air we breathe.
Whatever else is left undone, God has the first and foremost
right to our time.

The Word of God

For the word of God is full of living power.
HEBREWS 4:12

I find it a great help to use God's Word in my prayers. If the Holy Spirit impresses a certain text upon my mind, I plead the promise. This habit increases our faith, reminds us of God's promises, and brings us into harmony with God's will. We learn to pray according to God's will and understand that we can only expect an answer when our prayers are in accordance with that will (1 John 5:14).

Prayer is like fire. Fire can only burn brightly if it is supplied with good fuel. That fuel is God's Word which must be studied carefully and prayerfully. His Word must be taken into the heart and lived out in the life.

We are all familiar with the characteristics of a seed—a small grain in which the life-power of a whole tree slumbers. If it is placed in the soil, it will grow and increase and become a large tree.

Each word or promise of God is a seed containing a divine life in it. If I carry it in my heart by faith, love it, and meditate on it, it will slowly, surely spring up and bring forth the fruit of righteousness.

The Holy Spirit uses both the Word and prayer. Prayer is the expression of our human need and desire. The Holy Spirit teaches us to use the Word as a guide to what God will do for us.

The Name of Christ

And whatever you do or say,
let it be as a representative of the Lord Jesus,
all the while giving thanks through him
to God the Father.
COLOSSIANS 3:17

At the close of your prayer time, it is always well to add a request for the Holy Spirit to "remind you of everything I [Jesus] have told you" (John 14:26) all through the day. Then the prayers of the morning will not be counteracted by the work of the day.

Read today's text once more, prayerfully. Have you ever realized that it is a command? Is it the aim of your life to obey it? This may be difficult, but it is not impossible or God would not have asked it of us. God's Word has a wonderful power to preserve the spirit of thanksgiving in our lives. When we get up in the morning let us thank God for the rest of the night in the name of the Lord Jesus. In His name at night, thank Him for the mercies of the day. The ordinary daily life full of most ordinary duties will be lightened by the thought of what God has done for us for Christ's sake. Each ordinary deed will lead to thankfulness that He has given us the power to perform it.

At first it may seem impossible to remember the Lord Jesus in everything, yet the mere endeavor will strengthen us. The love of Christ will enable us to live all day in His presence.

The Spirit Glorifies Christ

He will bring me glory by revealing to you
whatever he receives from me.
JOHN 16:14

To understand and experience the work of the Holy Spirit you must try to grasp the relationship of the Holy Spirit to the Lord Jesus. Our Lord said that the Spirit would come as a Comforter to the disciples. The Spirit would reveal Him in their hearts. The disciples held onto that promise—they would not miss their Lord but have Him with them always. This made them pray earnestly for the Holy Spirit, for they longed to have Jesus with them always.

This is the meaning of our text—"He will bring me glory by revealing to you whatever he receives from me." Where there is an earnest desire for the glory of Jesus in the heart of the believer, the Holy Spirit will preserve the presence of Jesus in our hearts. We must not weary ourselves with striving after God's presence. We must quietly endeavor to abide in fellowship with Christ, to love Him and keep His commandments, and to do everything in the name of Jesus. Then we will be able to count upon the secret but powerful working of the Spirit within us.

If our thoughts are always occupied with the Lord Jesus— His love, His joy, His peace—then the Holy Spirit will graciously bring the fruit of the Spirit to ripeness within us.

Praying in the Spirit

And continue to pray as you are directed
by the Holy Spirit.
Live in such a way that
God's love can bless you.

JUDE 20–21

Paul began the last section of the Epistle to the Ephesians with the words: "Be strong with the Lord's mighty power" (Ephesians 6:10). He speaks of the whole armor of God and closes by saying that this armor must be put on with prayer: "Pray at all times and on every occasion in the power of the Holy Spirit" (Ephesians 6:18). Just as we need to be strong in the Lord and wear God's protective armor all day, so we need to live always praying in the Spirit.

The Holy Spirit will not come to us nor work within us just at certain times when we think we need His help. The Spirit comes to be our life-companion. He wants us totally in His possession at all times; otherwise He cannot do His work in us.

When this truth is grasped, we will realize that it is possible to live always praying in the power of the Spirit. The Spirit will keep us in a prayerful attitude and make us realize God's presence. Our prayer will be the continual exercise of fellowship with God and His great love. But as long as we regard the work of the Spirit as restricted to certain times and seasons, it will remain an unsolved mystery and a possible stone of offense.

The Temple of God

*For God's temple is holy,
and you Christians are that temple.*
1 CORINTHIANS 3:17

From eternity it was God's desire to create man as a dwelling place through which to show His glory. Because of man's sin, this plan seemed to be a failure. God sought a means of carrying out His plan in His people Israel. He would have a house in the midst of His people—first a tabernacle and then a temple—in which He could dwell. This was but a shadow of the true indwelling of God in redeemed mankind who would be His temple to eternity.

Since the Holy Spirit has been given, He has His dwelling in each heart that has been cleansed by the Spirit. The message comes to each believer however weak he may be: "Don't you realize that all of you together are the temple of God?" How seldom this truth is experienced; and yet how true it is: "God's temple is holy, and you Christians are that temple."

Paul testified: "Christ lives in me" (Galatians 2:20). This is the fullness of the gospel which he preached: the riches of the glory of the mystery, Christ in you. This is what he prayed for so earnestly for believers: that God would strengthen them through His Spirit in the inner man. Yes, this is what our Lord Himself promised: "All those who love me will do what I say. My Father will love them, and we will come to them and live with them" (John 14:23). Why is it that Christians are so slow to receive this wonder of God's grace?

The Fellowship of the Spirit

The fellowship of the Holy Spirit be with you all.
2 CORINTHIANS 13:13–14

In this verse we have one of the main characteristics and activities of the Holy Spirit. It is through the Holy Spirit that the Father and Son are one and have fellowship with each other.

We also have fellowship with the Father and the Son through the Spirit. "Our fellowship is with the Father and with his Son, Jesus Christ" (1 John 1:3). "And we know he lives in us because the Holy Spirit lives in us" (1 John 3:24). Through the Spirit we know the fellowship of love with the Father and Son.

Through the Spirit we, as God's children, have fellowship with each other. With the child of God there should be no selfishness. We are members of one Body. Through the Spirit the unity of the Body must be maintained. One reason that the Spirit does not work with greater power in the church is that the unity of the Spirit is not sought after. At Pentecost, after ten days spent in united prayer, the one hundred and twenty seemed melted together into one body. They received the Spirit in fellowship with each other.

We have fellowship when we meet at the communion table; we also have fellowship one with another in the trials of other members of the Body. Our text reminds us: "The fellowship of the Holy Spirit be with you all."

In heaven there is an eternal fellowship of love between Father and Son through the Spirit. Do we really long to be filled with the Spirit?

With the Whole Heart

If you look for me in earnest,
you will find me when you seek me.
JEREMIAH 29:13

It's often been said that if one seeks to perform any great work, he must do it with his whole heart and with all his might. In business this is the secret of success. Above all in spiritual things it is indispensable, especially in praying for the Holy Spirit.

Let me repeat that the Holy Spirit desires to have full possession of you. He can be satisfied with nothing less if He is to show His full power in your life.

Do you realize when you pray for the Holy Spirit that you are praying for the whole Godhead to take possession of you? Have your prayers had a wrong motive? If you were expecting that God would do something in your heart but in other things you would be free to do your own will, that would be a great mistake. The Holy Spirit must have full possession.

You may not feel a burning, urgent desire for the Holy Spirit to have full control, and you do not see any chance of its becoming true in your life. God knows about this inability of yours; He has ordained that the Holy Spirit will work within you all you need. What God demands of us, He will work within us. On our part there must be earnest prayer each day and an acceptance of the Holy Spirit as our leader.

Child of God, the Holy Spirit longs to possess you wholly. Submit yourself in complete dependence on His promise.

The Love of God in Our Hearts

*For we know how dearly God loves us,
because he has given us the Holy Spirit
to fill our hearts with his love.*

ROMANS 5:5

God the Father fills our hearts with the Holy Spirit. Likewise, the Holy Spirit fills our hearts with the love of God. As truly as God has given us the Spirit, so truly is the love of God given by the Spirit.

Why do we so seldom experience this? Simply because of our unbelief. It takes time to believe in the divine mighty working of the Holy Spirit. We need time to get away from the world and its interests for our souls to rest in the light of God so that the eternal love may take possession of our hearts. If we believe in the infinite love of God and the divine power with which He takes possession of the heart, then we will receive what we ask for—the love of God filling our hearts by the Holy Spirit. God desires His children to love Him with all their hearts and all their strength. He knows that is impossible in our own strength. For that very reason He has given the Spirit to fill our hearts with His love.

If you long for this, draw near to God. Abide with Him in quiet worship and adoration, and you will know the love of God in Christ which passes all knowledge.

Walk in the Spirit

Live according to your new life in the Holy Spirit. . . .
If we are living now by the Holy Spirit,
let us follow the Holy Spirit's leading
in every part of our lives.
GALATIANS 5:16, 25

The Christian in his daily walk must follow the leading of the Spirit. That will be the sign of a spiritual person who serves God in the Spirit and does not trust in his own abilities.

The Spirit is not needed just when we pray or just for our work for God's kingdom. God gives us His Spirit to be in us the whole day. We need Him most in the middle of our daily work because there the world has such power to lead us away from God. We need to ask the Father every morning for a fresh renewal of His Spirit. During the course of the day, let us remind ourselves that the Spirit is with us.

Paul says: "Now, just as you accepted Christ Jesus as your Lord, you must continue to live in obedience to him" (Colossians 2:6). Again: "Put on the Lord Jesus Christ" (Romans 13:14 KJV). Just as we put on a coat when we go out, so we must put on the Lord Jesus. We must show by our conduct that Christ lives in us and that we walk by the Spirit.

"Live according to your new life in the Holy Spirit. Then you won't be doing what your sinful nature craves" (Galatians 5:16). If we are not under the guidance of the Holy Spirit, we will do things in our own strength. The Spirit is given to teach us that we may walk by the Spirit at all times.

The Spirit Promised to the Obedient

> *If you love me, obey my commandments.*
> *And I will ask the Father,*
> *and he will give you another Counselor,*
> *who will never leave you.*
> JOHN 14:15–16

Christ would ascend to heaven and ask the Father to send the Comforter, the Holy Spirit. He would not do this only once, but it would become part of His intercessory work. He would "live forever to plead with God on their behalf" (Hebrews 7:25).

The Lord tells us in John 14 on what conditions He will send the Spirit: if we love Him and keep His commandments, "I will ask the Father." The Holy Spirit is given to enable us to do the will of the Father. The conditions are reasonable and just. As we keep the commandments through the Spirit, the Spirit will be granted to us in fuller measure. Let us say to God that we will strive to keep His commands.

Do not listen to the whispers of Satan or give way to unbelief. Surrender yourself unreservedly to the Lord who has said: "If you love me, obey my commandments." Love will enable you to do it. Trust the Lord Jesus with childlike faith and give yourself completely to do His will—that is all that is necessary. Then the beauty of the divine agreement that He makes with us will become reality: "When you obey me, you remain in my love" (John 15:10). The Father will send the Holy Spirit anew each day.

The Spirit of Wisdom

I pray for you constantly, asking God. . .
to give you spiritual wisdom and understanding,
so that you might grow in your knowledge of God.
EPHESIANS 1:16–17

In the Word of God we find a wonderful combination of the human and the divine. Anyone who has a good understanding of language can grasp the meaning of the words and the truths contained in them. But this is all that can be done in the power of human understanding.

There is a divine side in which the holy God expresses His deepest thoughts to us. We cannot understand them or comprehend them, for they must be spiritually discerned. Only through the Holy Spirit can the Christian apply the divine truth contained in God's Word.

Much of our religion is ineffectual because people accept the truths of God's Word with their intellect and strive to put them into practice in their own strength. Even a young student in a theological seminary may accept the truths of God's Word as head knowledge, but the Word has little power in his heart to lead to a life of joy and peace in the Lord Jesus. Paul teaches us that when we read God's Word we should pray, "Father, give me spiritual wisdom and understanding." As we do this each day we will find that God's Word is living and powerful and will work in our hearts and lives.

The Spirit of Sanctification

God the Father chose you long ago,
and the Spirit has made you holy.
As a result, you have obeyed Jesus Christ
and are cleansed by his blood.

1 PETER 1:2

In the New Testament the word "holy" is attributed to the Holy Spirit. Christ set Himself apart for us that we might be holy. The great work of the Holy Spirit is to glorify Christ in us by purifying us.

Have you really understood this truth? The main object for which the Holy Spirit is given is to purify you! If you do not accept this truth, then the Holy Spirit cannot do His cleansing work. If you only want the Spirit to help you to be a little better and to pray a little more, you will not get very far. But when you understand that the Holy Spirit was given in order to impart God's holiness and will cleanse you completely, then you will begin to realize that the Holy Spirit dwells in your heart.

And what will be the result? You will want Him to be in complete control of your life each day.

Your whole life and conversation must be in the Spirit. Your prayer, your faith, your fellowship with the Father, and all your work in God's service must be completely under His control. As the Spirit of holiness, He is the Spirit of your purification.

This is a deep, eternal truth. But it will be of no consequence if we do not wait upon God to grant us the Spirit of divine wisdom and a vision of what God has intended for us—the Spirit of purification. Each morning pray:

Abba, Father, for this new day renew within me the gift of Your Holy Spirit. Amen.

Rivers of Living Water

If you believe in me, come and drink!
For the Scriptures declare that rivers of
living water will flow out from within.
JOHN 7:38

Jesus, in His conversation with the Samaritan woman, said: "The water I give them takes away thirst altogether. It becomes a perpetual spring within them, giving them eternal life" (John 4:14). In John 7:38 the promise is even greater: rivers of living waters flowing from him, bringing life and blessing to others. John says that this refers to the Holy Spirit who would come when Christ had been glorified.

What do we need in order to experience the rivers of living water? Just one thing: the inner connection to Christ—the unreserved surrender to fellowship with Him. We have the firm assurance that His Spirit will work in us what we cannot do. We need a faith that rejoices in the divine power and love. We need a faith that depends on Him day by day to grant us grace that living water may flow out from us.

If the water from a reservoir is to flow into a house all day, one thing is necessary: The connection must be perfect. Then the water passes through the pipe of its own accord. So the connection between us and Christ must be uninterrupted. Our faith must accept Christ and depend on Him to sustain the new life.

Joy in God

For the Kingdom of God is not
a matter of what we eat or drink,
but of living a life of goodness and peace
and joy in the Holy Spirit.

ROMANS 14:17

A Christian man said to me shortly after his conversion: "I always thought that if I became religious, it would be impossible for me to do my worldly business. The two things seemed so contrary. I seemed to be a man trying to dig a vineyard with a bag of sand on his shoulders. But when I found the Lord I was so filled with joy that I could do my work cheerfully from morning till night. The bag of sand was gone; the joy of the Lord was my strength."

Many Christians do not understand that the joy of the Lord will keep them and enable them for their work. Read the Scriptures and see how the kingdom of God is pure joy and peace through the Holy Spirit. God will "keep you happy and full of peace as you believe in him. . .through the power of the Holy Spirit" (Romans 15:13).

Then try to realize that the Holy Spirit will give this joy and peace of Christ in our hearts. It is wrong to think of the Holy Spirit as a matter of grief and self-reproach, of disappointment, of something too high and holy. The great gift of the Father is meant to keep us in the joy and peace of Christ.

Listen attentively to the voice of the Spirit each day as He points to Jesus Christ, who offers you His wonderful fruit: love, joy, peace.

All the Day–Every Day

I will bless you every day.
PSALM 145:2

It is a step forward in the Christian life when you seek to have fellowship with God in His Word each day without fail. Perseverance will be crowned with success if you are really sincere. The experience may be somewhat as follows:

When you wake up in the morning, God will be your first thought. Set apart a time for prayer and resolve to give God time to hear requests and to reveal Himself. You may share all your desires with God and expect an answer.

Later on in the day, even if only for a few minutes, take time to keep up the fellowship with God. And again in the evening take time to reflect on the day's work and, with confession of sin, receive the assurance of forgiveness. Then commit yourself anew to God and His service.

Gradually you will get an insight into what is lacking in life and will be ready for uninterrupted fellowship with God through the Holy Spirit. You will gain the assurance through faith that the Holy Spirit, the Lord Jesus, and the Father Himself will give His presence and help all through the day.

Remember that you only need to live life one day at a time. You don't have to worry about tomorrow but rest in the assurance that He who has led you today will be even closer tomorrow.

The Spirit and the Cross

For by the power of the eternal Spirit,
Christ offered himself to God as
a perfect sacrifice for our sins.
HEBREWS 9:14

The connection between the cross and the Spirit is inconceivably close and meaningful. The Spirit brought Christ to the cross and enabled him to die there. The cross gave Christ the right to bring down the Holy Spirit on earth because there He made reconciliation for sin. The cross gave Christ the right and the power to grant us the power of the Spirit because on it He set us free from the power of sin.

Christ could not have attained to the heavenly life or poured out the Holy Spirit, if He had not first died to sin, to the world, and to His own life. He died to sin that He might live to God. And that is the way the Holy Spirit brings the cross into our hearts. It is only as we have been crucified with Christ that we can receive the full power of the Spirit. When we do not realize how necessary it is to die to all earthly things, the Spirit cannot gain full possession of us.

If we as Christians rely only on our human understanding, we cannot understand or experience that the fellowship of the Spirit is a fellowship of the cross. Wait on God to teach you divine truths through the Spirit.

The Spirit and the Blood

So we have these three witnesses—
the Spirit, the water, and the blood—
and all three agree.
1 JOHN 5:7–8

Baptism by water is an external sign of inner renewing and purifying through regeneration. The Spirit and the blood are spiritual expressions, working together in regeneration: the blood for the forgiveness of sins, the Spirit for the renewal of the whole nature.

There is spiritual oneness in the Spirit and the blood. Through the blood we obtain the Spirit, as through the blood we are redeemed and purified to receive the Spirit. Only through the blood can we pray with confidence to receive the Spirit.

There may be some sin in your life of which you are hardly conscious but which grieves the Spirit and drives Him away. The only way to avoid this is to believe that "the blood of Jesus, his Son, cleanses us from every sin" (1 John 1:7). Your only right to approach God is through the blood of the Lamb. Come with every sin, known or unknown, and plead the blood of Christ as your only claim to forgiveness.

But do not be content with just the forgiveness of sins. Accept the fullness of the Spirit which comes by the blood of Christ. Do not for a moment doubt that you have a right through the blood to the fullness of the Spirit.

As one who has been redeemed by the blood, give yourself to God as His purchased possession—a vessel ready for Him to use, a dwelling-place of the Holy Spirit.

The Spirit in Preacher and Hearer

> *For when we brought you the Good News,*
> *it was not only with words but also with power. . .*
> *So you received the message with*
> *joy from the Holy Spirit.*
>
> 1 THESSALONIANS 1:5–6

Paul more than once reminds his converts that the chief characteristic of his preaching was the supernatural power of the Holy Spirit. This is one of the most important lessons in the spiritual life. We as hearers are accustomed to listening attentively to the sermon to see what it has to teach us. But we may forget that the blessing of our church-going depends on two things. First, it depends on the prayer for the preacher that "the Holy Spirit [will be] powerful"; then prayer for ourselves that we may receive the word not from people, but as God's Word which "continues to work in you who believe" (1 Thessalonians 2:13). How often there is no manifestation of the Spirit when both the speaking and the hearing are mainly the work of human understanding or feeling.

We should pray earnestly that God will reveal to both minister and people "spiritual wisdom and understanding" (Ephesians 1:17) that we may discover what place the Holy Spirit really should have in our lives. As God gives us wisdom we will understand what Christ meant when He said: "Do not leave Jerusalem until the Father sends you what he promised. . . . But when the Holy Spirit has come upon you, you will receive power and will tell people about me everywhere. . .to the ends of the earth" (Acts 1:4, 8).

The Full Gospel

You must turn from your sins and turn to God,
and be baptized in the name of Jesus Christ. . . .
Then you will receive the gift of the Holy Spirit.
ACTS 2:38

When John the Baptist preached, "Turn from your sins and turn to God, because the Kingdom of Heaven is near" (Matthew 4:17), he also said: "Someone is coming soon who is greater than I am. . .He will baptize you with the Holy Spirit and with fire" (Luke 3:16). When Christ preached the gospel of the kingdom, He said: "And I assure you that some of you standing here right now will not die before you see me, the Son of Man, coming in my Kingdom" (Matthew 16:28). This is what happened at the outpouring of the Holy Spirit.

Peter preached on the Day of Pentecost the full gospel of repentance, forgiveness of sins, and the gift of the Holy Spirit. This is indispensable in preaching the gospel, for only then is it possible for a Christian to live in the will of God and to please Him in all things. The continuous joy of which Christ speaks can only be obtained through the power of the Holy Spirit.

How often only half the gospel is preached—conversion and forgiveness of sins. The appropriation of the life of the Spirit is not mentioned. No wonder so many Christians fail to understand that they must depend each day on the Spirit.

Accept this truth for yourself. The daily enjoyment of the leading of God's Spirit is indispensable for a joyous life of faith. Ask the Father to grant you the gift of the Holy Spirit anew each day.

The Ministry of the Spirit

Clearly, you are a letter from Christ prepared by us.
It is written not with pen and ink,
but with the Spirit of the living God.
It is carved not on stone, but on human hearts.

2 CORINTHIANS 3:3

The Corinthians' Church was a "letter of recommendation" for Paul, showing how much he had done for them. Although he claimed nothing for himself, God had enabled him as a "minister of the Spirit" to write in their hearts "with the Spirit of the living God."

What a wonderful example of the work of a minister for his people! A preacher prepared to be a minister of the Spirit, with power to write in the hearts of his people the name and the love of Christ. No wonder Paul speaks of how "all of us have had that veil removed so that we can be mirrors that brightly reflect the glory of the Lord. And as the Spirit of the Lord works within us, we become more and more like him and reflect his glory even more" (2 Corinthians 3:18).

May God restore the ministry of the gospel to its original power! If only ministers and church-members would unite in the prayer that God, by the working of His Spirit, would give the ministry of the Spirit its right place. We need to pray that God will teach the people to believe that when Christ is preached to them, they are seeing as in a mirror the glory of the Lord and may be changed into the same image by the Spirit of the Lord!

The Spirit from Heaven

*And now this Good News has been announced by
those who preached to you in the power of
the Holy Spirit sent from heaven.*
1 PETER 1:12

Christ has taught us to think of God as our own Father in heaven
who is ready to give His blessings to His children on earth. Our
Lord Himself was taken up into the glory of heaven, and we are
told that we are seated with Him in the heavenly places in
Christ. The Holy Spirit comes to us from heaven to fill our
hearts with the light, the love, the joy, and the power of heaven.

Those who are truly filled with the Spirit have a heavenly life
in themselves. They are in daily fellowship with the Father and
with the Son and seek the things that are above. Their main
characteristic is heavenly-mindedness. They carry with them the
marks of their eternal, heavenly destiny.

How can we cultivate this heavenly disposition? By allowing
the Holy Spirit, sent from heaven, to do His heavenly work in
our hearts and to bring to maturity in our lives the fruit of the
Spirit. The Spirit will lift our hearts to daily fellowship with God
in heaven. The Spirit makes the glorified Christ in heaven pres-
ent in our hearts and teaches us to dwell in His presence.

The Spirit and Prayer

The truth is,
you can go directly to the Father
and ask him, and he will grant your request
because you use my name.

JOHN 16:23

In Jesus' farewell discourse (John 13–17), He presented life in the Spirit in all its power and attractiveness. Through the Holy Spirit God's children can go directly to the Father and ask God to bless the world. Seven times we have the promise repeated: "You can ask for anything in my name, and I will do it" (John 14:13–14; 15:7, 16; 16:23–24, 26). Read these passages over so that you may come to understand how urgently and earnestly our Lord repeated the promise.

During the ten days before Pentecost the disciples proved this. In response to their continuous united prayer, the heavens were opened. The Spirit of God descended to earth, filling them with His life. They received the power of the Spirit that they might impart it to thousands. That power is still the pledge of what God will do. If God's children will agree with one accord to wait for the promise of the Father each day, there is no limit to what God will do for them.

Christian, remember that the Holy Spirit will dwell in you with divine power, enabling you to testify for Him. But it also means that you may unite with God's children to ask in prayer greater and more wonderful things than the heart can imagine.

With One Accord in Prayer

They all met together continually for prayer.
ACTS 1:14

Jesus gave the command to His disciples: "Go into all the world and preach the Good News to everyone, everywhere" (Mark 16:15). He added the promise: "And be sure of this: I am with you always" (Matthew 28:20). This command and this promise were not meant only for the disciples but also for us.

Before His ascension Christ gave His last command with a promise. The command was: "Do not leave Jerusalem until the Father sends you what he promised" (Acts 1:4). The promise was: "When the Holy Spirit has come upon you, you will receive power and will tell people about me everywhere. . .to the ends of the earth" (Acts 1:8). This command and promise are also meant for us. As irrevocable as the command to preach the gospel is the command to wait for the Father to send what He promised—"When the Holy Spirit has come upon you, you will receive power."

For ten days the disciples pled in one accord and their prayer was answered. The Church of our day has tried to carry out the first command to preach the gospel, but it has often forgotten the second command to wait for the Father to send what He promised. The power of the first disciples lay in the fact that they, as one body, were prepared to forget themselves and to pray for the Holy Spirit.

Whatever you may have learned from reading this book, learn one more lesson. Daily prayer in fellowship with God's children is indispensable if the Spirit is again to come in power. Pray for power.

Pray at All Times

Pray at all times and on every occasion
in the power of the Holy Spirit.
Stay alert and be persistent in your prayers
for all Christians everywhere. And pray for me, too.
EPHESIANS 6:18–19

Pray at all times. Who can do this? How can we do it when we are surrounded by the cares of daily life? How can a mother love her child at all times? I can breathe and feel and hear at all times because all these are the functions of a healthy, natural life. If our spiritual life is healthy, under the power of the Holy Spirit, praying at all times will be natural.

Pray at all times. Does it refer to continual acts of prayer, in which we are to persevere until we receive an answer, or to the spirit of prayerfulness that should animate us all day? It includes both. Jesus gives us an example of this. We have to spend special times of prayer in private. We are also to walk all day in God's presence with our focus on heavenly things. Without set times of prayer the spirit of prayer will be dull. Without the continual prayerfulness the set times will not be effective.

Pray at all times. Does it refer to prayer for ourselves or for others? It refers to both, but too often we confine it to ourselves.

The death of Christ brought Him to the place of everlasting intercession. Our death with Him to sin and self sets us free from selfishness and elevates us to the dignity of intercessor—one who can get life and blessing from God for others.

Becoming Educated

I urge you. . .to pray for all people.
As you make your requests,
plead for God's mercy upon them, and give thanks.
Pray this way for. . .all. . .who are in authority.
1 TIMOTHY 2:1–2

Pray without ceasing. How can we learn to do that? The best way of learning to do a thing—in fact the only way—is to do it. Begin by setting apart some time every day, say ten or fifteen minutes, in which you say to God and to yourself that you come to Him now as intercessor for others. It can be in the morning, in the evening, or any other time. Do not worry if you cannot set aside the same time every day. Just see that you do it. Christ chose you and appointed you to pray for others.

If at first you do not feel any special urgency, faith, or power in your prayers, do not let that hinder you. Quietly tell the Lord Jesus of your weakness. Believe that the Holy Spirit is in you to teach you to pray. Be assured that, if you begin, God will help you. God cannot help you unless you begin and keep on.

Pray at all times. How do I know what to pray for? Once you begin to think of all the needs around you, you will soon find enough to pray for. But to help you, each day for the next few weeks we will concentrate on subjects and hints for prayer. Use and reuse these ideas until you know more fully to follow the Spirit's leading and have learned, if need be, to make your own list of subjects. These days can be a time of becoming educated in this matter of praying at all times.

How to Pray

The Holy Spirit prays for us with groanings
that cannot be expressed in words.

ROMANS 8:26

If only topics for prayer were given, one might fall into the routine of mentioning names and things before God and prayer would become a burden. Therefore "how to pray" hints are included. They are meant to remind us of the spiritual nature of prayer and of the need for divine help. They will encourage our faith in the certainty that God, through the Spirit, will give us grace to pray and will also hear our prayer. It takes time to learn to pray with boldness and to dare to believe that you will be heard.

Take a few moments each day to listen to God's voice reminding you of how certainly even you will be heard. Listen to Him calling you to pray with faith in your Father and to claim and take the blessing you plead for. Let these words about how to pray enter your hearts and thoughts at other times, too. The work of intercession is one of Christ's great works on earth, entrusted to Him because He gave Himself a sacrifice to God for us. The work of intercession is the greatest work a Christian can do. Give yourself as a sacrifice to God for others, and intercession will become your glory and your joy, too.

What to Pray

Pray for each other.
JAMES 5:16

Scripture calls us to pray for many things: for all Christians, for all men and women, for all in government, and for all who are in adversity. It tells us to pray for sending missionaries, for those in the ministry of the gospel, for believers who have fallen into sin, for those in our own circle of friends. The Church is now much larger than when the New Testament was written. The number of ministries and workers is much greater. The needs of the Church and the world are so much better known that we must take time to see where prayer is needed and to what our heart is most drawn.

The scriptural calls to prayer demand a large heart, taking in all saints, and all men and women, and all needs. An attempt will be made these next days to indicate what the chief subjects are that need prayer and that ought to interest every Christian.

It may be difficult to pray for such large spheres as are sometimes mentioned. Where one subject appears of more special interest or more urgent than another, spend some time day after day to pray about that. If you really give time to intercession and the spirit of believing intercession is cultivated, the object is accomplished. While the heart must be enlarged at times to take in all, the more pointed and definite our prayer can be, the better.

Answers to Prayer

Do not leave. . .
until the Father sends you
what he promised.
ACTS 1:4

When we pray for all believers, or for missions in general, it is difficult to know when or how our prayer is answered, or whether our prayer had any part in bringing the answer. To remind us that God hears us, we should take note of what answers we look for and when they come. On the day of praying for all believers, take those in your congregation or in your prayer group and ask for a revival among them. In connection with missions, take some special location or missionary you are interested in and pray for blessing. Record definite requests with regard to individuals or special areas and look for the answers. Expect and look for God's answers so that you may praise Him.

When committing to persistent, meaningful prayer—prayer that expects answers—it may be helpful to have a small prayer group. You may meet for prayer once a month with some special topic introduced for every day. You may meet for a year or longer with the aim of strengthening each other in the grace of intercession. If you were to invite some of your believing friends to join for some special requests along with printed topics for prayer or to unite in prayer for revival, some might join you in the great privilege of intercession who now stand idle because no one has invited them.

God Is Sufficient

My gracious favor is all you need.
2 CORINTHIANS 12:9

Who is sufficient for real intercession? The more we study and try to practice the grace of intercession, the more we feel overwhelmed by its greatness and our weakness. Let that feeling lead you to hear: "My gracious favor is all you need," and to answer truthfully, "Our only power and success come from God" (2 Corinthians 3:5).

Take courage; you are called to take part in the intercession of Christ. The burden and the agony, the triumph and the victory, are all His. Learn from Him; to know how to pray, yield to His Spirit in you. He gave Himself as a sacrifice to God for us that He might have the right and power of intercession. "He bore the sins of many and interceded for sinners" (Isaiah 53:12).

Let your faith rest boldly on His finished work. Let your heart identify with Him in His death and His life. Like Him, give yourself to God a sacrifice for others. It is your highest calling, your true and full union with Him.

Come and give your whole heart and life to intercession, and you will know its blessedness and its power. God asks nothing less; the world needs nothing less; Christ asks nothing less; let nothing less be what we offer to God.

The Power of the Holy Spirit

I pray that. . .
he will give you mighty inner strength
through his Holy Spirit.
EPHESIANS 3:16

Pray for the full manifestation of the grace and energy of the Holy Spirit to remove all that is contrary to God's revealed will. Do this so that we do not grieve the Holy Spirit. Then He can work with mightier power in the Church for the exaltation of Christ and for our blessing.

All prayer unites in the one request—the power of the Holy Spirit. Make it your prayer.

Pray as a child asks a father. "You fathers—if your children ask for bread, do you give them a stone? . . .If you sinful people know how to give good gifts to your children, how much more will your heavenly Father give the Holy Spirit to those who ask him" (Luke 11:11, 13).

Ask as simply and trustfully as a child asks for food. You can do this because "God has sent the Spirit of his Son into your hearts, and now you can call God your dear Father" (Galatians 4:6). This Spirit is in you to give you childlike confidence. Have faith in the fact that He is praying in you. In that faith ask for the power of the Holy Spirit everywhere. Mention places or groups where you especially desire it to be seen.

The Spirit of Prayer

I will pour out a spirit of grace and prayer.
ZECHARIAH 12:10

The evangelization of the world depends first of all upon a revival of prayer. It is needed more than personal witness or missionaries. Deep down at the bottom of our spiritless life is the need for the forgotten secret of persistent, worldwide prayer.

Every child of God has the Holy Spirit in him to pray. God waits to give you the Spirit in full measure.

Pray in the Spirit as Paul taught us: "Pray at all times and on every occasion in the power of the Holy Spirit" (Ephesians 6:18). Jude also wrote: "Continue to pray as you are directed by the Holy Spirit" (Jude 20).

On His Resurrection day our Lord gave His disciples the Holy Spirit to enable them to wait for the full outpouring on the day of Pentecost. It is only as we acknowledge and yield to the power of the Spirit already in us that we can pray for His full manifestation.

Pray for All Saints

*Pray at all times and on every occasion
in the power of the Holy Spirit.
Stay alert and be persistent in your prayers
for all Christians everywhere.*

EPHESIANS 6:18

Every member of a body is interested in the welfare of the whole and exists to help and complete the others. Believers are one body and ought to pray, not so much for the welfare of their own church, but for all saints. This large, unselfish love is proof that Christ's Spirit and love are teaching us to pray. Pray first for all believers and then for those around you.

Pray in the love of the Spirit. Jesus said, "Your love for one another will prove to the world that you are my disciples" (John 13:35). He taught us that we are to have the unity that comes from love. "My prayer for all of them is that they will be one. . . and the world will believe you sent me" (John 17:21).

Paul taught us to pray from love. "Dear brothers and sisters, I urge you in the name of our Lord Jesus Christ to join me in my struggle by praying to God for me. Do this because of your love for me, given to you by the Holy Spirit" (Romans 15:30). And Paul's teaching was reinforced by Peter. "Most important of all, continue to show deep love for each other" (1 Peter 4:8).

If we are to pray, we must love.

The Spirit of Holiness

Make them pure and holy by
teaching them your words of truth.
JOHN 17:17

God is the Holy One. His people are a holy people. He speaks: "I, the Lord, am holy, and I make you holy" (Leviticus 21:8). Christ prayed: "Make them pure and holy by teaching them your words of truth" (John 17:17). Paul prayed: "Christ will make your hearts strong, blameless, and holy when you stand before God" (1 Thessalonians 3:13). "May the God of peace make you holy in every way" (1 Thessalonians 5:23).

Pray for all the believers—God's holy ones—throughout the Church. Pray that the Spirit of holiness may rule them. Especially pray for new converts. Pray for the believers in your own neighborhood or congregation, especially for any you are interested in. Think of their special need, weakness or sin, and pray that God may make them holy.

Pray, trusting in God's omnipotence. The things that are impossible with men are possible with God. Often when we ask for great things, we think there is little likelihood of their happening. Prayer is not only wishing or asking, but believing and accepting. Be still before God and ask Him to allow you to know Him as the Almighty One and leave your requests with Him who does wonders.

Kept from the World

Holy Father, keep them and care for them. . .
I'm not asking you to take them out of the world,
but to keep them safe from the evil one.
JOHN 17:11, 15

Pray that God's people may be kept from the world. The night before He was crucified, Christ asked three things for His disciples: 1) that they might be kept and cared for as those who are not of the world; 2) that they might be purified; 3) that they might be one in love. You cannot do better than to pray just as Jesus prayed. Ask that God's people may be kept separate from the world and the evil one. Pray that they, by the Holy Spirit, may live as those who are not of the world.

Pray with confidence before God. "Dear friends, if our conscience is clear, we can come to God with bold confidence. And we will receive whatever we request because we obey him and do the things that please him" (1 John 3:21–22).

Memorize that verse. Get the words into your heart. Join the ranks of those who, like John, draw near to God with an assured heart that does not condemn them. Learn to have confidence toward God. In the quiet confidence of an obedient child, pray for those believers who sin (1 John 5:16). Pray for all to be kept from the evil one. And say often, "What we ask, we receive, because we keep and do."

The Spirit of Love in the Church

When the Holy Spirit controls our lives,
he will produce this kind of fruit in us: love.
GALATIANS 5:22

"That they may be one, as we are—I in them and you in me. . . . Then the world will know that you sent me and will understand that you love them as much as you love me. . .that your love for me may be in them and I in them" (John 17:22–23, 26). Believers are one in Christ, as He is one with the Father. The love of God rests on them and can dwell in them. Pray that the power of the Holy Spirit will put this love in believers so that the world may see and know God's love in them. Pray consistently for this.

Pray as one of God's reminders: "I have posted watchmen on your walls; they will pray to the Lord day and night for the fulfillment of his promises. Take no rest, all you who pray" (Isaiah 62:6).

Study these words until your whole soul is filled with the realization: I am appointed as an intercessor. Enter God's presence with that faith. Approach the world's need with this thought: It is my job to intercede. Meditate on the fact that the Holy Spirit will teach you how to pray and what to pray for. Let it be a constant awareness: My great life work, like Christ's, is intercession. My purpose is to pray for believers and those who still do not know God.

The Holy Spirit and Ministers

I urge you. . .to join me in my struggle
by praying to God for me.
ROMANS 15:30

Paul and Timothy emphasized their need for prayer as ministers of Christ. "He will rescue us because you are helping by praying for us" (2 Corinthians 1:11). There are a lot of ministers in Christ's Church and they need prayer. They would have a mighty ministry if they were all covered with the power of the Holy Spirit. Pray for this in earnest. Think of your own minister and ask for the Holy Spirit's power especially for him. Ask that ministers everywhere be filled with the Spirit. Plead for them the promise, "Stay here. . .until the Holy Spirit comes and fills you with power from heaven" (Luke 24:49). "When the Holy Spirit has come upon you, you will receive power" (Acts 1:8).

Pray in private. "When you pray, go away by yourself, shut the door behind you, and pray to your Father secretly" (Matthew 6:6). Jesus "went up into the hills by himself to pray" (Matthew 14:23; see John 6:15).

Take time to be alone with God to intercede for His servants. Don't think that you have no influence or that your prayers don't count. Your prayer and your faith will make a difference. Go away by yourself and pray to God for His ministers.

Christian Workers

He will rescue us because you are
helping by praying for us.
2 CORINTHIANS 1:11

There are multitudes of Christian workers ministering in connection with our churches and missions, schools and colleges, our publishers and bookstores, our public service and government offices, young men and young women, children and youth, our worship in music, our military personnel, hospitals and clinics, prisons, and our poor. Praise God for this! How much more they could accomplish if each were living in the fullness of the Holy Spirit! Pray for them; it makes you a partner in their work. You will praise God each time you hear of blessings anywhere.

Pray with definite requests. Jesus asked the blind beggar, "What do you want me to do for you?" (Luke 18:41). The Lord knew what the man wanted, and yet He asked him. Verbalizing our wish gives meaning to our transaction with God. It awakens faith and expectation.

Being definite in your requests also helps you to know what answer you are looking for. Ask those you are praying for what they need. If they have prayer letters, use them as guides. Intercession is not mere words and pious wishes. Its aim is to receive and bring down blessing through believing, persevering prayer.

Mission Work

*One day as these men were worshiping the Lord and fasting,
the Holy Spirit said, "Dedicate Barnabas and Saul
for the special work I have for them."*

ACTS 13:2

The evangelization of the world depends, first of all, upon a revival of prayer. The need for the forgotten secret of prevailing, worldwide prayer is greater than the need for missionaries.

Pray that our missions work may all be done in this spirit: waiting on God, hearing the voice of the Spirit, sending out men and women with fasting and prayer. Pray that in our churches our mission interests may be in the power of the Holy Spirit and of prayer. It is a Spirit-filled, praying church that will send out Spirit-filled missionaries, mighty in prayer.

Take time when you pray. The psalmist said, "I give myself unto prayer" (Psalm 109:4 KJV). The early church leaders agreed. "We can spend our time in prayer" (Acts 6:4). Solomon in his God-given wisdom said, "Don't make rash promises to God. . . . Let your words be few" (Ecclesiastes 5:2).

Time is one of the main standards to measure value. The time we give is proof of the interest we feel. We need time with God—to know His presence and to wait for Him to make Himself known. We need time to consider and feel the needs we pray for. We need time to pray until we can believe that we have received.

Missionaries

When the Holy Spirit has come upon you,
you will receive power and will tell people
about me everywhere.
ACTS 1:8

Missionaries today need an outpouring of God's Spirit in their lives and ministries. God always gives His servants power equal to the work He asks of them. There are difficult times in this work of casting out Satan from his strongholds. Pray that everyone who takes part in it may receive and act in the power of the Holy Spirit. Think of the specific difficulties of your missionaries and pray for them.

Pray, trusting in God's faithfulness. "God can be trusted to keep his promise. . . . [Abraham] believed that God would keep his promise" (Hebrews 10:23; 11:11).

Just think about God's promises to His Son concerning His kingdom, His promises to the Church concerning the unbelievers, and His promises to His servants concerning their work. Think of His promises to you concerning your prayer. Then pray in the assurance that He is faithful and only waits for prayer and faith to fulfill them. "God, who calls you" (to pray), "is faithful; he will do this" (what He has promised) (1 Thessalonians 5:24).

Pray for individual missionaries, making yourself one with them, until you know that you are heard. Begin to live for Christ's kingdom as the one thing worth living for!

More Workers

So pray to the Lord who is in charge of the harvest;
ask him to send out more workers for his fields.

MATTHEW 9:38

It is remarkable that Jesus seeks help from His disciples in getting the need for workers supplied. What an honor put upon prayer. It is also proof that God wants prayer and will hear it.

Pray for students in theological seminaries and Bible schools that God will prepare them and send them out. Pray that all believers may be ready to go or to pray for those who go.

Pray by faith, doubting nothing. "Jesus said to the disciples, 'Have faith in God. I assure you that you can say to this mountain, "May God lift you up and throw you into the sea," and your command will be obeyed. All that's required is that you really believe and do not doubt in your heart' " (Mark 11:22–23).

Have faith in God! Ask Him to make Himself known to you as the faithful, mighty God. You will be encouraged to believe that He can give suitable and sufficient workers however impossible this seems. But remember, He does so in answer to prayer and faith.

Apply this to every opening where a good worker is needed. The work is God's. He can give the right person, but He must be asked.

Convincing the World of Sin

I will send [the Counselor] to you.
And when he comes,
he will convince the world of its sin.
JOHN 16:7–8

The one object of Christ's coming was to take away sin. The first work of the Spirit in the world is conviction of sin. Without that no real conversion is possible. Pray that the gospel may be preached in such power that men may see that they have rejected and crucified Christ and come to know His saving grace.

Pray most earnestly for a mighty power of conviction of sin wherever the gospel is preached.

Take hold of God's strength when you pray. Read what Isaiah wrote. "These enemies will be spared only if they surrender and beg for peace and protection" (Isaiah 27:5). "Yet no one calls on your name or pleads with you for mercy" (Isaiah 64:7). Paul adds, "Fan into flames the spiritual gift God gave you" (2 Timothy 1:6).

First, take hold of God's strength. God is a Spirit. I cannot take hold of Him except by the Spirit. Take hold of God's strength and hold on until He has done for you what He has promised.

Second, by the Holy Spirit's power in you, fan the flame of intercession in you. Give your whole heart and will to it.

The Spirit of Burning

He will cleanse. . .
by a spirit of judgment
that burns like fire.
ISAIAH 4:4

A washing by fire! A cleansing by judgment! Those that have passed through this will be called holy. The power of intercession and blessing for the world depends upon the spiritual state of the Church. Judgment must begin at the house of God; there must be conviction of sin for sanctification. Plead with God to give His Spirit as a spirit of judgment and a spirit of burning— to discover and burn out sin in His people.

Pray in the name of Christ, for He said, "You can ask for anything in my name, and I will do it. . . . Yes, ask anything in my name, and I will do it!" (John 14:13–14).

Ask in the name of your Redeemer God who sits upon the throne. Ask what He has promised—what He gave His blood for—that sin may be put away from among His people. Ask— the prayer is after His own heart—for the spirit of deep conviction of sin to come to His people. Ask for the spirit of burning. Ask in the faith of His name—the faith of what He will and of what He can do. Then look for the answer. Pray that the Church may be blessed and be a blessing in the world.

The Church of the Future

So [each generation] will not be like their ancestors—
stubborn, rebellious, and unfaithful,
refusing to give their hearts to God.
PSALM 78:8

Pray for the next generation who are to come after us. Isaiah
wrote, "I will pour my spirit and my blessings on your children"
(Isaiah 44:3). Think of the young men and young women and
children today and pray for all the special organizations that
work with them. Pray that wherever they are Christ may be hon-
ored and the Holy Spirit get possession of them.

Pray with your whole heart. "May [the Lord] grant your
heart's desire" (Psalm 20:4). "You have given him his heart's
desire" (Psalm 21:2). "I pray with all my heart; answer me,
Lord!" (Psalm 119:145).

God listens to every request with His whole heart. Each time
we pray the whole infinite God is there to hear. He asks that in
each prayer the whole person will be there, too, and that we pray
with our whole heart. If once we seek God with our whole heart,
the whole heart will be in every prayer with which we come to
God. Pray with your whole heart for our young people.

Schools and Colleges

These words I have given you . . .
will be on your lips and on the lips of your children
and your children's children forever.
ISAIAH 59:21

The future of the Church and the world depends on today's education. The Church may be seeking to evangelize unbelievers but is giving up her own children to secular and materialistic influences. Pray for schools and colleges and for godly teachers. The Church also has a duty to care for its children.

Do not limit God in your prayers. It is a fearful thing to do so. "They tested God's patience and frustrated the Holy One of Israel" (Psalm 78:41). Jesus "did only a few miracles there because of their unbelief" (Matthew 13:58). However, apart from such unbelief, God is not limited. "Is anything too hard for the LORD?" (Genesis 18:14). "O Sovereign LORD! You have made the heavens and earth by your great power. Nothing is too hard for you. . . . I am the LORD. . . . Is there anything too hard for me?" (Jeremiah 32:17, 27).

Beware of limiting God in your prayer, not only by unbelief but also by pretending that you know what He can do. Expect unexpected things, greater than all we ask or think. Each time you intercede, be quiet first and worship God. Acknowledge what He can do and expect great things.

Sunday Schools

*The captives of warriors will be released
and the plunder of tyrants will be retrieved.
For I will fight those who fight you,
and I will save your children.*
ISAIAH 49:25

Every part of the work of God's Church is His work. He must do it. Prayer is acknowledging that He will. It is the surrender of ourselves into His hands to let Him work in us and through us. Pray for hundreds of thousands of Sunday school teachers who know God that they may be filled with His Spirit. Pray for your own Sunday school. Pray for the salvation of the children.

Pray boldly. "We have a great High Priest. . .Jesus the Son of God. . . . So let us come boldly to the throne of our gracious God" (Hebrews 4:14, 16).

As we have been thinking about the work of intercession, what is it doing for us? Does it make us aware of our weakness in prayer? Thank God for this. It is the very first lesson we need on the way to praying the "earnest prayer of a righteous person [that] has great power and wonderful results" (James 5:16). Let us persevere taking each item boldly to the throne of grace. As we pray, we shall learn to pray, to believe, and to expect with increasing boldness. Hold fast your confidence; it is at God's command you come as an intercessor. Christ will give you grace to pray as you should.

Kings and Rulers

Pray for all people. As you make your requests,
plead for God's mercy upon them, and give thanks.
1 TIMOTHY 2:1

Our text is an example of real faith in the power of prayer! A few weak and despised Christians are to influence the mighty Roman emperors and help secure peace and quietness. Prayer is a power that is honored by God in His rule of the world. Let us pray for our country and its rulers, for all the rulers of the world, for rulers in cities or districts in which we are interested. When God's people unite, they can count upon their prayer affecting the unseen world more than they know.

Prayer is an incense before God. "Then another angel with a gold incense burner came and stood at the altar. And a great quantity of incense was given to him to mix with the prayers of God's people to be offered on the gold altar before the throne. The smoke of the incense, mixed with the prayers of the saints, ascended up to God from the altar where the angel had poured them out. Then the angel filled the incense burner with fire from the altar and threw it down upon the earth; and thunder crashed, lightning flashed, and there was a terrible earthquake" (Revelation 8:3–5).

The same incense burner brings the prayers of the saints before God and throws fire upon the earth. The prayers that go up to heaven have their share in the history of this earth. Be assured that your prayers enter God's presence.

Pray for Peace

[He] causes wars to end throughout the earth.
PSALM 46:9

The military armaments in which the nations find their pride are a terrible sight! The evil passions that may at any moment bring on war are a terrible thought! The suffering and desolation that comes from war are a sad prospect!

"I urge you, first of all, to pray. . .for kings and all others who are in authority, so that we can live in peace and quietness, in godliness and dignity. This is good and pleases our Savior" (1 Timothy 2:1–3). God can, in answer to the prayer of His people, give peace. Let us pray for it and for the rule of righteousness.

When you pray, pray with the understanding. "I will pray in the spirit, and I will pray in words I understand" (1 Corinthians 14:15).

We need to pray in the Spirit if we are to take hold of God in faith and power. We need to pray with understanding if we are really to enter deeply into the needs we bring before Him. Be careful to understand the nature, the extent, the urgency of the request. Comprehend the certainty of God's promise as revealed in His Word. Let the mind affect the heart. Pray with understanding and in the Spirit.

The Mistake

Remain in me, and I will remain in you.
JOHN 15:4

A person thinks, *I have my business, family, and community responsibilities. In addition I am to serve God in order to keep from sin. I hope God will help me.*

That is not right. When Christ came He bought you with His blood. In those days there was slavery. If someone bought a slave, the slave was required to take orders from his master. The slave lived as if he had no will or interests of his own. His one responsibility was to promote the well-being of his master.

In a similar manner, I have been purchased with the blood of Christ. I am to live every day with one thought, "How can I please my Master?"

We find the Christian life so difficult because we seek for God's blessing while we live life according to our own desires. We make our own plans and choose our own work. Then we ask the Lord to help us not to go too far wrong. Instead, our relationship with Jesus should be that we are entirely at His disposal. We should ask Him daily, "Lord, is there anything in me that is not according to Your will, that is not entirely surrendered to You?"

If we will wait patiently for His guidance there will spring up a relationship between us and Christ so close that we will be amazed. He will take actual possession of us and give us unbroken fellowship.

The Unreached

See, my people will return from far away, from. . .
as far south as Egypt.
ISAIAH 49:12

Will the unreached come to Christ? Does God have such a plan? "Let Egypt come with gifts of precious metals; let Ethiopia bow in submission to God" (Psalm 68:31). "I, the LORD, will bring all to pass at the right time" (Isaiah 60:22).

Pray for those who are yet without the Word: China with her hundreds of millions without Christ; India with its millions; millions each year living in darkness. If Christ gave His life for them, you can give yourself up to intercede for them.

If you have not started to intercede, begin now. God's Spirit will draw you on. Persevere, however hesitant you are. Ask God to give you some country or people group to pray for. Can anything be nobler than to do as Christ did—to give your life for the unreached?

Pray with confident expectation of an answer. "Ask me and I will tell you some remarkable secrets about what is going to happen here" (Jeremiah 33:3). "This is what the Sovereign LORD says: I am ready to hear Israel's prayers. . .and I am ready to grant them their requests" (Ezekiel 36:37). Both texts refer to promises definitely made, but their fulfillment would depend upon prayer.

God's Spirit on Israel

*Then I will pour out a spirit of grace and prayer
on the family of David and on all the people of Jerusalem.
They will look on me whom they have pierced.*

ZECHARIAH 12:10

"Dear brothers and sisters, the longing of my heart and my prayer to God is that the Jewish people might be saved" (Romans 10:1). Paul states his desire for the well-being of Israel. Pray for them. Their return to the God of their fathers stands connected, in a way we cannot understand, with wonderful blessing to the Church and with the coming of our Lord Jesus. Don't think that God has foreordained all this and that we cannot hasten it. In a divine and mysterious way God has connected the fulfillment of His promise with our prayer. His Spirit's intercession in us is God's forerunner of blessing. Pray for Israel and the work done among them. Pray, too: "Amen! Come, Lord Jesus!" (Revelation 22:20).

Pray with the intercession of the Holy Spirit. "We don't even know what we should pray for, nor how we should pray. But the Holy Spirit prays for us with groanings that cannot be expressed in words" (Romans 8:26).

In our ignorance and weakness we can believe in the secret intercession of the Holy Spirit within us. Habitually yield yourself to His life and leading. He will help your weakness in prayer. Plead the promises of God even where you do not see how they are to be fulfilled. God knows the mind of the Spirit because "the Spirit pleads for us believers in harmony with God's own will" (Romans 8:27). Pray with the simplicity of a little child; pray with the holy awe and reverence of one in whom God's Spirit dwells and prays.

The Suffering

Share the sorrow of those being mistreated,
as though you feel their pain in your own bodies.
HEBREWS 13:3

We live in a world of suffering! The persecuted believers in Islamic countries, the famine stricken millions, those in poverty and wretchedness, refugees from armed conflict—and so much more. In our smaller circles, in thousands of homes and hearts, there is great sorrow! In our own neighborhood, how many need help or comfort? Let us have a heart for the suffering. Jesus sacrificed all and identified Himself with our suffering! Let us in our measure do so, too. It will stir us to pray, to work, to hope, to love more. And in a way and time we do not understand, God will hear our prayers.

Pray always without giving up. "Jesus told his disciples a story to illustrate their need for constant prayer and to show them that they must never give up" (Luke 18:1).

Have you begun to feel that prayer is really the help needed for this sinful world? The very greatness of the task makes us despair! What can our ten minutes of intercession accomplish? It is okay that we feel this: It may be the way in which God is calling and preparing us to give more of our time to prayer. Give yourself wholly to God, pour out your heart to others in love, and look to God in dependence and expectation. To a heart thus led by the Holy Spirit, it is possible to pray always and not give up.

The Spirit in Your Own Work

I work very hard at this, as I depend on Christ's mighty power that works within me.
COLOSSIANS 1:29

You have your own special work; make it a work of intercession. Paul worked hard, depending on God's power working in him. Remember, God not only created us but works in us. You can do your work only in His strength—by Him working in you through the Spirit.

Intercede often for those you work with and for other believers, too. Pray in God's very presence. "Draw close to God, and God will draw close to you" (James 4:8).

The nearness of God gives rest and power in prayer. The nearness of God is given to those who make it their first aim to "draw close to God." Seek His nearness, and He will give it. "He will draw close to you." Then it becomes easy to pray in faith.

Remember that when first God takes you into the school of intercession, it is almost more for your own sake than that of others. You have to be trained to love and wait and pray and believe. Only persevere. Learn to place yourself in His presence, to wait quietly for the assurance that He draws near. Enter His holy presence, wait there, and bring your concerns before Him.

The Local Church

Beginning in Jerusalem.
LUKE 24:47

Most of us are connected with some church congregation—a community of believers. They are to us the part of Christ's body with which we come into most direct contact. They have a special claim on our intercession. Let it be a settled matter between God and you that you are to intercede on their behalf. Pray for the minister and all leaders and workers. Pray for the believers according to their needs. Pray for conversions. Pray for the power of the Spirit to manifest itself. Join with others in specific prayer. Let intercession be a definite work, carried on as systematically as preaching or Bible studies. And pray, expecting an answer.

Pray continually. Read the Scriptures. "Watchmen. . .will pray to the LORD day and night. . . . Take no rest, all you who pray" (Isaiah 62:6). ". . . His chosen people who plead with him day and night" (Luke 18:7). "Night and day we pray earnestly for you" (1 Thessalonians 3:10). "But a woman who is a true widow, one who is truly alone in this world, has placed her hope in God. Night and day she asks God for help and spends much time in prayer" (1 Timothy 5:5).

When the glory of God and the love of Christ and the needs of others are revealed to us, the fire of this unceasing intercession will begin to burn in us for those who are near and those who are far away.

The Salvation of Souls

> *Therefore he is able, once and forever,*
> *to save everyone who comes to God through him.*
> *He lives forever to plead*
> *with God on their behalf.*
> HEBREWS 7:25

Christ's power to save depends on unceasing intercession. "Then we can spend our time in prayer and preaching and teaching the Word. . . . God's message was preached in ever-widening circles. The number of believers greatly increased" (Acts 6:4, 7). After the apostles spent time away in continual prayer, the number of the disciples multiplied greatly.

As we spend time in intercession, we will see more conversions. Christ is exalted as sinners repent. The Church exists with the divine purpose and promise of conversions. Don't be ashamed to confess our sin and weakness and pray to God for more conversions both here and in other countries. Plead for the salvation of sinners.

Pray in deep humility. "Yes, Lord. . .but even dogs are permitted to eat crumbs. . . . Woman. . .your faith is great. Your request is granted" (Matthew 15:27–28).

True humility proves its integrity by not seeking for anything but simply trusting His grace. And so it is the strength of a great faith. Don't let your littleness hinder you for a moment.

Young Converts

As soon as [Peter and John] arrived,
they prayed for these new Christians
to receive the Holy Spirit.
The Holy Spirit had not yet come upon any of them.
ACTS 8:15–16

Many new converts remain weak, many fall into sin, and many backslide entirely. As you pray for the Church, its growth in holiness and devotion to God, pray especially for the young converts. Many stand alone, surrounded by temptation. Many have no teaching on the Spirit in them and the power of God to establish them. They don't know the promise of Scripture: "It is God who gives us, along with you, the ability to stand firm for Christ. . . . He has identified us as his own by placing the Holy Spirit in our hearts" (2 Corinthians 1:21–22). Many are in other countries, surrounded by Satan's power. Pray for the power of the Spirit in the Church and especially that every young convert may know the fullness of the Spirit.

Pray without ceasing. "As for me, I will certainly not sin against the LORD by ending my prayers for you" (1 Samuel 12:23).

It is sin against the Lord to stop praying for others. Once we begin to see how indispensable intercession is—just as much a duty as loving God—we will feel that to stop intercession is sin. Ask for grace to fill the role of intercessor with joy and give our life to bring down the blessings of heaven.

Realize Our Calling

I will bless you. . .and. . .make you a blessing to others. . . .
All the families of the earth will be blessed through you.
GENESIS 12:2–3

Abraham was only blessed that he might be a blessing to all the earth. Israel prays for blessing that God may be known among all nations. Every believer, just as much as Abraham, is blessed so that he may carry God's blessing to the world. "May God be merciful and bless us. May his face shine with favor upon us. May your ways be known throughout the earth, your saving power among people everywhere" (Psalm 67:1–2).

Plead with God that His people may know that every believer is only to live for the interests of God and His kingdom. If this truth were preached and believed and practiced, it would bring dramatic changes in our mission work. We would have a host of willing intercessors.

Pray as one who has accepted for himself what he asks for others. "The Holy Spirit fell on them, just as he fell on us at the beginning. . . . God gave these Gentiles the same gift he gave us" (Acts 11:15, 17).

As you pray for the Holy Spirit to take entire possession of God's people for God's service, yield yourself to God and claim the gift anew in faith. As the blessing comes to others, you, too, will be helped.

Know the Holy Spirit

*Don't you know that your body is
the temple of the Holy Spirit?*
1 CORINTHIANS 6:19

The Holy Spirit is the power of God for the salvation of men. He only works as He dwells in the Church. He is given to enable believers to live as God wants them to live—in the full experience and witness of Him who saves completely.

Ask God for every one of His people to know the Holy Spirit! They cannot expect to live as their Father desires without having Him in His fullness, without being filled with Him! Pray that all God's people may learn to say: "I believe in the Holy Spirit."

Pray earnestly. "Epaphras, from your city. . .sends you his greetings. He always prays earnestly for you, asking God to make you strong and perfect, fully confident of the whole will of God" (Colossians 4:12).

To a healthy man work is a delight; he works earnestly in what interests him. The believer who is in good spiritual health, whose heart is filled with God's Spirit, prays earnestly. For what?—that believers may stand perfect and complete in all the will of God, that they may know what God wills for them, and walk by the Holy Spirit.

The Spirit of Intercession

I chose you. I appointed you to go and produce fruit. . .
so that the Father will give you whatever you ask for,
using my name.

JOHN 15:16

Often our intercession lacks power because we have not prayed in the name of Jesus. He promised His disciples that when the Holy Spirit came upon them, they could ask for anything in His name. Let us intercede today for all God's children that Christ may teach them that the Holy Spirit is in them. May He teach us what it is to live in His fullness and to yield ourselves to His work of intercession within us. The Church and the world need nothing as much as a mighty Spirit of intercession to bring down the power of God on earth. Pray for the Spirit of intercession to bring a great prayer revival.

Pray, joined to Christ. "If you stay joined to me and my words remain in you, you will ask any request you like, and it will be granted" (John 15:7).

Our acceptance with God—our access to Him—is all in Christ. As we consciously abide in Him we have the liberty to ask what we will in the power of the new nature, and it will be done.

The Word of God

It was not only with words but also with power,
for the Holy Spirit gave you full assurance
that what we said was true.

1 THESSALONIANS 1:5

Many Bibles are being circulated. Many sermons on the Bible are being preached. Many Bibles are being read. The blessing comes not just in words only. The blessing and power comes in the Holy Spirit, when it is preached with the Holy Spirit. "This Good News has been announced by those who preached to you in the power of the Holy Spirit sent from heaven" (1 Peter 1:12).

Pray for the power of the Spirit through the Word in all the world wherever it is being read or heard. Let every mention of the Word of God call us to intercession.

Be alert and pray. "Devote yourselves to prayer with an alert mind and a thankful heart. Don't forget to pray for us, too, that God will give us many opportunities to preach" (Colossians 4:2–3).

Do you see how everything depends upon God and prayer? As long as He lives and loves and hears and works, as long as there are hearts closed to the Word, as long as there is work to be done in carrying the Word—pray at all times.

Christ in His People

> *Yes, I am the vine;*
> *you are the branches. . . .*
> *But if you stay joined to me*
> *and my words remain in you,*
> *you may ask any request you like,*
> *and it will be granted.*
> JOHN 15:5, 7

As branches we are to be so like the vine, so entirely identified with it, that everyone may see that we have the same nature and life and spirit. When we pray for the Spirit, let us not only think of a Spirit of power, but the very attitude of Christ Jesus. Ask and expect nothing less for yourself and all God's children.

What must we be or do that will enable us to pray as we should and to receive what we ask? The answer is this: It is the branch life that gives power for prayer. We are branches of Christ, the living vine. We must simply live like branches and abide in Christ; then we shall ask what we will and it shall be done for us.

Struggle in prayer. "Join me in my struggle by praying to God for me" (Romans 15:30). "I want you to know how much I have agonized for you" (Colossians 2:1).

All the powers of evil seek to hinder us in prayer. Prayer is a conflict with opposing forces. It needs our whole heart and all our strength. May God give us grace to struggle in prayer until we have victory.

The Lost Standard

Do not leave Jerusalem until
the Father sends you what he promised. . . .
In just a few days you will be baptized with the Holy Spirit.
ACTS 1:4–5

After Jesus had given the command to go into all the world and preach the gospel to every creature, He added His very last command: "Do not leave Jerusalem until the Father sends you what he promised. . . . In just a few days you will be baptized with the Holy Spirit."

Christians agree that the command to preach the gospel was not only for the disciples but is for us, too. But not everyone considers that this last command is also for us. The Church appears to have lost possession of its secret—the awareness that it is only by living in the power of the Holy Spirit that the gospel can be preached in power. Because of this there is a lot of preaching and working with very few spiritual results. There is little prayer that brings down God's power.

For the next several days we will study the secret of Pentecost as it is found in the words and deeds of our Master and His disciples. They continued with one accord in prayer until the promise was fulfilled. Then they became full of the Holy Spirit and proved what the power of God could do.

The Kingdom of God

During the forty days after his crucifixion,
he appeared to the apostles from time to time. . . .
On these occasions he talked to them
about the Kingdom of God.

ACTS 1:3

When Christ began to preach, He repeated the message of John that the kingdom of heaven was near. Later He said: "Some of you standing here right now will not die before you see the Kingdom of God arrive in great power!" (Mark 9:1). That could not happen until the King had taken His throne. Then His disciples were ready to receive the gift of the Holy Spirit, bringing down the kingdom of God in its heavenly power.

Our text tells us that all the teaching of Jesus after the Resurrection dealt with the kingdom of God. Luke sums up all the teaching of Paul at Rome: He proclaimed the kingdom of God (Acts 28:31).

Christ, seated upon the throne, was now King and Lord of all. He had entrusted to His disciples the announcement of the kingdom. The prayer He had taught them, "Our Father in heaven. . .may your kingdom come soon" (Matthew 6:9–10), now had a new meaning for them: The Kingdom of God as seen in heaven came down in the power of the Spirit. There was now on earth good news of the kingdom of God ruling and dwelling with men, even as in heaven.

JULY 3

Characteristics of the Kingdom

You will receive power
and will tell people about me everywhere.
ACTS 1:8

"Do not leave Jerusalem until the Father sends you what he promised. . . . In just a few days you will be baptized with the Holy Spirit. . . . When the Holy Spirit has come upon you, you will receive power and will tell people about me everywhere—in Jerusalem, throughout Judea, in Samaria, and to the ends of the earth" (Acts 1:4, 5, 8). In this last command Jesus gave to His disciples we find the essential characteristics of the kingdom presented in great power.

1. The King—the crucified Christ.
2. The disciples—His faithful followers.
3. The power for their service—the Holy Spirit.
4. Their work—testifying for Christ as His witnesses.
5. Their aim—the ends of the earth.
6. Their first duty—waiting on God in united unceasing prayer.

If we are to continue the prayer of the disciples, it is essential to have a clear and full understanding of all that Christ said to them in that last moment, and what it meant for their inner life and all their service.

Christ as King

*I assure you that some of you standing here right now
will not die before you see
the kingdom of God arrive in great power!*

MARK 9:1

Christ said that it would be in the lifetime of some who heard
Him that the kingdom would come in power. That meant that
when He, as King, had ascended the throne of the Father, the
kingdom would be revealed in the hearts of His disciples. In the
kingdom of heaven God's will is always being done. Christ's dis-
ciples would do His will even as it was done in heaven.

We can see in the King the mark of what a kingdom is.
Christ was now on the throne of the Father. On earth its power
is seen in the lives of those it rules. Only in them the united
Body can be seen. Jesus Himself taught how close the relation-
ship would be. "On that day you will realize that I am in my
Father, and you are in Me, and I am in you."

This is our first lesson. We must know that Christ rules in
our hearts as King. We must know that in His power we are able
to accomplish all that He wants us to do. Our whole life is to be
devoted to our King and the service of His kingdom. This
comes only through consistent daily prayer.

Jesus the Crucified

God has made this Jesus whom you crucified
to be both Lord and Messiah.
ACTS 2:36

Our King is none other than the crucified Jesus. All that we know of Him—His divine power, His abiding presence, His wonderful love—does not teach us to know Him fully unless we are deeply conscious that our King is the crucified Jesus. Even the hosts of heaven adore Him. We worship the crucified Jesus as a King.

Christ's cross is His highest glory. Through it He conquered every enemy and gained His place on the throne of God. When Paul wrote "I have been crucified with Christ. . .Christ lives in me" (Galatians 2:19–20), he taught us that it was as the crucified One that Christ ruled on the throne of his heart.

The disciples had been crucified to the world. We also need to experience this fellowship with Christ in His cross if the Spirit of Pentecost is really to take possession of us. It is as we "share in His death" (Philippians 3:10) that we can become worthy servants of a crucified King.

The Apostles

*In one of these meetings as he was
eating a meal with them,
he told them, "Do not leave Jerusalem until
the Father sends you what he promised."*

ACTS 1:4

The second mark of the Church is found in the disciples who received His Spirit and were called to be His witnesses.

What was there in these disciples that enabled them to have such powerful, effectual prayer? They were simple, uneducated men with many faults, whom the Lord had called to forsake all and follow Him. They had done this as much as they could. Though there was much sin in them and so far they had no power to completely deny themselves, their hearts were committed to Him. Even though they stumbled, they still followed Him to the cross. They shared with Him His death; unconsciously but in reality they died with Him to sin and were raised with Him in a new life. It was this that prepared them for the power in prayer.

Have we surrendered to the fellowship of Christ's sufferings and death? Have we crucified our own life and received the power of Christ's life in us? If so, this will give us freedom to believe that God will hear our prayer and give us His Holy Spirit to work in us. Above everything we seek that intimate fellowship with Him that will enable us to pray the prayer of Pentecost and receive its answer.

Not of This World

And the world hates them because
they do not belong to the world,
just as I do not.
They are not part of this world any more than I am.
JOHN 17:14, 16

In His last night Jesus took pains to make clear to His disciples the impassable gulf between Him and the world and also between them and the world (John 16:16–21). He had said of the Spirit: "The world at large cannot receive him, because it isn't looking for him and doesn't recognize him" (John 14:17). "The world would love you if you belonged to it, but you don't. I chose you to come out of the world, and so it hates you" (John 15:19).

One great mark of the disciples was to be as little a part of the world as Christ was. Christ and the disciples had become united in the cross and the Resurrection; they both belonged to another world, the kingdom of heaven.

Why is it that faith in the Holy Spirit is practiced so little by Christians? The world rules too much in the lives of Christians. The "world offers only the lust for physical pleasure, the lust for everything we see, and pride in our possessions" (1 John 2:16)— all this robs the heart of its desire for that true self-denial necessary for receiving the Holy Spirit.

Obedience

> *If you love me, obey my commandments.*
> *And I will ask the Father,*
> *and he will give you another Counselor,*
> *who will never leave you.*
> JOHN 14:15–16

We have learned how the disciples were trained for the baptism of the Spirit. We have seen what was needed for them to continue with one accord in prayer for the power of the Spirit. Christ was everything to them—even before the cross, but much more after it. With the Resurrection He was their life, their one thought, their only desire.

Was this something special just for the disciples? Or is it something that the Lord asks from all who desire to be filled with the Spirit? God expects it of all His children. The Lord has need of people now as much as then, to receive His Spirit and His power, to minister here on earth and, as intercessors, to link the world to the throne of God.

Is Christ something, nothing, or everything to us? For the average Christian, Christ is something; for the true Christian, Christ is all. When we pray for the power of the Spirit, we must say: "I yield myself with my whole heart to the leading of the Spirit." Full surrender is the question of life or death—an absolute necessity.

The Holy Spirit

You will be baptized with the Holy Spirit.
But when the Holy Spirit has come upon you,
you will receive power.
ACTS 1:5, 8

The third mark of the Church is the power for service through the Holy Spirit. Since the time of Adam's fall when he lost the spirit God had breathed into him, God's Spirit had worked with people and worked in some with power. But He had never been able to find His permanent home in them.

It was only when Christ had come, had broken the power of sin by His death, and had won a new life for men in the Resurrection, that the Spirit of God could come and take possession of the whole heart.

Nothing less than this could be the power—in the disciples and in us—by which sin could be overcome and prisoners set free. This Spirit is the Holy Spirit. In the Old Testament He was called the Spirit of God. But in the cross of Christ the holiness of God was magnified, and Christ has purified us that we might be pure like Him.

He is the Spirit of the Son. On earth He led the Son and Christ yielded Himself implicitly to the leading of the Spirit, even to the Crucifixion. The Spirit now reveals Christ in us as our life and our strength, for a perfect obedience.

The Power from on High

> *But stay here. . .*
> *until the Holy Spirit comes*
> *and fills you with power from heaven.*
> LUKE 24:49

The Lord said to the disciples: "Apart from me you can do nothing" (John 15:5). Why is it that He chose these weak men to go out to conquer the world for Him? It was so they would yield themselves to Him and give Him the opportunity to show His power working through them. As the Father had done all the work in Christ when He was on earth, so Christ would now be the great worker, proving in the disciples the power that had been given to Him in heaven and on earth. Their place would be to pray, to believe, and to yield themselves to the mighty power of Christ.

The Holy Spirit would not be in them a power they could possess, but He would possess them. Their work really would be the work of the almighty Christ. Their whole posture would be that of unceasing dependence and prayer and of confident expectation.

The Apostles had learned to know Christ intimately. They had seen His mighty works; they had received His teaching; they had gone with Him through His sufferings. And they had known Him in the power of His Resurrection. They had experienced that resurrection life in their own hearts. Yet they were not capable of making Him known as they should until He Himself had taken possession of them by His Spirit dwelling in them.

Everything calls the Christian to be content with nothing less than the indwelling life and power of the Holy Spirit.

My Witnesses

You will tell people about me everywhere.
ACTS 1:8

The fourth mark of Christ's Church: His servants are to be witnesses to Him, testifying of His love, of His power to redeem, of His abiding presence, and of His power to work in them.

This is the only weapon that the King allows His redeemed ones to use. Without claiming authority, power, wisdom, or eloquence, without influence or position, each one is called by words and action to be living proof of what Jesus can do.

This is the only weapon they are to use in conquering men and bringing them to the feet of Christ. This is what the first disciples did. It was in this power that those who were scattered abroad by persecution went out preaching in the name of Jesus. And a multitude believed. They had no commission from the apostles, they had no special gifts or training, but out of the fullness of the heart they spoke of Jesus Christ.

This is the secret of a flourishing Church: every believer a witness for Jesus. And this is the cause of the weakness of the Church: so few willing to testify daily that Jesus is Lord.

What a call to prayer!

The Gospel Ministry

But I will send you. . .
the Spirit of truth. He will. . .
tell you all about me.
And you must also tell others about me.
JOHN 15:26–27

Tell others—that not only refers to all believers but especially to all ministers of the gospel. This is the only power of the preacher of the gospel—to be a witness for Jesus in everything.

This gives us two great truths. First, with all that the preacher teaches from the Word of God or according to the need of his congregation, he must first preach Christ Himself. This is what the first disciples did. "And every day, in the Temple and in their homes, they continued to teach and preach this message: 'The Messiah you are looking for is Jesus' " (Acts 5:42). And Paul writes: "I decided to concentrate only on Jesus Christ and his death on the cross" (1 Corinthians 2:2).

The minister of the gospel must never forget that he has been set apart to be, with the Holy Spirit, a witness for Christ. It is as he does this that sinners will find salvation and that God's children will be sanctified and prepared for His service.

The second thought is just as important. The teaching must always be a personal testimony from experience to who Christ is and what He can do. The Holy Spirit carries the message as a living reality to the heart. It is this that will build up believers so that they can walk in fellowship with Jesus Christ. And it is this that will lead them to the knowledge of the indispensable secret of spiritual health—the prayer life in daily fellowship, in child-like love, with the Father and the Son.

The Whole World

You will receive power and will
tell people about me everywhere. . .
to the ends of the earth.
ACTS 1:8

Here we have the fifth mark of Christ's Church—the whole world.

How can this be? The man who, in His absolute humanity, had been crucified by His enemies speaks of the ends of the earth as His dominion! What foolishness is expressed by those who speak of Christ as being nothing but a man. How could it have entered the mind of any writer to prophesy that by the disciples He should conquer the world? No human mind could have formed such a conception. It is the thought of God.

The word that Jesus spoke to His disciples, "When the Holy Spirit has come upon you, you will receive power" (Acts 1:8), gave them the assurance that the Holy Spirit would maintain in them Christ's divine power. Christ assured His disciples that He Himself would work all their works in them from the throne of heaven. They could ask anything and it would be done to them. In the strength of that promise the Church of Christ can make the ends of the earth its aim.

The Earth Filled with His Glory

Bless his glorious name forever!
Let the whole earth be filled with his glory.
Amen and Amen!
PSALM 72:19

What a prospect—this earth, now under the power of the evil one, renewed and filled with the glory of God. Though it is hard to believe, it surely will come to pass; God's Word is the pledge of it. God's Son, by His blood and death, conquered the power of sin. The power of God is working out His purpose and the whole earth will be filled with His glory!

But it is a difficult work. It is two thousand years since Christ ascended the throne, and yet hundreds of millions have never learned the name of Jesus. Of the rest, there are millions called by His name, yet they don't even know Him. This work of bringing the knowledge of Christ to every creature has been entrusted to a Church that thinks little of its responsibility and of the consequence of its neglect. Will the work ever be done? God's power and faithfulness are pledges that one day we shall see it—the whole earth filled with the glory of God.

What a wonderful prayer! For it is a prayer: "Let the whole earth be filled with his glory. Amen and Amen!" Every believer is called to this prayer. How wonderful to know that true prayer will indeed be answered! What joy to seek God's face and, with confidence, pray with perseverance until the earth is full of His Glory!

The First Prayer Meeting

They all met together continually for prayer,
along with Mary the mother of Jesus,
several other women, and the brothers of Jesus.
ACTS 1:14

The sixth mark of the early Church—waiting on the promise of the Father in united prayer.

It is difficult to adequately understand the enormous importance of this first prayer meeting, a prayer meeting which was the simple fulfilling of the command of Christ. It was the first example of the one condition on which His Spirit would be known in power. In it we have the secret key that opens the storehouse of heaven.

Christ had prayed that the disciples might be one, even as He and the Father were one, so the world would know that God loved them as He loved Christ. The disciples were far from such a state when Christ prayed the prayer. We see it in the conflict among them at the Last Supper as to who would be chief.

It was only after Christ had gone to heaven that they would spend ten days in united prayer and be brought to that place of love and purpose which would make them the unified Body of Christ, prepared to receive the Spirit in all His power. What a prayer meeting! The fruit of Christ's training during His three years with them was evident there.

This prayer meeting gives us the law of the kingdom. Where Christ's disciples are linked to each other in love and yield themselves completely to Him, the Spirit will be given from heaven to show God's approval. Christ will show His mighty power.

The Unity of the Spirit

Always keep yourselves united in the Holy Spirit. . . .
We are all one body, we have the same Spirit.
EPHESIANS 4:3–4

We learn from Paul how the Christian communities in different places ought to remember each other in the fellowship of prayer. He writes more than once of how the ministry of intercession glorifies God.

Today there still is a great need for Christians to be drawn close together in the awareness of their being chosen by God. We need to understand our role as a holy priesthood ministering continually the sacrifice of praise and prayer. What can be done to foster the unity of the Spirit?

Nothing will help so much as the separation to a life of more prayer, praying specifically that God's people will demonstrate their unity in a life of holiness and love. That will be a living testimony to the world of what it means to live for God. Paul names one of the essential differences between God's people and the world: "Pray at all times and on every occasion in the power of the Holy Spirit. Stay alert and be persistent in your prayers for all Christians everywhere" (Ephesians 6:18).

Earnestly desire to bear this mark of the children of God. Resolve to carry this great distinction of the Christian—a life of intercession. Join with others who are committed to praying down a blessing upon His Church. Don't hesitate to give a quarter of an hour every day for meditation on some promise of God to His Church—and then plead with Him for its fulfillment. Unobservedly, slowly, but surely, you will become one with God's people, and receive the power to pray the prayer that accomplishes much.

Unity Is Strength

After this prayer. . .
they were all filled with the Holy Spirit. . . .
All the believers were of one heart and mind.
ACTS 4:31–32

We see the power of union everywhere in nature. How tiny is a drop of rain as it falls. But when many drops are united in one stream, the power quickly becomes irresistible. Such was the prayer at Pentecost. And our prayer can be like that if we unite all our forces in pleading the promise of the Father. When the world comes in like a flood, it can be overcome in the power of united prayer.

Because of the many mountains in Natal, the streams often flow down with great force. The Zulus join hands when they want to pass through a stream. The leader has a strong stick in the right hand and gives his left hand to some strong man who comes behind him. And so they form a chain and help each other cross the current. When God's people reach out their hands to each other in the spirit of prayer, there will be power to resist the terrible influence that the world can exert. In that unity God's children will have power to triumph with God.

Christ's followers stayed ten days in the upper room until they truly had become one heart. When the Spirit of God descended, He not only filled each individual but took possession of the whole group as the Body of Christ. It is in the fellowship of loving and believing prayer that our hearts can be melted into one. Then we will become strong to believe and to accept what God has promised us.

Prayer in the Name of Christ

You can ask for anything in my name,
and I will do it,
because the work of the Son
brings glory to the Father.
JOHN 14:13

The link between our prayers and the work of Christ in heaven is wonderful. Much prayer on earth brings Him much glory in heaven. Little prayer means, as far as we are concerned, little glory to the Father. What an incentive to pray. Our prayer is indispensable to glorifying the Father.

Christ desired that His disciples learn to believe in the power of His name and to benefit from His promise of a sure answer. His desire was so strong that we find the promise repeated seven times. He longs to stir in us a confident faith and to teach us to look upon intercession as the most certain way of bringing glory to God.

If we think that prayer is not easy, we need to remember what Christ told His disciples: when the Holy Spirit came they would have power to pray. He promises us, "Ask, using my name, and you will receive, and you will have abundant joy" (John 16:24), to encourage us to yield ourselves to the control of the Spirit. As we believe in the power of the Spirit, intercession will become to us the joy and strength of our service.

When Paul wrote "Whatever you do or say, let it be as a representative of the Lord Jesus, all the while giving thanks through him to God the Father" (Colossians 3:17), he reminds us how everything in life is to bear the signature of the name of Jesus. As we learn to live in that name, we will pray with the confidence that our prayer in Jesus' name will be answered.

Your Heavenly Father

Our Father which art in heaven.
LUKE 11:2 KJV

This invocation which Christ teaches us to pray is so simple. Yet it is inconceivably rich in meaning and in the fullness of the love and blessing it contains.

A book could be written of all the memories here of wise and loving fathers. Think of what this world owes to fathers who have made their children strong and happy by giving their lives to look out for the welfare of others. All this is but a shadow of what the Father in heaven is to His children on earth.

Christ gave us a gift when He gave us the right to say: "Father, our Father, my Father." We count it a great privilege as we bow in worship to know that the Father comes near to us where we are here on earth. But we soon begin to feel the need of rising up to enter into His holy presence in heaven. As we leave earth behind in the power of thought and imagination, and as we enter the holiest of all in the power of the Holy Spirit, the words "heavenly Father" get new meaning.

We can only bow in reverent, loving adoration to "Father, our Father, my Father." Joy and power can come to us as we rest rejoicing in Jesus' words: "How much more will your heavenly Father give the Holy Spirit to those who ask him" (Luke 11:13).

The Power of Prayer

The earnest prayer of a righteous person
has great power and wonderful results.
JAMES 5:16

Prayer is effective with God. It affects the history of His Church and people. Prayer is the one power the Church can exercise in securing the working of God's omnipotence in the world.

The prayer of a righteous person is powerful and effective. A righteous person lives as the servant of righteousness (see Romans 6:16, 19). The Lord loves the righteous and their prayers have power (see Psalm 66:18–19; 1 John 3:22). When Christ gave His great prayer promises, it was to those who keep His commandments. "If you love me, obey my commandments. And I will ask the Father, and he will give you another Counselor, who will never leave you" (John 14:15–16). "But if you stay joined to me and my words remain in you, you may ask any request you like, and it will be granted!" (John 15:7).

When the righteous commit their whole being to take hold of God, prayer is powerful and effective. As Jacob said: "I will not let you go unless you bless me" (Genesis 32:26).

Then comes the earnest prayer of many righteous people together. When two or three agree, there is the promise of an answer. God will display His power even more when hundreds and thousands unite in earnest prayer.

Prayer and Sacrifice

I want you to know how much I have agonized for you.
COLOSSIANS 2:1

People who undertake a great venture have to prepare themselves and direct all their abilities to that end. Likewise, we as Christians need to prepare ourselves to pray just as God's Word tells us to love God: "with all your heart, all your soul, all your strength, and all your mind" (Luke 10:27). This is the law of the kingdom. Prayer needs sacrifice of comfort, of time, of self. Sacrifice is the secret of powerful prayer.

Christ Jesus, the great Intercessor, was an example of sacrifice in prayer. It is written of Him, "When he sees all that is accomplished by his anguish, he will be satisfied. . . . I will give him the honors of one who is mighty and great, because he exposed himself to death" (Isaiah 53:11–12). In Gethsemane "he offered prayers and pleadings, with a loud cry and tears, to the one who could deliver him out of death" (Hebrews 5:7). Prayer *is* sacrifice. David said: "Accept my prayer as incense offered to you, and my upraised hands as an evening offering [sacrifice]" (Psalm 141:2).

Our prayer receives its worth from being rooted in the sacrifice of Jesus Christ. As He gave up everything in His prayer, "Your will be done," our attitude must always be the offering up of everything to God and His service.

When we are reluctant to make the needful sacrifice in waiting upon God, we lack power in our prayer. Christ—the Christ we trust in, the Christ that lives in us—offered Himself a sacrifice to God. It is as this spirit lives and rules in us that we will receive power to pray the earnest prayer that accomplishes much.

Intercession of the Spirit for Saints

The Father who knows all hearts knows
what the Spirit is saying,
for the Spirit pleads for us believers
in harmony with God's own will.

ROMANS 8:27

These words shed light on the life of prayer of the saints! We do not know what we should pray for. This often hinders our prayer or hinders the faith that is essential to its success. But here we are told that the Holy Spirit prays for us: "The Spirit pleads for us believers in harmony with God's own will."

What hope this gives us! Where and how does the Spirit pray for the saints? In the heart which does not know what to pray He secretly and effectually prays what is in harmony with the will of God. This of course implies that we trust Him to do His work in us and that we spend time with God even when we do not know what to pray.

What a difference it would make in the life of many of God's children if they realized this! We not only have Jesus, the great High Priest, ever living to intercede for us; we not only have the liberty of asking in faith what we desire and the promise that it shall be given to us; but we have in very deed the Holy Spirit to intercede for us in harmony with the will of God.

This calls us to separate ourselves from the world and to yield ourselves wholeheartedly to the leading and praying of the Spirit within us!

That They All May Be One

Holy Father, keep them and care for them—
all those you have given me—
so that they will be united just as we are.
JOHN 17:11

Jesus continues, "I am praying not only for these disciples but also for all who will ever believe in me because of their testimony. My prayer for all of them is that they will be one, just as you and I are one, Father—that just as you are in me and I am in you, so they will be in us, and the world will believe you sent me. I have given them the glory you gave me, so that they may be one, as we are—I in them and you in me, all being perfected into one. Then the world will know that you sent me and will understand that you love them as much as you love me" (John 17:20–23).

Notice how the Lord refers to "being one" five times in this text. It is as if He felt the need to strongly emphasize these words so we would really realize the main thought of His High Priestly prayer. He longs that the words have the same place in our hearts that they have in His. As He was on the way to go to the Father through the cross, He wanted us to understand that He took this desire with Him to heaven. He wanted us to know that He will make it the object of His unceasing intercession there.

He entrusted the words to us that we should take them into the world and make them the object of our unceasing intercession too. That alone would enable us to fulfill the last new command which He gave: that we should love each other as He loved us so that we would be full of joy.

One with All Believers

I in them and you in me,
all being perfected into one.
Then the world will know that you sent me
and will understand that you love them
as much as you love me.

JOHN 17:23

The Lord Jesus entrusted these words to us so that we would make them the object of our persistent intercession. Only that would enable us to carry out the last command which He gave: that we should love our brothers and sisters in Christ as He loved us so that our joy would be full.

Our churches today are not always marked by a fervent, affectionate love for all the saints of whatever name or denomination. As a part of our daily fellowship with God, let us pray "that we may be one."

It would be simple if once we connected the words, "our Father," with all the children of God throughout the world. Each time we used the words we would only have to expand this little word "our" into all the largeness of God's Father-love. Just as we say "Father" with the thought of our love to Him, we can say "our" with the childlike affection for all the saints whoever and wherever they be. The prayer that "we may be one" would then bring joy and strength, a deeper bond of fellowship with Christ Jesus and all His saints, and an offering of sweet savor to the Father of love.

The Disciples' Prayer

They all met together continually for prayer.
ACTS 1:14

What a lesson it would be to us in the school of prayer to have a clear understanding of what continually meeting for prayer meant to the disciples.

The disciples knew from the words of Jesus that "it is actually best for you that I go away, because if I don't, the Counselor won't come" (John 16:7). They knew that the Spirit would give the glorified Christ to their hearts in a way they had never known Him before. It would be He Himself, in the mighty power of God's Spirit, Who would be their strength for the work to which He had called them.

With strong confidence they expected the fulfillment of the promise. Had not the Master given them the assurance of what He would send to them from the throne of the Father in heaven?

The disciples prayed with intensity and persistence in the full assurance that, however long the answer might be delayed, He would most assuredly fulfill their desires. Let us realize that the very same promise that was given to the disciples is given to us. Even though we have to cry day and night to God, we can count on the Father to answer our prayers.

As believers we also may unite as one in presenting our requests, even though we cannot be together in one place. We can claim the promise that we, too, will be filled with the Holy Spirit.

Paul's Call to Prayer

*Pray at all times and on every occasion
in the power of the Holy Spirit.
Stay alert and be persistent in your prayers
for all Christians everywhere.
And pray for me, too.*
EPHESIANS 6:18–19

Paul had a sense of the deep unity of the Body of Christ and of the actual need of constant prayer for all members of the Body. He did not mean this to be an occasional thing but the unceasing exercise of life. This is evident from the words he uses, "Pray at all times and on every occasion." He expects believers to be filled with the consciousness that they are in Christ and, through Him, united to the whole Body. Their highest aim would always be the welfare of the Body of Christ.

Paul counted on them being filled with the Spirit so that it would be perfectly natural for them to pray for all who belong to the Body of Jesus Christ. As natural as it is for each member of my body to be ready to do what is needed for the welfare of the whole, even so, where the Holy Spirit has entire control, union with Christ will be accompanied by consciousness of the unity and the love of all the members.

Isn't this what we need in our daily life? Just as war brings to light the intensity with which millions of citizens sacrifice their all for their country, so the saints of God will live for Christ their King and also for all the members of that Body of which He is the Head.

Paul's Request for Prayer

And pray for me, too.
Ask God to give me the right words
as I boldly explain God's secret plan.. . .
pray that I will keep on speaking boldly for him,
as I should.
EPHESIANS 6:19–20

These words, "pray for me, too," indicate Paul's faith in the ab-
solute necessity and the wonderful power of prayer. Listen to
how he asks them to pray: "But pray that I will keep on speaking
boldly for him, as I should." Paul had been a minister of the
gospel for more than twenty years. You would think that he had
such experience that it would come naturally for him to speak
boldly. But his conviction of his own weakness is so deep and his
dependence on divine power is so absolute, that he feels he can-
not do the work as it should to be done without the direct help
of God. His total dependence upon God is the ground of all his
confidence.

But there is more. Because of his deep spiritual insight into
the unity of the Body of Christ, and because of his own depend-
ence on the prayers of others, he pleads for their prayers in the
Spirit. Paul could not do without the prayers of the believers.

May we realize anew that Christ is our Intercessor in heaven,
and all saints here on earth are engaged in one mighty contest.
We must cultivate the gift of unceasing prayer for the power of
God's Spirit in all His servants.

Prayer for All Saints

Devote yourselves to prayer with an alert mind
and a thankful heart.
Don't forget to pray for us, too.
COLOSSIANS 4:2–3

Prayer for all saints—it will take time, thought, and love to realize what is included in that expression. It means thinking of the saints you know, thinking of your whole country, thinking of the nations of the world and the saints to be found in each of them, and thinking of the saints of God living in persecuted places.

All of these have different circumstances and varying needs for God's help. Pray for many of God's saints who are walking in the dark because of ignorance or laziness or an evil heart.

Think of so many who are in earnest and yet conscious of a life of failure, with little or no power to please God or to serve others. Then think of those whose one aim is to serve the Lord and to be light to those around them. Think of them especially as joining in pleading for the great promise of the Holy Spirit and the love and unity which He alone can give.

This is not the work of one day or one night. It needs a heart which will commit to do serious intercession for the Body of Christ. Once we begin we will find abundant reason for persevering in praying for the love of God to fill the hearts of His people and for the power of the Holy Spirit to accomplish God's work in this world.

Prayer by All Saints

We are confident that he will continue to deliver us.
He will rescue us because
you are helping by praying for us.
2 CORINTHIANS 1:10–11

Prayer calls us to think of all saints throughout the world from a different standpoint. If we are to ask God to increase the number and the power of those who pray, we will form some impression of whom we are praying for.

Our first thoughts will naturally turn to the multitude of saints who think very little about the duty or the joy of interceding for the Body of Christ. We will also remember many that do intercede for the power of His Spirit, but their thoughts are chiefly limited to spheres of work that they are directly interested in.

That will leave us with a limited number who will be ready to take part in the prayer for the unity of the Body and the power of the Spirit, though this prayer ought to be sent up by the whole Church.

Prayer meets a long-felt need: that it is an unspeakable privilege to make Christ's last prayer, "that they will be one" (John 17:21), the daily supplication of our faith and love. Maybe in time believers will band together in helping to encourage those around them to take part in the great work of prayer for all saints.

This message is given to all who seek to prove their consecration to their Lord in the unceasing daily supplication for the power of His love and Spirit to be revealed to all His people.

Prayer for the Fullness of the Spirit

> *Bring all the tithes into the storehouse. . . .*
> *If you do. . .*
> *I will pour out a blessing so great*
> *you won't have enough room to take it in!*
>
> MALACHI 3:10

This last promise in the Old Testament tells us how abundant the blessing is to be. Pentecost was only the beginning of what God was willing to do. The promise of the Father still waits for its perfect fulfillment. Try to realize how much liberty we have to ask and expect great things.

The great command to go and preach the gospel was not only meant for the disciples but for us, too. So the very last command, "Stay here. . .until the Holy Spirit comes and fills you with power from heaven" (Luke 24:49), is also for us. "Do not leave Jerusalem until the Father sends you what he promised. . . . In just a few days you will be baptized with the Holy Spirit" (Acts 1:4–5). We have confident assurance that our prayer with one accord will be heard.

Take time to think of what a cry of need there is throughout the whole Church. There is only one remedy to be found to enable us to gain victory over the powers of this world. It is the manifest presence of our Lord. Let us take time to think of the state of all the Churches throughout Christendom until we are brought to the conviction that nothing will be accomplished except by the supernatural intervention of our Lord Himself. Only He can call His hosts for the great battle against evil. Our main prayer should be for the power of God on all His people— to give them power from on high to make the gospel in very deed the power of God unto salvation.

Every Day

Give us our food day by day.
LUKE 11:3

There are some Christians who are afraid to promise to pray every day. They believe it is beyond them, and yet they pray to God to give them their food day by day. If a child of God has yielded his whole life to God's love and service, he should count it a privilege to come into God's presence every day.

There are many of us who desire to live wholly for God. We acknowledge that Christ gave Himself for us and that He watches over us without ceasing. We admit that the measure of the love of Christ for us is to be the measure of our love for Him. We want to devote our lives to Christ's kingdom and to the prayer that can bring down God's blessing.

Our invitation to pray day and night for His power on His people and on this needy world may come as a new and unexpected opportunity. Think of the privilege of being allowed to plead every day with God on behalf of His saints for the outpouring of His Spirit and for the coming of His kingdom. If you have not understood the privilege and solemn duty of waiting on God in prayer, the invitation will be most welcome.

Believers Meeting Together

On the day of Pentecost. . .
the believers were meeting together in one place.
And everyone present was filled with the Holy Spirit.
ACTS 2:1, 4

We have gained wonderful new insights into the solidarity of the whole Body of Christ and the need to cultivate the slumbering talents of intercession. We know of the tens of thousands of His children who pray daily for some portion of God's kingdom. But in many cases prayers are limited to the work that they take interest in. There is a lack of a large-hearted love that takes all the saints of God in its embrace. There is not the boldness and the strength that comes from the awareness of being part of a conquering army under the leadership of our King.

In the British Army during war, with its millions of soldiers, each detachment not only throws its whole heart into its work, but it takes new courage from every report of the bravery of the farthest members of the one great army. That is what we need in the Church of Christ. Enthusiasm for the King and His kingdom and confident faith in Him should make us pray every day with a large-hearted love that grasps the whole Body of Christ and pleads for the power of the Holy Spirit on all its members.

The strength unity gives is something inconceivable. The power of each individual is increased by the inspiration of fellowship with a large and conquering host. Nothing can help us to an ever-larger faith as much as the awareness of being one Body in Christ Jesus.

A Personal Call

We learned not to rely on ourselves,
but on God who can raise the dead.

2 CORINTHIANS 1:9

When we plead with Christians to pray without ceasing there are a large number who quietly decide that such a life is not possible for them. They think they do not have any special gift for prayer. They may not have an intense desire for glorifying Christ in the salvation of souls; they have not yet learned to live not for themselves but for Him who died and rose again for them.

And yet to them we bring the call to offer themselves to live entirely for Christ. We ask them whether they are not ashamed of the selfish life that simply uses Christ as a convenient escape from hell and to secure a place in heaven. We come to them with the assurance that God can change their lives and fill their hearts with Christ and His Holy Spirit. We plead with them to believe that with God all things are possible. He is eager to restore them to the joy of the Father's presence and service.

One step to accomplish this is to listen to the call to live in the power of Christ's abiding presence and in the spirit of unceasing prayer. This is nothing less than a duty, a sacrifice that Christ's love has a right to claim.

The person who accepts the call and draws near to God in humble prayer for the needed grace will have taken the first step to the path that leads to fellowship with God. It will lead to a new faith in Christ Jesus and to a prayer life that will help bring Pentecost again into the hearts of God's people.

Absolute Dependence

Yes, I am the vine; you are the branches. . . .
For apart from me you can do nothing.
JOHN 15:5

The Christian life is a life of absolute dependence. At Hampton Court there was a vine that sometimes bore a couple thousand clusters of grapes. People were amazed at its productivity. Later the secret was discovered. Not too far from Hampton Court flows the River Thames. The vine had stretched its roots hundreds of yards under the ground until it came to the riverbed. There, in all the nutrients of the river bottom, it found rich nourishment and moisture. The roots drew the sap all that distance to the branches.

The vine had the work to do. The branches simply had to depend upon the vine and receive what it gave.

That is exactly what Christ desires you to understand. Christ desires that in all your work, the very foundation should be the simple acceptance that Christ must care for all.

As you depend on Him He supplies your needs by sending down the Holy Spirit. Jesus wants you to be dependent as you serve Him. Day by day, hour by hour, in everything you do, simply abide before Him. Live in the total helplessness of one who can do nothing.

Absolute dependence upon God is the secret of power in work. You and I have nothing unless we receive it from Jesus.

Inspiration

*You are to be perfect even as your
Father in heaven is perfect.*
MATTHEW 5:48

"It is a mistake to confine inspiration to extraordinary messengers of God. The common Christian desires to be led and inspired by God. Though all are not called to be prophets, all are called to be perfect as their heavenly Father is perfect. The holiness of the Christian is always stirring in us. If we are called to this inward holiness, then a perpetual operation of the Spirit of God within us is absolutely necessary" (William Law).

To know this truth—to be inspired by God to inward holiness—we must experience the Spirit of God, the spirit of love, and the spirit of prayer. The Holy Spirit must dwell in the Christian, bringing us to the full experience of the life of God.

The spirit of love is shown in God's delight in making us partakers of His love. Our nature has fallen into selfishness. Nothing but the death of self can fit us for receiving the love which God seeks to give.

The spirit of prayer comes when we turn away from the vanity of time into the riches of eternity. Self keeps us from prayer, but our hearts can be prepared for prayer by hungering for God and by denying the world. Then the Holy Spirit can do His work and reveal Christ in our inner life.

Our Total Dependence on God

"Why ask me about what is good?"
Jesus replied. "Only God is good."
MATTHEW 19:17

Goodness and virtue in our lives is nothing else but the goodness of God manifesting itself in us. Goodness can only belong to God. It is essential to Him and inseparable from Him. All that is glorious and happy in our spirits is only the glory and blessedness of God dwelling in us. The relationship of unalterable dependence on God is the basis of true faith. It is a continual receiving of every degree of goodness and happiness from God alone.

The angels are full of pure love because the glory, the love, and the goodness of God is all that they see and know. Their adoration in spirit and in truth never ceases because they acknowledge their total dependency on God and His centrality to all of creation.

This is the true religion of heaven and this is the one true religion on earth. Nothing in religion can be good unless the power and presence of God really is living and working in it. Mankind must have all its religious goodness wholly and solely from God's immediate activity.

Continual Inspiration

If your sinful nature controls your mind,
there is death.
But if the Holy Spirit controls your mind,
there is life and peace.
ROMANS 8:6

True religion is an essential union and communion of our spirit with the Spirit of the Creator: God in us, and we in God, one life, one light, one love. Divine inspiration and divine religion are inseparable.

Our human nature has none of the truth or power of divine worship in it. Self-love, self-esteem, and self-seeking are all we can be in the natural man. No one can be in a higher state than this, until something supernatural is found in it. This supernatural something is called in Scripture the Spirit or inspiration of God. It is from that alone that we can have good thoughts about God or the power to let the Holy Spirit control us.

No one can reach God's love unless he is inspired with the spirit of love with which God loved from all eternity. This is the only love that can draw us to God. We have no power to live for Him or adore Him except by His spirit of love. Therefore the continual inspiration or operation of the Holy Spirit is the one only possible ground of our continually loving God.

Let us meditate and pray until this blessed truth begins to get possession of our heart.

The Ministry of the Spirit

It is actually best for you that I go away,
because if I don't,
the Counselor won't come.
JOHN 16:7

A natural life can exist only while it is under the power of the root from which it sprang. Likewise nothing but obedience to the Spirit can possibly keep us from sin. Only the ministry of the Spirit reveals the truth of the gospel.

When Christ told His disciples: "It is actually best for you that I go away," He taught them to understand their great need and joyfully expect the coming of something better. Christ's teaching in human language was changed into the inspiration and operation of the Counselor, the Holy Spirit.

Two basic truths are demonstrated. First, the perfection of the gospel could not take place until Christ was glorified. His kingdom on earth became an on-going ministry of the Spirit.

Secondly, no one can have true knowledge of the spiritual blessings of Christ's redemption, nor have a divine capacity to bear witness of them to the world, except by the Holy Spirit.

It is not easy for us to yield ourselves wholly to this truth. The continual inspiration of the Holy Spirit is absolutely needed, is promised by God, and is made possible to us. Let us make this the one aim of our desire and prayer.

Humility

If you want to be my follower
you must love me more than your own
father and mother, wife and children,
brothers and sisters—
yes, more than your own life.
LUKE 14:26

The gifts of human learning and wisdom often assert themselves in Christians, instead of that entire dependence upon the Holy Spirit of which Christ spoke. Exaltation of self is the consequence. The Church demonstrates the difference between pride in the power of human learning and humility with absolute dependence on the teaching of the Holy Spirit. Without humility we become self-sufficient and cease from persevering in prayer.

Our minds, by the Fall, are self-sufficient and require self-denial. We need to know two things: 1) Our salvation consists of being saved from ourselves or from that which we are by nature; 2) this salvation was given to us in great humility by God, who manifested Himself in human form. The first stipulation of this Savior to fallen man is: "If you want to be my follower you must love me more than. . .your own life." To show that this is only the beginning of man's salvation, Jesus also says: "Let me teach you, because I am humble and gentle, and you will find rest for your souls" (Matthew 11:29).

What a light is here for those who love the light. Self is the whole evil of the fallen nature; self-denial enables us to become a follower of Jesus, our example of humility.

The Humility of Christ

Let me teach you, because I am humble and
gentle, and you will find rest for your souls.
MATTHEW 11:29

All the vices of fallen angels and men have their birth and power in the pride of self, or I may better say, in the atheism and idolatry of self. Self is both atheist and idolater. It is atheist because it has rejected God. It is an idolater because it is its own idol.

On the other hand, all the virtues of the heavenly life are the virtues of humility. Joy, glory, and praise in heaven are results of humility. Only in humility do we depend on prayer. It is humility alone that bridges the impossible gulf between heaven and hell. This is the most plain truth of the gospel. There never was, nor ever will be, a better example of humility than that of Christ.

In the life of faith, humility has a far deeper place than we think. It is not only one among other virtues, but it is the first and chief need of the soul. It leads us to know the absolute and entire inability in ourselves to do any good. It leads us to look to the humility of our Lord Jesus as being a virtue He has prepared in His life for us and will work in us in response to our faith.

AUGUST 10

The Kingdom of Heaven

The Kingdom of God is near.
MARK 1:15

"May your Kingdom come soon. May your will be done here on earth, just as it is in heaven" (Matthew 6:10). God's kingdom in heaven is the manifestation of what God is and does in His heavenly creatures. How is His will done there? Through His Holy Spirit who is the life, the power, and mover of all who live there.

We pray this prayer, "May your kingdom come," daily—knowing that only God can do what we have prayed. Where can God's kingdom come except where every other power but His has ended? How can only His will be done except through the Spirit?

This is the truth of the kingdom of God come unto humanity. This is the birthright privilege of all that are members of it. They can be delivered from their own natural spirit which they had from Adam and from the spirit and wisdom of this world. Throughout their whole lives they only need to say, to do, and to be what the Spirit of their Father works in them.

Much has been written about what the kingdom of heaven means, but here we have what it really is. As God rules in His kingdom in heaven, likewise when the kingdom is in our hearts, He lives and rules there. The kingdom of God consists of the people in whom God rules as He does in heaven.

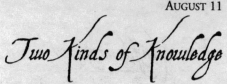

Two Kinds of Knowledge

The old way ends in death; in the new way,
the Holy Spirit gives life.
2 CORINTHIANS 3:6

Every kind of virtue may be brought into us by two different ways. They may be taught us outwardly by men, by rules and precepts; and they may be inwardly born in us as the genuine birth of our own renewed spirit.

The former at best change our outward behavior, putting our passions under a false restraint. This way of learning goodness, though imperfect, is necessary. But all this outward instruction, whether from good men or the Scripture, makes nothing perfect.

The Scriptures have no good or benefit except as they lead to salvation. This salvation is not from the Scriptures themselves but from faith in Christ Jesus. Scripture is to teach us where to find the source of all light and knowledge and can only direct us to something better.

If you learn virtue and goodness only from men or books, you will be virtuous according to time and place and outward forms. You may do works of humility and love. But the inward virtues are only to be obtained by the operation of the Holy Spirit—not outwardly teaching but inwardly bringing forth a newborn spirit within us.

Key to the Treasures in Heaven

Whatever is good and perfect comes
to us from God above.
JAMES 1:17

We have been sent into the world with an important errand: by prayer to rise out of the vanity of time into the riches of eternity. We have access to all that is great and good and happy and carry within ourselves a key to the treasures of heaven.

God is not an absent God. He is more present in our souls than our own bodies. We are strangers to heaven and without God because we are void of the spirit of prayer. It opens heaven and the kingdom of God within us. A plant living in the best climate is not so sure of its growth as a person whose spirit aspires after all that God wants to give him.

We are the offspring of God. "In Him we live and move and exist" (Acts 17:28). The first man had the breath and spirit of God breathed into him. He was in the image and likeness of God because the Holy Trinity had breathed its own nature into him. The spirit breathed into man brought heaven into man.

The lesson that we find here is one of the deepest truths of God's Word. As willing as the sun is to shine its light on the waiting earth, so is the living God waiting to work in the heart of His child.

The Goodness of God

For God so loved the world that he gave his only Son,
so that everyone who believes in him
will not perish but have eternal life.

JOHN 3:16

The goodness of God was the cause of the creation. In all eternity God's only thought or intent has been to communicate good to His creation. As the sun gives the blessings of life, so our holy God pours forth the riches of divine perfection upon everything that has capacity to receive them.

This is the love of God. He is the unchangeable, overflowing fountain of good. He is love itself—the unmixed immeasurable love doing nothing but from love, giving nothing but gifts of love. He requires nothing of all His creatures but the fruit of that love which brought them into being. Oh, how marvelous is this contemplation of the height and depth of the riches of divine love.

Look at every part of our redemption—from Adam's sin to the resurrection of the dead—and you will find nothing but successive mysteries of that first love which created angels and men. All the mysteries of the gospel are proofs of God's desire to make His love triumph over sin and disorder from all nature.

As God's children we need to wait before God in quiet till His light shines on us. Unless we take time enough with God for His light to shine into the depths of our hearts, it is useless for us to expect that His immeasurable love can enter our hearts and fill our lives.

AUGUST 14

The Kingdom of Self

The law no longer holds you in its power,
because you died to its power when
you died with Christ on the cross.
ROMANS 7:4

Mankind has fallen from a life in God into a life of self—a life of self-love, self-esteem, and self-seeking. God's creatures chose to concentrate on the perishing pleasures of the world. All sin, death, and hell are nothing else but this kingdom of self.

On the Day of Pentecost a new dispensation of God came forth. On God's part it was the operation of the Holy Spirit in gifts and graces upon the Church. On our part it was the adoration of God in spirit and in truth. All this was to make way for the continual operation of God to enable us, baptized with the Holy Spirit, to absolutely renounce self. We are to use our minds and all the outward things of the world only as enlightened and inspired by the Holy Spirit.

The kingdom of self is the fall of man and the great apostasy from the life of God. The kingdom of Christ is the Spirit and power of God manifesting itself in the birth of a new inward person. When the call of God to repentance comes in your soul, be quiet before God in prayer and humbly attentive to the new life within you. Disregard the workings of your own will and reason. Then you will know the power and love of God in its fullness.

The Sinful Nature

The LORD. . .saw that all their thoughts
were consistently and totally evil.
GENESIS 6:5

Our sinful nature makes necessary the denial of all our senses, appetites, tempers, passions, and judgments. Our own life is to be rejected. The reason is plain: There is nothing lovely in it. We must own our own insignificance and inability. We must recognize that our only capacity for good is by receiving it from God. When we come to this, our self will be wholly denied and its kingdom destroyed.

As believers we know we are to die to self and live for Christ. Therefore look upon every day as lost that does not encourage both this death and this life. Through God's mercy, desire that every moment of your life may be given to Him. Pray from the bottom of your heart that the spark of life that had so long been smothered under earthly rubbish might breathe and come to life in you.

Keep this thought in mind: To make way for the continual operation of God through the power of the Holy Spirit in us, we need to renounce self and yield our whole being to God. This self-denial is indispensable if God's redeeming love is to display its power and blessing in our lives.

Prayer: A State of the Heart

Everything else is worthless when compared
with the priceless gain of knowing Christ Jesus my Lord.
PHILIPPIANS 3:8

Jesus, though He had all wisdom, only gave us a small number of moral teachings. This is because He knew that the desire of our hearts is focused on this world. Nothing can set us right but turning the desire of our hearts to God. Therefore He calls us to a total denial of ourselves and the life of this world. He calls us to a faith in Him as the one who gives a new birth and a new life. He teaches us every reason for renouncing ourselves and for loving our redemption as the greatest joy and desire of our heart.

We see that our will and our heart are everything. True religion is only the religion of the heart. We see that a spirit of longing after the life of this world made us the poor pilgrims on earth that we are. Only the spirit of prayer, or the longing desire of the heart after Christ and God and heaven, breaks our bondage and lifts us out of the miseries of time into the riches of eternity.

When the spirit of prayer is born in us, it is no longer confined to a certain hour but is the continual breathing of the heart after God. The spirit of prayer, as a state of the heart, becomes the governing principle of the soul's life.

A Continual Relationship

Don't worry about anything;
instead, pray about everything.
PHILIPPIANS 4:6

Seeing and knowing our selfish condition calls us to prayer. The desire of our heart becomes the spirit of prayer. What characteristics of prayer should distinguish the Christian?

At times an honest person may show honesty by actions. At other times there is no special situation to confirm this honesty. But honesty is, all the same, the inward living principle of that person's heart. Just so the spirit of prayer may quietly possess the heart without interruption and at other times may have certain hours of prayer. But prayer that has its own life and spirit is vastly superior to any ritual form. It is independent and has no particular hours or forms of work.

It would be worthwhile to study the place that the word "continual" ought to have in our life: continual joy of the infinite love of God towards us; continual unalterable dependence upon God every hour of our life; the continual receiving of goodness and happiness from God alone; the continual denial of our evil nature; the continual and immediate inspiration of the Holy Spirit maintaining the life of Christ in us; the continual breathing of the heart after God in prayer; and then the continual loving Him with our whole heart.

The Despair of Self

*If we love our Christian brothers and sisters
it proves that we have passed
from death to eternal life.*
1 JOHN 3:14

When the truth of God touches our hearts, we know we cannot overcome the hardness of heart and pride just by the force of our own reason. It is only through death to ourselves that we can pass into life. There is no real conversion from the life of sin until we realize that our whole nature must be parted with, but we discover that in ourselves we cannot do it.

Through this despair we lose all our life to find a new one in God. Here faith, hope, and true seeking for God are born. But up to this point, faith and hope and turning to God in prayer have been practiced only by obligation and method. They are not living qualities of a new birth until we have stopped feeling any confidence in ourselves.

We must feel within the reach of divine love. We must feel that God created us to be a habitation of His own life and Holy Spirit. In dealing with us, love is God's bait. It will put its hook into the heart and make us realize that nothing is so strong, so irresistible, as divine love.

The Practice of Prayer

> *Those who belong to Christ Jesus*
> *have nailed the passions and desires*
> *of their sinful nature to his cross*
> *and crucified them there.*
>
> GALATIANS 5:24

The best preparation for the spirit of prayer is thinking about our miserable fall and our glorious redemption. These things fill us with a dislike of our present earthly desires and create in us an honest longing after perfection. Prayer can only be taught by having a true sense of who we are and who we should be. Then we are filled with a continual longing for God and can pray only for what is pleasing to God.

We should expect nothing from ourselves but in everything depend on God to enable us to nail the passions and desires of our sinful natures to His cross. When we see our inability to have goodness of our own, then our attitude becomes true trust in the work of God's Spirit.

It is strange that our highest privilege—fellowship with God in prayer—is sometimes a burden and a failure. Learn to expect nothing from ourselves. Expect everything from God. These two thoughts lie at the root of all true prayer.

A Touchstone of Truth

*God sets himself against the proud, but
he shows favor to the humble.*
JAMES 4:6

There is an infallible touchstone that will teach you the spirit of
prayer. Pull away from the world and all activities. Stop the for-
mer workings of your heart and mind. With all your strength,
spend all this month as continually as you can in one kind of
prayer to God. Offer it frequently on your knees but, whether
sitting, standing, or walking, always be inwardly longing and
earnestly praying this one prayer to God. Pray that He would
show you and take from your heart every form of pride. Pray
that He would awaken in you the depths of humility so that you
will be open to His light and His Holy Spirit. Reject every
thought except that of praying in this matter from the bottom
of your heart.

The painful sense and feeling of what you are, kindled by the
light of God within you, is the fire and light from which your
spirit of prayer proceeds. At first nothing is found or felt but
pain and darkness. But as this prayer of humility is met by the
divine love, the mercy of God embraces it. Then your prayer is
changed into songs and thanksgiving.

Prayer of Humility

*When you bow down before the Lord
and admit your dependence on him,
he will lift you up and give you honor.*
JAMES 4:10

The first prayer of humility is nothing else but a sense of repentance and confession. Acknowledging our sin and need drives us to total dependence upon God for His light and the power of the Holy Spirit.

When this earnest prayer has melted away all earthly passions and desires so that we delight in God alone, then our prayer changes again. Now we come so near to God and have found such union with Him that we do not so much pray as live in God. Prayer is not any particular action confined to times or words or places. It is the work of the whole being which continually stands in fullness of faith, in purity of love, in absolute willingness to do and be what pleases God. This is the spirit of prayer and is the highest union with God in this life.

Prayer is not merely bringing certain requests to God. Prayer is the highest revelation of our fitness for fellowship with God. It begins with the deep humility and has no desire but to meet God in the fellowship of His love. Then our whole being desires continually to live in absolute surrender to do and be what pleases the Lord.

The Spirit of Prayer

Pray at all times and on every occasion
in the power of the Holy Spirit.
EPHESIANS 6:18

The spirit of the soul is in itself nothing but a spirit breathed from God. He created it for this end only: that the life of God, the nature of God, the working of God might be manifested in it.

The spirit of prayer is stretching with all our desire after the life of God. It is leaving, as far as we can, our own spirit and receiving a Spirit from above to be one life, one love, one spirit with Christ. This prayer is an emptying of ourselves and our own lusts and desires. It is opening ourselves for the light of God to enter into it. It is the prayer in the name of Christ, to which nothing is denied.

The love of God, His never-ceasing desire to enter and dwell in us and give birth to His Spirit in us, waits no longer once the door of our heart opens. Nothing can hinder God's holy union with the soul except the decision of the heart that is turned away from Him. The life of the soul in itself is nothing but a working will. Wherever the will works, there the soul lives, whether it be in God or in the creature.

Our Prayer of the Heart

> *As the deer pants for streams of water,*
> *so I long for you, O God.*
> PSALM 42:1

Turning to God according to our inward feeling, want, and action of heart and turning to God in love, in trust, in faith of having from Him all that we want and need—this turning to God, with or without words, is the best form of prayer in the world.

Prayers not formed according to the real condition of your heart are like prayers pulled out of a deep well when you are not in it.

When the heart really pants after God, its prayer is moved and animated by the Spirit of God. Its prayer is the breath or inspiration of God, stirring and opening itself in the heart. Nothing ever had, or can have, the least tendency to ascend to heaven unless it first came down from heaven. Therefore, every time a truly good desire stirs in one's heart, that heart sends a good prayer that reaches God. That prayer is the fruit and work of His Holy Spirit.

When the heart continually wants to have that which may be expressed in but few words—it is the reality, the steadiness and the continuity of the desire that is the goodness and perfection of the prayer.

The Step of Prayer

Keep on praying.
1 THESSALONIANS 5:17

If you have already taken the first step in the spiritual life, you have devoted yourself absolutely to God to live wholly for His will. You have chosen to be under the light and guidance of His Holy Spirit.

The next step is to continually give yourself to God. This second step cannot be taken except by prayer. Nothing else has power here but prayer. This prayer must come from your heart and your relationship with God. Consider this prayer an infallible guide to heaven. As a person who has some great responsibility turns from everything that is not related to it, so your heart will focus on its own state of prayer as soon as God is its objective.

Our times of prayer are meant to lead us on to a life of prayer. Just as the eye can rejoice all the day in the sunshine which gives it light, so the heart will continually live and rejoice in God's presence. Let us believe that God, who is able to do exceeding abundantly above all that we ask or think, is indeed able and willing to lead us into a life of prayer. By the power of His Holy Spirit, He will strengthen us for this life of unceasing prayer as we walk in the light of His countenance.

The Image of God

> Then God said,
> "Let us make people in our image,
> to be like ourselves."
>
> GENESIS 1:26

Genesis 1 gives us the first thought of people—their origin and destiny entirely divine. God undertook the amazing work of making creatures, who are not God, to be perfect likenesses of Him. God's glory, His holiness, and His love were to dwell in them and shine out through them.

When sin did its terrible work and spoiled the image of God, the promise of a Redeemer was given, in whom the divine purpose would be fulfilled. "The Son reflects God's own glory, and everything about him represents God exactly" (Hebrews 1:3). God's plan would be carried out in Him. His image would be revealed in human form.

The New Testament continues the thought of Creation: "For God knew his people in advance, and he chose them to become like his Son" (Romans 8:29). The promise is then given: "We do know that when he comes, we will be like him, for we will see him as he really is" (1 John 3:2).

Let us keep our hearts set on the glory of the image of God in Christ, with the assurance that the Spirit will change us into that same image day by day.

The Obedience of Faith

The Lord appeared to [Abram] and said,
"I am God Almighty;
serve me faithfully and live a blameless life.
I will make a covenant with you."
GENESIS 17:1–2

In Abraham's life we see not only how God asks for faith but also how He develops faith by the gracious training that He gives. When God first called Abraham, He gave the great promise, "All the families of the earth will be blessed through you" (Genesis 12:3). When he reached the land, God promised that the land would be his. Before the birth of Isaac, in the words of our text, God sought to strengthen Abraham's faith. Step by step, God led him until his faith was perfected for full obedience in the sacrifice of Isaac. From the very beginning, Abraham obeyed God and believed His promises, even when his circumstances seemed to be in conflict with those promises.

God makes great demands on our faith as well. If we are to follow in Abraham's footsteps, we, too, are to live in the land of spiritual promise with nothing but His Word to depend on. Bow in prayer before God until He speaks to you, too: "I am God Almighty; serve me faithfully and live a blameless life." When Abraham heard this, he fell on his face and God talked with him. There you have the secret birthplace of the power to trust God for everything that He promises.

The Love of God

And you must love the Lord your God
with all your heart,
all your soul, and all your strength.

DEUTERONOMY 6:5

Moses taught Israel what the first and great commandment was: to love God with all their heart. It has its foundation in the relationship between God as the loving Creator and His creation as the object of that love. People find their life, destiny, and happiness as they love God with all their heart and strength.

Moses said that because "The Lord chose your ancestors as the objects of his love" (Deuteronomy 10:15). Such a God was infinitely worthy of being loved. All our faith in God and obedience to Him is to be inspired by this one thought: We are to love God with all our heart and all our strength. Every day our first duty should be to live out this command.

How little Israel was able to obey the command we all know so well. This is true of us even today. We are content in the thought that such love is impossible for us to produce. We forget that it is the Holy Spirit that enables us to love God and walk in His ways.

A perfect heart that loves God is what He claims and what He is completely worthy of. As we pray, expect the fulfillment of God's promises as we love Him with our whole heart.

The Joyful Sound

Happy are those who hear the joyful call to worship,
for they will walk in the light of your presence, Lord.
PSALM 89:15

"The joyful sound" consists of God's people walking in His light and rejoicing in His name. They have undisturbed fellowship and neverending joy.

In every well-ordered family one finds the father delighting in his children and the children rejoicing in their father's presence. This mark of a happy home on earth is what the heavenly Father has promised as we rejoice in His name. It has been made possible in Christ through the Holy Spirit filling our hearts with the love of God. It is the heritage of all who truly seek to love God with all their heart and strength.

Yet there are many of God's children who simply give up hope that a life of rejoicing in God's presence is possible. Yet Christ promised it so definitely: "I have told you this so that you will be filled with my joy. Yes, your joy will overflow!" (John 15:11).

The Father longs to have the perfect confidence and love of His children. Through prayer we can have the Father's presence every moment of the day for our happiness and strength. Let us be content with nothing less than the joyful sound: "They will walk in the light of your presence, Lord. They rejoice all day long in your wonderful reputation" (Psalm 89:15–16).

The Thoughts of God

*For just as the heavens are higher than the earth,
so are my thoughts higher than your thoughts.*

ISAIAH 55:9

God reminds us that as high as the heavens are above the earth, so high His thoughts are above ours. They are altogether beyond the power of our comprehension. When God laid out all His promises to Abraham, they were indeed thoughts higher than the heavens.

God tells us that we are made in His image. By grace we are actually renewed again into that image. As we gaze upon God's glory in Christ, we are changed into the same image by His Spirit. These, too, are thoughts beyond our comprehension— our minds cannot take them in.

God, by His Holy Spirit, conveys to our hearts the life and the light that can make us feel at home with these thoughts dwelling in us. But we need daily, prayerful fellowship with God if we are to enter into His mind and to have His thoughts make their home in us. It is by faith that God will not only reveal the beauty and the glory of these thoughts but will actually work in us their divine reality.

Just think of what Paul writes: "No eye has seen, no ear has heard, and no mind has imagined what God has prepared for those who love him" (1 Corinthians 2:9). But as we pray God will reveal them through His Spirit.

The New Covenant in Jeremiah

I will make a new covenant with
the people of Israel and Judah. . . .
I will put my laws in their minds,
and I will write them on their hearts.
JEREMIAH 31:31, 33

When God made the first covenant with Israel at Sinai, He said, "If you will obey me and keep my covenant, you will be my own special treasure from among all the nations of the earth" (Exodus 19:5). But Israel did not have the power to obey. Their whole nature was carnal and sinful. In the covenant there was no provision for the grace that would make them obedient. The law only served to show them their sin.

In our text God promised to make a new covenant in which He would enable men to live a life of obedience. In this new covenant, the law was to be put in their minds and written on their hearts—not with ink but with the Spirit of the living God. As Jeremiah puts it, "I will make an everlasting covenant with them. . . . I will put a desire in their hearts to worship me, and they will never leave me" (Jeremiah 32:40).

This promise ensures a continual, whole-hearted obedience as the mark of the believer who takes God at His Word and fully claims what the promise secures. Bow in deep stillness before God and believe what He says. Then His law, and our delight in it, will take possession of our inner life with all its power.

The New Covenant in Ezekiel

> *I will sprinkle clean water on you,*
> *and you will be clean. . . .*
> *And I will put my Spirit in you so you will obey.*
>
> EZEKIEL 36:25, 27

As in Jeremiah, God again outlines His new covenant in Ezekiel: "And I will put my Spirit in you so you will obey my laws and do whatever I command." In contrast with the old covenant in which there was no power to keep God's law, the new covenant promises a divine power which enables us to keep His laws. Obeying God's law is now possible because He has cleansed our hearts from sin and, by His Spirit, has given us new hearts.

Paul, who had complained of the power that brought him into captivity under the law of sin, thanks God that he is now in Christ Jesus. In Romans 8 we read that the law of the Spirit of life in Christ Jesus has now made us free from the law of sin and death.

Why are there so few today who claim God's promise of cleansing? What must be done to receive it? Just one thing is needed: faith in an omnipotent God who will do what He has promised. "I will sprinkle clean water on you, and you will be clean." As we pray, let us believe all that God promises. Then let those promises build our faith as we believe them.

The New Covenant: Prayer

For I, the Lord, have promised this,
and I will do it. . . .
I am ready to hear Israel's prayers,
and I am ready to grant them their requests.
EZEKIEL 36:36–37

The fulfillment of the great promises of the new covenant depends on prayer. In answer to the prayer of Jeremiah, God had said: "I will put a desire in their hearts to worship me, and they will never leave me" (Jeremiah 32:40). And to Ezekiel He had spoken: "I will put my Spirit in you so you will obey my laws and do whatever I command" (Ezekiel 36:27).

Often in our unbelief we do not expect these promises to be truly fulfilled. We do not believe that God means them to be literally true. We do not have the faith in the mighty power of God that is waiting to make His promise true in our experience.

God has said that without such faith our experience will only be partial and limited. However, He has graciously showed us the way in which such faith can be found. It is in the discipline of fervent prayer. "Ask me and I will tell you some remarkable secrets about what is going to happen here" (Jeremiah 33:3). When individual men and women prayerfully turn to God with their whole hearts to plead for these promises, He will fulfill them.

We need to pray that the power of the Holy Spirit may be deeply felt and that our faith may be strengthened to claim and to expect His mighty working.

The New Covenant in Hebrews

And I will forgive their wrongdoings, and I will never again remember their sins.

HEBREWS 8:12

In this Epistle of Hebrews, Christ is called the Mediator of a better covenant, based upon better promises (8:6). In Him the two parts of the covenant find their complete fulfillment. First of all, He came to atone for sin so that its power over man was destroyed. And with that came the fuller blessing—a new heart, with God's Holy Spirit breathing into it delight in God's law and the power to obey it.

These two parts of the covenant may never be separated. There are so many who put their trust in Christ for the forgiveness of sin and yet never think of claiming the fullness of His promised blessings.

Jesus Christ is the Mediator of the new covenant with the forgiveness of sin in the power of His Spirit. Just as surely as complete pardon of sin is assured, the complete fulfillment of God's promises should be expected, too.

To appropriate the new covenant, it requires a strong desire for a life wholly given to Christ. As we pray let us be willing to accept our place with Him—crucified to the world, to sin, and to self. It means a readiness to follow Him at any cost. It means a simple, whole-hearted acceptance of Christ as Lord and Master and a surrender of our heart and life to Him.

The Trial of Faith

But [Naaman's] officers tried to reason with him and said. . .
"You should certainly obey him when he says simply
to go and wash and be cured!"
2 KINGS 5:13

In Naaman we have a striking Old Testament illustration of the part faith plays in God's dealing with man. It gives us a wonderful picture of what faith really is.

Think first of how intensely Naaman desired healing. He appealed to the king of Syria and the king of Israel for help. He undertook a long journey. He humbled himself before the prophet who didn't even bother to come out to see him. In this intensity of desire for blessing, we have the root of a strong faith.

The second mark of faith is that it gives up all its preconceived notions and simply obeys the word of God. This was more than Naaman was willing to do, and he turned away in a rage. It was a good thing his faithful servant gave him better advice.

Then comes the third mark of faith. It submits implicitly to the word of God: "Wash and be cured." At first all appears useless, but faith proves itself in obedience. Naaman obeyed, not once or twice, but seven times, believing that the mighty miracle would be performed.

In the quietness of prayer let us believe that a simple, determined surrender of our whole will to God's promise will indeed bring the heart-cleansing we need.

Faith in Christ

You trust God, now trust in me.
JOHN 14:1

When Christ was about to leave His disciples, He taught them that they were to believe in Him with the same perfect confidence with which they had believed in God. "Just believe that I am in the Father. . . . Anyone who believes in me will do the same works I have done" (John 14:11–12). Here on earth He had not been able to make Himself fully known to His disciples. But in heaven, the fullness of God's power would be His. Jesus would do greater things in and through His disciples than He had ever done here on earth.

This faith must focus itself on the person of Christ in His union with the Father. The disciples were to have perfect confidence that all God had done could now be done by Jesus, too. The deity of Christ is the rock on which our faith depends. God's power has worked in Christ through His resurrection from the dead. Christ can also, in His divine power, work in us all that we need.

Take time in prayer to worship Jesus in His divine omnipotence as one with the Father. Bow in deep humility before the Lord Jesus and worship Him as Thomas did: "My Lord and my God!" (John 20:28). Let the Savior you have known and loved become, as never before, the Mighty God. Let Him always be your confidence and your strength.

Christ's Life in Us

For I will live again, and you will, too.
JOHN 14:19

There is a great difference in the teaching of the first three Gospels and that of John. John's special relationship with Jesus allows him to understand the Master better than the others. The others speak of repentance and the pardon of sin as the first great gift of the New Testament, but they say little of the new life in Christ.

It is John who records what Christ taught about His very own life really becoming ours. We are united with Him just as He was with the Father. The other Gospels speak of Christ as the Shepherd seeking and saving the lost. John speaks of Him as the Shepherd who gives His life for the sheep—His very life becoming ours. "My purpose is to give life in all its fullness" (John 10:10).

And so Christ says here in John, "I will live again, and you will, too." The disciples were to receive from Him the resurrection life in the power of its victory over death. From now on He would always dwell in them. This promise applies to all who will accept it in faith.

Take time to pray and let Christ's wonderful promise of a new life take possession of your heart. Be content with nothing less than full salvation—Christ living in you, and you living in Christ.

The Obedience of Love

When you obey me you remain in my love.
JOHN 15:10

The question is often asked: How can I abide in Christ and live wholly for Him? In our text the Lord gives the simple but far-reaching answer: obey Him. This is the only way to remain in Him. "When you obey me you remain in my love, just as I obey my Father and remain in his love" (John 15:10). Loving obedience is the way to enjoy His love.

In John chapter 15 Jesus frequently connected keeping His commandments with loving Him. "If my words remain in you, you may ask any request you like, and it will be granted" (15:7). "When you obey me, you remain in my love" (15:10). "You are my friends if you obey me" (15:14). The love that keeps His commandments is the only way to remain in His love. In our whole relationship to Christ, love is everything. Christ's love to us and our love to Him is proved in our love to each other.

The power of Christ's life through the Holy Spirit is pledged to those who truly love Him and keep His commands. This is the great secret of remaining in Christ and of having Him dwell in us. Then the divine power of our prayer will bring down God's blessing.

The Promise of the Spirit

If I do go away, [the Counselor] will come because
I will send him to you. He will bring me glory by
revealing to you whatever he receives from me.
JOHN 16:7, 14

From out of the glory of heaven the crucified Christ sent the Holy Spirit into the hearts of His disciples. The Spirit of Christ became their life in fellowship with Him and their power for His service. The Spirit comes to us, too, as the Spirit of the divine glory. We are to welcome Him and yield ourselves absolutely to His leading.

Yes, the Spirit of Christ came to dwell in the disciples and to make them the conscious possessors of the presence of the glorified Christ. It was this Spirit who was their power for a life of loving obedience. He was their teacher and leader in praying down from heaven the blessing that they needed. It was in His power that they conquered God's enemies and carried the gospel to the ends of the world.

The Spirit is God. As God, He claims to have possession of our whole being. Our heart and life are to be entirely and unceasingly under His control. In prayer we are to be led by the Spirit every day and every hour. In His power our life is to be a direct and continual abiding in the love and fellowship of Jesus. The Spirit who searches the deep things of God claims the very depths of our being and reveals Christ as Lord and Ruler.

In Christ

> *When I am raised to life again,*
> *you will know that I am in my Father,*
> *and you are in me, and I am in you.*
> JOHN 14:20

Our Lord spoke of His life in the Father in John 14:11: "Just believe that I am in the Father and the Father is in me." He and the Father were not two persons next to each other; they were in each other. Even as a man on earth, Jesus lived in the Father. All He did was what the Father did in Him.

This picture of Christ in God and God in Christ is the pledge of what our life in Christ is to be here on earth. We must always live in the faith that we are in Christ and yield ourselves to His power. Then we will learn that, even as the Father worked in Christ, so Christ will also work in us.

As the Father worked in Christ because He lived in the Father, so Christ worked in the disciples as they lived in Him. Their life in Him was the reflection of His life in the Father. But this did not happen until the Holy Spirit came. They had to wait until they were clothed with the power of the Spirit. Then by daily fellowship and prayer He did in them the greater works He had promised.

The secret of our power is to be found in nothing less than where Christ found it—abiding in the Father and His love.

Remaining in Christ

Remain in me,
and I will remain in you.
JOHN 15:4

Jesus illustrated and enforced the truth of His being in the Father by the wonderful parable of the branch and the vine. He gave the parable to drive home to the apostles the absolute necessity of a daily life in full communion with Him: "Remain in me."

Jesus points to Himself and to the Father—"Just as I am fully in the Father, so you are in Me." Then He points to the vine—"Just as truly as the branch is in the vine, you are in Me. Remain in Me!"

Wait on the Lord Jesus in the power of His Spirit until these two great truths get the complete mastery of your mind. The result will be: "My true disciples produce much fruit" (John 15:8). Fruit, more fruit, much fruit is what Christ seeks. It is what He will give to the one who trusts Him.

To the weakest of God's children Christ says: "Remain in Me." The same applies to the strongest of His children: "Remain in Me, and you will produce much fruit." Take time to let the Holy Spirit renew in you the secret of remaining in Him so you will understand the full meaning of His words: "Remain in Me."

The Power of Prayer

If you stay joined to me and my words remain in you,
you may ask any request you like,
and it will be granted.
JOHN 15:7

Before Jesus went to heaven, He taught His disciples two great lessons in regard to their relationship to Him in the work they had to do.

The one was that, in heaven, Jesus would have much more power than He had here on earth. He would now use that power through His disciples for the salvation of men.

The other was that without Him they could do nothing. Their first and chief work would therefore be to bring everything they wanted done to Him in prayer. In His farewell discourse, Jesus repeats the promise seven times: "Remain in me, pray in my name." "Ask any request you like and it will be granted." You can count on it!

With these truths written in their hearts, He sent the disciples out into the world to accomplish His work. The disciples on earth always looked up to Him in prayer, fully confident that He would hear their prayer. The first and only condition is an unflinching confidence in the power of His promise.

The same condition applies for us today. Close, abiding fellowship with Christ begins with deep dependence and unceasing prayer. It is only then that we can do our work in the full assurance that God has heard our prayer and will be our source of strength.

The Mystery of Love

My prayer for all of them is that they will be one,
just as you and I are one, Father. . . .
Then the world will know that you sent me.
JOHN 17:21, 23

When Christ spoke the last evening before His death, He especially pressed the thought of the disciples being in Him and remaining in Him. But in His prayer as High Priest, He gives more emphasis to the thought of His being in them, just as the Father was in Him. "That they will be one, just as you and I are one, Father. . . . Then the world will know that you sent me and will understand that you love them as much as you love me."

God seeks to convince the world that He loved His disciples as He loved His Son. It is through believers today that He accomplishes this. The world will know that we are in Christ when they see the living unity of our love for each other. The Father's love to Christ, brought by Christ to us, must flow out from us to each other and to all men.

Prayerfully claim the promise: "My Father will love them, and we will come to them and live with them" (John 14:23). As this becomes a reality in our lives, the world will be compelled by the love that God's children have for each other. In this way, God's Word will be fulfilled: "I [Jesus] will do this so that your love for me may be in them and I in them" (John 17:26).

Christ Our Righteousness

Now God in his gracious kindness declares us not guilty.
He has done this through Christ Jesus,
who has freed us by taking away our sins.

ROMANS 3:24

The first three Gospels speak of redemption as a pardon of sin, or justification. John speaks of it as a life which Christ is to live in us, or regeneration.

In the book of Romans we find both truths in their beautiful connection and harmony. Early in his epistle Paul speaks of justification. But then he goes on from there to speak of the life that we have in our union with Christ. In Romans 4 he tells us that we find both of these truths in the life of Abraham. God first of all counted Abraham's faith as righteousness. Then He empowered him to believe in Him as the God who can give life to the dead.

As believers we know that justification comes at the moment of conversion. But that is only the beginning. Gradually the believer must understand that his calling now is to remain in Christ and to let Christ remain and work in him.

Most Christians have learned from Abraham the first lesson: to believe in God Who justifies the ungodly. But they fail to go beyond that because they do not prayerfully yield themselves to Christ to maintain His life in them. The grace of pardon is only the beginning. Growing in grace leads to a fuller experience of what it means to be in Christ, to live in Him, and to grow in Him.

Christ Our Life

All who receive God's wonderful,
gracious gift of righteousness will live in triumph over sin
and death through this one man, Jesus Christ.
ROMANS 5:17

Paul teaches that faith in Christ as our righteousness is to be followed by faith in Him as our life from the dead. He now asks: "Have you forgotten that when we became Christians and were baptized to become one with Christ Jesus, we died with him?" (Romans 6:3). We are now to consider ourselves as truly "dead to sin and able to live for the glory of God" (verse 11).

The new life in us is an actual participation in and experience of the risen life of Christ. Our death to sin in Christ is also a spiritual reality. It is only when we see how we were one with Christ on the cross in His death and in His Resurrection that we will understand that "death no longer has any power over us" (Romans 6:9). This is the true life of faith.

Being in Christ and having Him live His life in us can only come true as the full power of the Holy Spirit is experienced. Paul says in Romans 8:2 that "The power of the life-giving Spirit has freed you through Christ Jesus from the power of sin that leads to death." And he then adds: "that the requirement of the law would be fully accomplished for us who no longer follow our sinful nature but instead follow the Spirit" (Romans 8:4). Through the Spirit we enter into the glorious liberty of the children of God.

Crucified with Christ

I have been crucified with Christ.
I myself no longer live,
but Christ lives in me.
GALATIANS 2:19–20

As in Adam we died out of life and into sin, so in Christ we are made partakers of a new spiritual death—a death to sin and into the life of God. To Paul this was such a reality that he was able to say: "I have been crucified with Christ. I myself no longer live, but Christ lives in me." He had indeed died to the old nature and to sin and had been raised up into the power of the living Christ dwelling in him.

It was the crucified Christ who lived in Paul. He lived in all practicality as a crucified man. The very mind of Christ worked in him because the crucified Christ lived in him.

Christ's death on the cross was the highest exhibition of His holiness and victory over sin. The believer who receives Christ is made partaker of all the power and blessing that the crucified Lord has won. As believers learn to accept this by faith, they learn that the mystery of the cross opens the entrance into the fullest fellowship with the living Christ. Plumb the depth of its meaning and prayerfully dare to say: "I am crucified with Christ. I myself no longer live, but Christ lives in me."

The Faith-Life

So I live my life in this earthly body
by trusting in the Son of God,
who loved me and gave himself for me.
GALATIANS 2:20

What does Paul mean when he says that he no longer lives but Christ lives in him? What now is his part in living that life? He gives us the answer: "I live my life in this earthly body by trusting in the Son of God, who loved me and gave himself for me." Faith was the power that possessed and permeated his whole being and his every action.

Here we have the simple but full statement of what the secret of the true Christian life is. It is not faith only in certain promises of God or in certain blessings that we receive from Christ. It is a faith that has a vision of how entirely Christ gives Himself to us.

As essential as continuous breathing is to the support of our physical life, equally essential is the faith that trusts Christ to maintain the life of the Spirit within us. Faith rests on that infinite love in which Christ gave Himself totally for us—to be ours in the deepest meaning of the word—and to live His life in us.

Faith, led and taught by God's Holy Spirit, gains the confidence to prayerfully claim: "I can do everything with the help of Christ who gives me the strength I need" (Philippians 4:13).

Full Consecration

*Yes, everything else is worthless when
compared with the priceless gain
of knowing Christ Jesus my Lord.*
PHILIPPIANS 3:8

What was it that made just the disciples worthy of the high honor of being baptized with the Holy Spirit? The answer is simple. When Christ called them they gave up everything and followed Him. They denied themselves and, in obedience, submitted to Christ's commands. They followed Him to Calvary. And even as Christ suffered and died, their hearts clung to Him alone.

Just as Jesus Christ had to sacrifice all to be a perfect offering to God, so we His people must give up everything to follow God's divine leading. This was true for Paul, too. To count all things but loss for Christ was the keynote of his life. It must be ours also if we are to fully share in the power of His Resurrection.

As the merchant who found the treasure in the field had to sell all he had to purchase it, we must relinquish our whole heart, life, and strength in order to claim Christ. It is only then that we can share with Him in His victory through the power of the Holy Spirit. The law of the kingdom is unchangeable; "Everything else is worthless when compared with the priceless gain of knowing Christ Jesus my Lord." It is in this that we find the path to the fullness of the Spirit.

Entire Sanctification

Now the God of peace make you holy in every way. . . .
God, who calls you, is faithful;
he will do this.
1 THESSALONIANS 5:23–24

What a promise! Just listen: God, the God of peace Himself, promises to sanctify us completely in Christ. It is God who is doing the work. It is in close, personal fellowship with God Himself that we become holy.

This should make us rejoice, but it is as if the promise is too great, and so it is repeated and amplified: "Now the God of peace make you holy in every way, and may your whole spirit and soul and body be kept blameless until that day when our Lord Jesus Christ comes again." To prevent the possibility of any misconception, the words are added: "God, who calls you, is faithful; he will do this."

Yes, God has said: "I the LORD have spoken! I will do what I have said" (Ezekiel 22:14). All that He asks is that we prayerfully stay in close fellowship with Him every day. As the heat of the sun shines on the body and warms it, the fire of God's holiness will burn in us and make us holy.

Child of God, beware of unbelief. It dishonors God; it robs your soul of its heritage. Let every thought of your high and holy calling respond: "God, who calls you, is faithful; he will do this." Yes, He will do it; and He will give you the grace to stay close to Him.

The Exceeding Greatness of His Power

I pray for you constantly, asking God. . .
to give you spiritual wisdom. . .
I pray that you will begin to understand
the incredible greatness of his power.
EPHESIANS 1:16–17, 19

This is one of the great texts that will make our faith strong and bold. Paul was writing to believers who had been sealed with the Holy Spirit. Yet he felt the need to pray for them for the enlightening of the Holy Spirit. They needed to know that it was the mighty power of God that was working in them. It was the very same power by which God raised Christ from the dead.

When Christ died on the cross, He died under the weight of the sin of the world and its curse. When He descended into the grave, it was under the weight of all that sin that He was buried. The power of death had apparently conquered Him. But the mighty power of God raised Christ from the dead to a place of honor at God's right hand.

It is that very same power that is working in us every day of our lives. The God Who said to Abraham, "Is there anything too hard for the LORD?" (Genesis 18:14), pledges to work His power in us, too, if we will learn to trust Him.

Pray in faith to God and trust His Holy Spirit to enable us to claim nothing less than the exceeding greatness of this Resurrection power working in us.

The Indwelling Christ

I pray that Christ will be more and more at home
in your hearts as you trust in him.
EPHESIANS 3:17

The great privilege that separated Israel from other nations was this: They had God dwelling in their midst. He made His home in the tabernacle and the temple. In the New Testament we see God dwelling in the heart of the believer. Jesus said: "All those who love me will do what I say. My Father will love them, and we will come to them and live with them" (John 14:23). Or, as Paul says of himself, "Christ lives in me" (Galatians 2:20).

The gospel is the dispensation of the indwelling Christ. In Ephesians 3:14–19 Paul teaches how we can experience this blessing of the Christian life.

1. "I fall on my knees and pray to the Father." The blessing must come from the Father to the praying believer.
2. "I pray that from his glorious, unlimited resources he will give you mighty inner strength through his Holy Spirit."
3. "I pray that Christ will be more and more at home in your hearts as you trust in him." It is in the very nature of Christ to desire to live in the heart of faith.
4. "May your roots go down deep into the soil of God's marvelous love."

Prayerfully meditate on what Christ, through the Holy Spirit, has chosen to do. He has chosen to make His home in our hearts!

Christian Perfection

And now may the God of peace. . .
equip you with all you need for doing his will.
May he produce in you. . .
all that is pleasing to him.

HEBREWS 13:20–21

The book of Hebrews wonderfully explains the redemption that Christ worked out for us in His death. The writer closes his teaching with a benediction. Listen: "The God of peace. . . equip you with all you need for doing his will. May he produce in you. . .all that is pleasing to him." Can we possibly desire more?

All that God has done for our redemption has one purpose: that He might now have free reign to work out in us that redemption which Christ had accomplished. All that we have learned about the completeness of salvation in Christ is consummated in the promise that God Himself will equip us to do what is pleasing in His sight. And this is accomplished through Jesus Christ.

The thought of being totally equipped to please Him is too high; the promise is too large. And yet the promise remains, stimulating our faith. It calls us to take hold of this truth—the everlasting God works in me every hour of the day through Jesus Christ. I have just one thing to do: to yield myself into God's hands for Him to work and not to hinder Him by any of my efforts. In silent prayer and adoring faith, be assured that God Himself will work in us all that is well-pleasing in His sight. Lord, increase our faith!

The God of All Grace

After you have suffered a little while,
he will restore, support, and strengthen you,
and he will place you on a firm foundation.
1 PETER 5:10

Peter picks up the theme of our being perfectly equipped in Christ with these words: "He will restore, support, and strengthen you, and he will place you on a firm foundation." God Himself must be the one object of our hope and trust in our work, our needs, and our desires.

Just as God is the center of the universe, the one guide that orders and controls its movements, so God must have the same place in the life of the believer. With every new day our first thought should be: Only God can enable me this day to live as He would have me to live.

What should be our attitude towards this God? Shouldn't we humbly place ourselves in His hands and confess our absolute helplessness? We must yield ourselves in childlike surrender to receive from Him the fulfillment of His promise: "The God of peace. . .equip you with all you need for doing his will" (Hebrews 13:20).

Some of us have learned how absolutely indispensable it is to meet with God every morning in prayer and to allow Him to take charge of our life for the day. This is exactly the point Peter is trying to get across. In light of what this day might hold for us, our hearts must rest on God and His Word to restore, support, and strengthen us.

Not Sinning

And you know that Jesus came to take away our sins,
for there is no sin in him.
So if we continue to live in him,
we won't sin either.

1 JOHN 3:5–6

In our text John teaches how we can be kept from sinning: "If we continue to live in him, we won't sin either." Though we are sinful by nature, living in the sinless Christ frees us from the power of sin and enables us to live a life pleasing to God. In John 8:29 the Lord Jesus said of the Father: "I always do those things that are pleasing to Him." And so John writes here: "Dear friends, if our conscience is clear, we can come to God with bold confidence. And we will receive whatever we request because we obey him and do the things that please him" (1 John 3:21–22).

Let the one who longs to be free from the power of sin take to heart these simple but far-reaching words: "there is no sin in him." He that establishes us in Christ is God. As I seek to live in Him in Whom there is no sin, Christ will indeed live out His own perfect life in me in the power of the Holy Spirit. I will then be equipped to do the things that are pleasing in His sight.

By faith claim these words: "If we continue to live in him, we won't sin either." God the Almighty has pledged to make this promise a reality.

Overcoming the World

*The ones who win this battle against the world are
the ones who believe that Jesus is the Son of God.*
1 JOHN 5:5

Early on in this epistle John teaches us what the real nature and
power of the world consists of: the lust for physical pleasure, the
lust for everything we see, and pride in our possessions. We find
these three marks of the world in the Garden of Eden. Through the
body, the eyes, and the pride of wisdom, the world acquired the
mastery over Eve and over us. Ever since the kingdom of God and
the kingdom of this world have been in deadly conflict.

The world still exerts a terrible influence over Christians who
do not know that in Christ they have been crucified to the
world. The power of this world proves itself in all the pleasures
of sin. And most Christians are either ignorant of the danger of
a worldly spirit or feel utterly powerless to conquer it.

Christ left us with this great far-reaching promise: "But take
heart, because I have overcome the world." As we abide in
Christ and seek to live a holy life in the power of the Holy Spirit,
we may confidently count on that power to overcome the world.
"The ones who win this battle against the world are the ones
who believe that Jesus is the Son of God." Prayerfully place your
trust in the mighty power of God as the only pledge of certain
and continual victory.

Author and Perfecter of Our Faith

I do believe, but help me not to doubt.
MARK 9:24

What a treasure of encouragement these words from Mark contain. Jesus had said to the father who had asked Him to heal his child: "Anything is possible if a person believes" (Mark 9:23). The father felt that Christ was throwing the responsibility on him. If he believed, the child could be healed. But he felt his faith was totally inadequate. Yet as he looked in the face of Christ, he felt assured that the love which was willing to heal would also be ready to help him with his weak faith. So he cried: "I do believe, but help me not to doubt." Christ heard the prayer, and the child was healed.

Christ will always accept the faith that puts its trust in Him. Remember the mustard seed. If it is put into the ground and allowed to grow, it becomes a great tree. The weakest faith is made strong and bold when it trusts Christ—the Author and Perfecter of our faith.

Take the hidden seed of little faith and plant it in your heart. Rest on God's promise as you bring it to Him in prayer. He will certainly embrace the trembling faith that clings to Him and will not let Him go. A weak faith in an almighty Christ will become the great faith that can remove mountains.

Prayer to Be Holy

Christ will make your hearts strong, blameless, and holy
when you stand before God our Father on that day
when our Lord Jesus comes.
1 THESSALONIANS 3:13

This is a prayer for holiness, which is the very nature of God, inseparable from His Being. We are in Christ, who is made of God our sanctification. The Spirit of God is the Spirit of holiness. We have been sanctified in Christ Jesus. The new nature we have from Him has been created in true holiness.

It is as we believe in God, through Christ and the Holy Spirit working in us, that the inflow of the holy life from above is renewed. And as we believe we have the courage and the power to live out that holy life.

Like the whole of salvation, the life of holiness is the result of cooperating with God in faith: First of all, our entire dependence on and surrender to God is the only source of goodness or strength. Then we must act out in life and conduct all that God has worked within us.

Believers, God desires your sanctification. Worship God in His holiness until every thought of God in His glory and grace is connected with the deep conviction that the blessed God wills my holiness. Do not rest until your will has surrendered unconditionally to the will of God and found its true destiny in receiving that divine will and working it out.

When, by God's grace, you will as God wills, when you have accepted God's will for sanctification as your own will, you can count on God working it. God wills it with all the energy of His divine being.

When Trouble Comes

Patient endurance is what you need now,
so you will continue to do God's will.
Then you will receive all that he has promised.

HEBREWS 10:36

The first concern of most Christians in trouble is to be delivered from it. However, perhaps this should not be the primary thing. Our one great desire ought to be that we do not fail in knowing or doing the will of God in anything. This is the secret of strength and true character in the Christian life.

When trials come, though, it is beyond human power to think of and do God's will first. It is indeed something beyond human power but not beyond the power of grace. It is just for this that our Lord Jesus came to earth—to do God's will. He went to the cross with the prayer to God: "Not My will, but Yours be done."

Ask God to renew your spirit and your mind and to show you how He would have you live wholly in His will. Yield yourself to that will in everything you know and do it. Yield yourself to that will in all its divine love and quickening power as it works in you and makes you partaker of its inmost nature. Pray, pray, pray, until you see increasingly in Jesus' life and death the promise and pledge of what God will work in you. Your abiding in Him and your oneness with Him mean nothing less than your being called to do the will of God as He did it.

SEPTEMBER 27

Praying to Please God

And now, may the God of peace,
who brought again from the dead our Lord Jesus,
equip you with all you need for doing his will.
HEBREWS 13:20

Hebrews 10:7–10 speaks about Christ doing God's will as the cause of our redemption, the deep root in which our life stands. Further along, Hebrews 10:36 speaks about us—Christians—patiently doing God's will even in the trials of this earth.

The prayer quoted above shows us how God's will can be done in our lives. The same God who demonstrated His will in Christ for our redemption is working out that will in us, too. What God did in Christ is the pledge of what He will do in us. Christ doing the will of God secures our doing that will, too.

All that is said about the Lord Jesus refers to the previous teaching of this epistle. It teaches about the covenant, the blood of the covenant, the exaltation of the throne, Christ as the Priest-King, the great Shepherd of the sheep. And now it says that the God of peace who did it all—who gave Christ to do His will and die on the cross, then raised Him from the dead—will equip us to do His will.

Surely this benediction, prayed for all of us, teaches us in a very practical way both how to pray and how to be prayed for.

Humble Praying Rests

Come unto me,
all of you who are weary
and carry heavy burdens,
and I will give you rest.
MATTHEW 11:28

When Jesus was on earth He did not mention meekness as one of several other virtues that were to be learned from Him, but rather as the one which was His primary characteristic—the one which we must learn if we are to find rest for our souls. He came to deliver us from the sins of self-exaltation and pride.

In heaven He humbled Himself as Son before the Father, that He might be sent as a servant into the world. He humbled Himself to become man. As man He humbled Himself to the death of the cross. He had to come into the world as the gentle Lamb of God to bring to earth the meekness of heart in which true submission to God is manifested.

There is no way to heaven except by meekness, by entirely dying to our pride, and by living entirely in the lowliness of Jesus. Pride gives no rest; it is from hell. It must die or nothing of heaven can live in us. As we come to Him in prayer, God will certainly bestow this meekness and by His Spirit work it out in the heart of everyone who surrenders his life entirely to the power of the blood of the Lamb.

The Spirit works as the Spirit of the Lamb. He works with a hidden but perfect power, breathing into the heart of His own people that which is the divine glory of the Lamb—His meekness.

Heavenly Praying

And they sang a new song. . .
"You are worthy. . .for. . .
your blood has ransomed people for God from every
tribe and language and people and nation."
REVELATION 5:9

When we prayerfully lay our gifts for the work of the Lord upon His altar, it should not be done from mere custom or without serious thought. Every penny—the same as every prayer—that comes into God's treasury has a value corresponding to the intention with which it is offered to Him. Only true love to Him and His work transforms our gifts into spiritual offerings.

Thus, it would be well for us to learn what God thinks and says about missionary work so that we may think and act according to His will.

What is prayer like in heaven? Do we have biblical insight? Our text tells us of a vision of things in "the heavenlies" which sheds the light of eternity upon the work of missions. We hear the redeemed praising the Lamb that He redeemed them to God by His blood. In praise of the power which the blood has exercised, there will be no kindred nor nation unrepresented and there will be no division caused by language or nationality, for every breech will have been healed. All will be united in one spirit of love as one spotless body before the throne of God.

What else is that vision but a revelation in heaven of the high calling and glorious result of mission work?

Silent Listening Before God

For we are the temple of the Living God.
2 CORINTHIANS 6:16

After worshiping God in prayer with praise and thanksgiving, prepare yourself for intercessory prayer by waiting on God in meditative, prayerful Bible study.

One reason why the discipline of prayer is not attractive is that people do not know how to pray. Their stock of words is soon exhausted, and they do not know what else to say. This happens because they forget that prayer is not a soliloquy where everything comes from one side, but it is a dialogue where God's child listens to what the Father says, replies to it, and then asks for the things he needs.

Read a few verses from the Bible. Do not concern yourself with the difficult parts in them; you can consider these later. Take what you understand, apply it to yourself, and ask the Father to make His Word light and power in your heart. Thus you will have material enough for prayer from the Word which the Father speaks to you. You will also have the liberty to ask for things you need.

Keep on in this way, and prayer will become at length, not a place where you sigh and struggle, but a place of living fellowship with the Father in heaven. Prayerful study of the Bible is indispensable for powerful prayer. The Word prayerfully read and cherished in the heart by faith will, through the Spirit, be both light and life within us.

Approaching God in Prayer

You love him even though you have never seen him.
Though you do not see him, you trust him; and. . .
are happy with a glorious, inexpressible joy.
1 PETER 1:8

When you pray, begin by thanking God for His unspeakable love which invites you to come to Him and communicate freely with Him.

If your heart is cold and dead, remember that worship is not simply a matter of feeling but has to do first with the will. Raise your heart to God and thank Him for the assurance you have that He looks down on you and will bless you. Through such an act of faith you honor God and draw your soul away from being occupied with itself. Think also of the glorious grace of the Lord Jesus who is willing to teach you to pray and to give you the desire to do so. Think, too, of the Holy Spirit who was purposely given to intercede for you in prayer. Five minutes spent this way will strengthen your faith for the work of prayer.

Once more I say, begin with an act of thanksgiving. Praise God for the inner chamber of prayer and His promise of blessing there.

It is a great thing to say, but it is the simple truth: God will make the place a Beth-El (house of God) where His angels shall ascend and descend and where you will cry out, "Yahweh will be my God." He will also make it Peni-El (face of God) where you will see the face of God, as a prince of God (Isra-El,) wrestling in overcoming-type prayer. It will become the most blessed place on earth.

Requests for Worrisome Needs

> *Don't worry about anything, instead,*
> *pray about everything.*
> *Tell God what you need,*
> *and thank him for all he has done.*
>
> PHILIPPIANS 4:6

Whenever we come in prayer to present our requests to God, our Lord instructs us to pause long enough to remember who He is: our King, our Righteousness. His word tells us of His kingdom—the realm in which His servants' requests are to be made.

If we don't acknowledge who He is, prayer is not prayer at all. Instead, the recitation of our worries is simply an attempt to worry God. God is already aware of our needs. He wants us to think over what we ask from Him. Do not be satisfied with going over the same things every day. No child goes on saying the same thing day after day to his earthly father.

Conversation with the Father is colored by the needs of the day. Let your prayer be something definite, rising out of the Word which you have read or out of the real soul—needs which you long to have satisfied. Let your prayer be so definite that you can say, "I know what I have asked for from my Father, and I expect an answer." It is a good plan sometimes to take a piece of paper and write down what you pray for. You might keep such a paper for a week or more and repeat the prayers until some new need arises.

No One to Intercede?

> The LORD. . .was amazed to see that
> no one intervened to help the oppressed.
> So he himself stepped in to save them.
> ISAIAH 59:15–16

To be an intercessor before God for others is greatly needed. But do not attempt it hastily or thoughtlessly, as though you know well enough how to pray. Prayer in our own strength brings no blessing. Take time to present yourself reverently and in quietness before God. Remember His greatness and holiness and love. After receiving God's Word into your heart, begin to pray for your own needs and the needs of others.

One reason why prayer does not bring more joy and blessing is that it is too selfish, and selfishness is the death of prayer. Remember your family, your own church, your own neighborhood, and the extended church. Let your heart be enlarged and remember the concerns of missions and of the Church throughout the whole world. Become an intercessor and you will experience for the first time the blessedness of prayer as you find that you have something to say to God. He will do things in answer to your prayers which otherwise would not have been done.

Intercessory Prayer

The Spirit pleads for us believers
in harmony with God's own will.
ROMANS 8:27

After we have humbled ourselves before God in praise and thanksgiving, have received His Word in personal communion with Him, and have made our requests for our own needs, God desires that we continue in prayer as intercessors before Him for the needs of others—to grow in our praying.

Children can ask their father for bread, but full-grown children converse with him about all the interests of his business and other areas of life. Weak children of God pray only for themselves, but persons growing in Christ understand how to consult with God over what must take place in the kingdom. Let your prayer list include the names of those for whom you pray—your minister, and all other ministers, and the different missionary affairs with which you are connected. Thus your prayer time will really become a wonder of God's goodness and a fountain of great joy.

More than one Christian who has desired to give himself to the ministry of intercession has wondered why he has found it so difficult to rejoice in it, to persevere, and to prevail. But we must confess that we have a nature perfectly adapted to do this work God has called us to do. We have been created in Christ to pray. It is our very nature as children of God. God's Spirit has been sent into our hearts to draw our hearts up to God in childlike prayer.

We must honor God the Holy Spirit, believe that He is praying within us, and yield to the strength and courage He brings to our praying in His power.

Spending Time in Prayer

One day. . .Jesus went to a mountain to pray,
and he prayed to God all night.
LUKE 6:12

Before the creation of the world time did not exist. God lived in eternity in a way which we hardly understand. Time began with Creation, and everything was placed under its power. God has placed all living creatures under a law of slow growth. Think of the length of time it takes for a child to become full grown in body and mind. Learning, wisdom, business, skills—even politics—all depend on patience and perseverance; everything needs time.

It is the same reality and principle in our cultivating the life of God in us daily and in witnessing what He wants to teach us and accomplish through our lives. There can be no communion with a holy God, no fellowship between heaven and earth, no power for salvation of others unless much time is set apart for it. Just as it is necessary for a child to grow and learn every day, so the life of grace depends entirely on the time we are willing to give to it day by day.

Was it not so with Jesus? Why must He, who had no sin to confess, sometimes spend all night in prayer? It was because the divine life in Him had to be strengthened in communication with the Father and the Spirit. His experience of a life in which He took time for fellowship with God has enabled Him to share that life with us.

Carefully Praying the Word

*And all who heard him [Jesus] were amazed
at his understanding and his answers.*

LUKE 2:47

In Jesus' time on earth He treasured the Word in His heart. In the temptation in the wilderness and on every opportunity that presented itself until His death on the cross, He showed that the Word of God filled His heart.

In Jesus' prayer life He manifested two things to us: first, God's Word supplies us with material for prayer and encourages us in expecting everything from God; second, it is only by prayer that we can live such a life so that every word of God can be fulfilled in us.

How can we come to the place where the Word and prayer may each have its undivided right over us? There is only one answer: Our lives must be wholly transformed.

We must, by faith in what God will do in us, appropriate the heavenly life of Christ as He lived it here on earth. We must have the certain expectation that the Spirit, who filled Jesus with the Word and prayer, will also accomplish that work in us.

Let us understand that God the Holy Spirit is essentially the Spirit of the Word and the Spirit of prayer; He is the Spirit of the Lord Jesus who is in us to make us truly partakers of His life. If we firmly believe this and set our hearts upon it, then there will come a change in our use of God's Word and prayer such as we could not have thought possible.

Receptive Praying

The disciples were meeting behind locked doors. . . .
Suddenly, Jesus was standing there among them! . . .
He. . .said. . ."Receive the Holy Spirit."
JOHN 20:19, 22

It is foolish to pray for the fullness of the Spirit if we have not first placed ourselves under the full power of the Cross! Just think of the disciples. The crucifixion of Christ had touched, broken, and taken possession of their entire hearts. They could speak or think of nothing else, and when the Crucified One had shown them His hands and His feet, He said unto them, "Receive the Holy Spirit."

Christ gave Himself up entirely to the cross. The cross demands this also from us; it would have our entire life. To comply with this demand requires nothing less than a powerful act of the will, for which we are unfit. It also requires a powerful act of God which will assuredly come to those who cast themselves unreservedly on Him.

The Spirit who is in you, in however limited a measure, is prepared to teach you, to lead you to the cross, and to make you know something of what the crucified Christ wills to do for you and in you. He wants you to spend time with Him, so that He may reveal the heavenly mysteries to you. He will teach you what is meant by the denial of self, taking up your cross, losing your life, and following Him.

Begin at the beginning. Be faithful in prayer. Although everything appears cold, dark, and strained, bow in silence before the loving Lord Jesus. Thank Him that you can count on Him to meet you there.

Prayer's Obedience of Faith

But if you stay joined to me
and my words remain in you,
you may ask any request you like,
and it will be granted! . . .
When you obey me,
you remain in my love.
JOHN 15:7, 10

If you make the morning hour holy to the Lord, the day with its duties will also be holy.

Do not forget the close bond between the inner chamber and the outer world. The attitude of prayer must remain with us all day. The object of the prayer is to so unite us with God that we may have Him always abiding with us.

Sin, thoughtlessness, and yielding to the flesh or to the world make us unfit for communion with God and bring a cloud over the soul. If you have stumbled or fallen, return to God in prayer. First invoke the blood of Jesus and claim cleansing by it. Do not rest till by confession you have repented of and put away your sin. Let the precious blood really give you a fresh freedom of approach to God.

Remember that the roots of your life in the inner chamber strike far out in body and soul so as to manifest themselves in daily life. Let the obedience of faith, in which you pray in secret, rule you constantly.

The inner chamber is intended to bind us to God, to supply us with power from God, to enable us to live for God alone. Thank God for the inner chamber and for the life which He will enable us to experience and nourish there.

Morning by Morning

Listen to my voice in the morning, LORD.
Each morning I bring my requests to you
and wait expectantly.
PSALM 5:3

Many Christians observe the morning watch, while others speak of it as the quiet hour, the still hour, or the quiet time. All these, whether they think of a whole hour or half an hour or a quarter of an hour, agree with the psalmist.

In speaking of the extreme importance of this daily time of quiet for prayer and meditation on God's Word, a well-known Christian leader has said: "Next to receiving Christ as Savior and claiming the baptism of the Holy Spirit, we know of no act that brings greater good to ourselves or others than the determination to keep the morning watch and spend the first half hour of the day alone with God."

At first glance this statement appears too strong. The firm determination to keep the morning watch hardly appears sufficiently important to be compared to receiving Christ and the baptism of the Holy Spirit. However, it is true that it is impossible to live our daily Christian life, or maintain a walk in the leading and power of the Holy Spirit, without a daily, close fellowship with God. The morning watch is the key to maintaining a position of total surrender to Christ and the Holy Spirit.

We as believers cannot stand for one moment without Christ. Personal devotion to Him refuses to be content with anything less than to abide always in His love and His will. This is the true scriptural Christian life. The importance, joy, and purpose of the morning watch can only be realized as our personal devotion becomes its chief purpose.

Time for Jesus

Jesus awoke long before daybreak. . .
to pray. Later. . .the others. . .said,
"Everyone is asking for you."
But he replied, ". . .I will preach to them, too,
because that is why I came."

MARK 1:35–38

Although our daily quiet time with God gives us a special time for prayer and Bible study, bringing us a certain measure of refreshment and help, this is not enough! The morning watch must not be regarded as an end in itself! The overriding, prime objective is not simply the personal discipline, no matter how beneficial this may be.

The clear, focused objective of the morning quiet time is to secure the presence of Christ for the whole day. Meditation and prayer and the Word are secondary to this purpose of renewing the link for the day between Christ and you in the morning hour.

Concern for the day ahead with all its possible cares, pleasures, and temptations may seem to disturb the rest I have enjoyed in my quiet devotion. This is possible, but it will be no loss.

True Christianity aims at having the character of Christ formed in us. Then in our most ordinary activities and relationships with people, it will be second nature for us to act like Him. All this is possible because Christ Himself lives in us.

As the morning watch begins to have its effects on the day, the day will respond to that time spent with God. Fellowship with Christ will have new meaning and power.

Nothing Separates Us from Jesus

Jesus said, ". . .I do nothing on my own,
but I speak what the Father taught me.
And the one who sent me is with me. . .
I always do those things that are pleasing to him."
JOHN 8:28–29

The above Scripture passage is the beloved apostle John's record of Jesus' unique "personal testimony." It represents the "gold standard" toward which we all should press.

Personal devotion to a friend or a pursuit means that they will always hold a place in our heart, even when other persons and things occupy our attention. Personal devotion to Jesus means that we allow nothing to separate us from Him for a moment. To abide in Him and His love, to be kept by Him and His grace, to be doing His will and pleasing Him—this cannot possibly be an irregular practice if we are truly devoted to Him.

The clearer the objective of our goal, the better we will be able to accomplish it. Consider the morning watch now as the means to this great end: I want to secure the presence of Christ all the day, to do nothing that can interfere with it. Our success during the day will depend upon the time we spend alone with Him in the morning.

Do not be disturbed if at first this goal appears too difficult and occupies too much of your time. The time you give to bring your daily concerns to the Lord will be richly rewarded. You will return to prayer and Scripture reading with new purpose and new faith.

Prayer's Wholehearted Determination

Daniel. . .prayed three times a day, just as he had always done.
DANIEL 6:10

As we seek to have unbroken fellowship with God in Christ throughout the day, we will realize that only a definite meeting time with Christ will secure His presence for the day. The essential thing to having a daily quiet time is wholehearted determination, whatever effort or self-denial it may cost. In academic study or athletics, every student needs determined purpose to succeed. Christianity requires, and indeed deserves, not less but more intense devotion. If anything, surely the love of Christ needs the whole heart.

When we make this decision to secure Christ's presence, we will overcome every temptation to be superficial in the keeping of our pledges. Our determination will make the morning watch itself a mighty force in strengthening our character and giving us boldness to resist self-indulgence. It will enable us to enter the inner chamber and shut the door for our communion with Christ. From the morning watch on, this firm resolution will become the keynote of our daily life.

Often we hear the statement that great things are possible to those who know what they want and will it with all their heart. If we have made personal devotion to Christ our goal, we will find the morning hour the place where daily insight into our holy calling is renewed. During this quiet time, we are fortified to walk worthy of His calling. Faith is rewarded by the presence of Christ who is waiting to meet us and take charge of us for the day.

We are more than conquerors through Him who loves us. Christ waits to meet us.

Prayer's Fellowship

But when you pray, go away by yourself,
shut the door behind you,
and pray to your Father secretly. Then your Father,
who knows all secrets, will reward you.
MATTHEW 6:6

Of more importance than all your requests is this one thing—the childlike, living assurance that your Father sees you and that you have now met Him face to face. With His eye on you and yours on Him, you are now enjoying actual fellowship with Him.

Fellowship is the living interchange of giving God your love, your heart, and your life and receiving from God His love, His life, and His Spirit. We were created for fellowship with Him. He made us capable of understanding and enjoying God, entering into His will, and delighting in His glory.

The greatest hindrance to fellowship is anything that keeps our heart and mind occupied instead of leading us to God Himself. What a difference it would make in the life of many Christians if everything were subordinate to the one decision to walk with God throughout the day. What encouragement when we can say: God has taken charge of me; He is going with me; I am going to do His will all day in His strength; I am ready for all that may come. Yes, what a change would come into our lives if secret prayer were not only an asking for knowledge of strength, but the giving of our lives for one day into the safekeeping of a faithful God.

Prayer's Unbroken Fellowship

When Moses came down the mountain. . .
he wasn't aware that his face glowed because
he had spoken to the LORD face to face.
EXODUS 34:29

Close and continued prayer fellowship with God will in due time leave its mark and be evident to those around us. Just as Moses did not know that his face shone, we ourselves will be unaware of the light of God shining from us. The sense of God's presence in us may often cause others to feel ill at ease in our company. However, true believers will prove by humility and love that they are indeed persons like those around them. And yet there will be the proof that they are people of God who live in an unseen world.

The blessings of communion with God can easily be lost by entering too deeply into communion with people. The spirit of inner prayer must be carried over into a holy watchfulness throughout the day. We do not know at what hour the enemy will come. This continuance of the morning watch can be maintained by quiet self-restraint, by not giving the reins of our lives over to our natural impulses.

When the abiding sense of God's presence has become the aim of the morning hour, then with deep humility and in loving conversation with those around us, we will pass on into the day's duties with the continuity of unbroken fellowship. It is a great thing to enter the inner chamber, shut the door, and meet the Father in secret. It is a greater thing to open the door again and go out to enjoy God's presence—which nothing can disturb.

OCTOBER 15

The Place of Prayer

Whenever Moses went into the Tabernacle
to speak with the LORD,
he heard the voice speaking to him from between
the two cherubim.
NUMBERS 7:89

When Moses went in to pray for himself or his people and to wait for instructions, he found One waiting for him. What a lesson for our morning watch.

We must get into the right place. Moses went into the tabernacle to speak with God. He separated himself from the people and went where he could be alone with God. He went to the place where God was to be found. Jesus has told us where that place is. He calls us to enter into our closet, shut the door, and pray to the Father who is in secret. Any place where we are really alone with God can be for us the secret of His presence. To speak with God requires separation from all else. It needs a heart intently set upon and in full expectation of meeting God personally and having direct dealings with Him. When we go there to speak to God will hear the voice of One speaking to them.

We must get into the right position. Moses heard the voice of One speaking from the mercy seat. Bow before the mercy seat where the awareness of your unworthiness will not hinder you, but will be a real help in trusting God. At the mercy seat you can have the assurance that your upward look will be met by His eye, that your prayer can be heard, that His loving answer will be given. Bow before the mercy seat and be sure that the God of mercy will see and bless you.

God's Word and Prayer

They have kept your word.
My prayer is not for the world,
but for those you have given me,
because they belong to you.

JOHN 17:6, 9

Prayer and God's Word are inseparably linked together: Power in the use of either depends upon the presence of the other. It is clear why this is so. Prayer and the Word have one common center—God. Prayer seeks God; the Word reveals God. In prayer, we ask God; in the Word, God answers us. In prayer, we rise to heaven to dwell with God; in the Word, God comes to dwell with us. In prayer, we give ourselves to God; in the Word, God gives Himself to us.

Little of the Word with little prayer is death to the spiritual life. Much of the Word with little prayer is unhealthy. Much prayer with little of the Word gives more life, but without steadfastness. A full measure of the Word and of prayer each day gives a healthy and powerful life.

In prayer and the Word, God must be all. Make God the center of your heart, the one object of your desire. Prayer and the Word will be a blessed fellowship with God, the interchange of thought and love and life—a dwelling in God and God in us. Seek God and live!

Prayer and God's Word

This is what the LORD says:
". . .I will bless those who have
humble and contrite hearts,
who tremble at my word."
ISAIAH 66:1–2

Many of us are so occupied with how much or how little we have to say in our prayers that the voice of One speaking is never heard because it is not expected or waited for. We need to get into the right frame of mind and have a listening attitude.

In regard to the connection between prayer and the Word of God in our private devotion, this expression has often been quoted: "I pray, I speak to God; I read the Bible, God speaks to me." We need to ask how our Scripture reading and praying can become true fellowship with God.

A prayerful spirit is the spirit to which God will speak. Prayer prepares the heart for receiving the Word from God Himself, for the teaching of the Spirit to give the spiritual understanding of it, for the faith that is made part of its mighty working.

In God's Word we read what God will do in me, how God would have me come to Him in prayer, assurance that I will be heard, and what God will do in the world. A prayerful spirit will be a listening spirit waiting to hear what God says. In true communion with God, His presence and the part He takes must be as real as my own.

Let us prepare ourselves to pray with a heart that humbly waits to hear God speak. The greatest blessing in prayer will be our ceasing to pray to let God speak.

The Will of God

Pray like this: Our Father in heaven,
may your name be honored.
May your Kingdom come soon.
May your will be done here on earth,
just as it is in heaven.
MATTHEW 6:9–10

Our secret communion with God is the place where we learn the great lessons concerning God's will. Desire is awakened in us for the life it promises, as the Holy Spirit reveals God's perfecting work through Jesus Christ. As we believe and receive it into our hearts according to His purposes, His will masters our hearts, giving us courage to be confident in God's assurance that we can do our part, so that our will on earth can correspond and cooperate with His will.

Let this be our heart's one desire—that in everything the will of God be done in us and by us, even as it is in heaven.

By God's grace every hour of our lives can be lived in complete harmony with the will of God. We need to maintain surrender—to do what God wills us to do. The God we worship asks of us perfect union of our wills with His will so that the will of God in its beauty and application to daily life can be truly known.

As we fellowship with God in the inner chamber of the morning watch, waiting and depending with a childlike attitude of trust on what He gives us, we receive the knowledge of His will as well as the power to perform it. In surrender to do all that He wills, the study of His Word and this time of prayer bring true and full blessing.

According to God's Will

And we can be confident that
he will listen to us whenever we ask him
for anything in line with his will.
1 JOHN 5:14

How can we know if we are praying according to God's will? That is an intensely practical question to ask as we take time to pray.

To properly understand 1 John 5:14, we must connect the words "in line with his will" with "ask"—not merely with "anything." Similarly, connect "he will listen" with "whenever we ask." Not only the thing asked for but also the disposition and character of the one asking must be in line with God's will. Both the thing asked for and the spirit of asking must be in harmony with God's will.

Jesus' teaching continually connected the answer to prayer with a life that was being lived according to God's will: trusting, forgiving, merciful, humble, believing, asking in His name, abiding in His love, observing/keeping His commands, and having His words abiding within. He also said that if they loved Him and kept His commands, then He would pray to the Father for them. Prayer has power according to the life! A life in line with God's will can ask according to God's will.

When you live according to God's will, you are spiritually able to discern what to ask for. A life yielded to and molded by the will of God will know what and how to pray. Boldness in prayer comes from the assurance that the spirit of asking and the thing asked are both according to the will of God.

Praying for Deliverance

> God knows how often I pray for you.
> Day and night I bring you and your needs
> in prayer to God.
>
> ROMANS 1:9

Paul had several prayer requests: (1) deliverance; (2) acceptable service; and (3) to get to Rome. He had no idea how he would get to Rome specifically. It is apparent that his clear purpose for sending this letter to the Christians in Rome was to request their prayers—and any assistance that the Spirit would enable them to give him for this journey he obviously believed God wanted him to take (Romans 1:7–13, 15; 15:13–16, 19–20, 22–29).

He intended first to visit Jerusalem but did not know how he would be delivered from the dangers to which he might be exposed through his adversaries among the Jews. We know from the Acts the dangers he faced. Men had vowed not to eat until they had killed him. Was it because of the prayers of the saints in Rome to whom he writes that the deliverance came?

We have the clear record of how Paul's life was protected during the two to three years that it subsequently took for the Roman government to "pay all his expenses" to get him to Rome; and how God the Holy Spirit authored so much more of the New Testament canon, through the instrumentality of Paul's writings, "than had already been recorded on parchment scrolls."

Let us pray for ministers and missionaries that the Holy Spirit may give us a new vision of the inconceivable power that prayer can exert.

Counting on Prayers

He will rescue us because you are helping by praying for us. . . .
Many will give thanks to God because so many people's
prayers for our safety have been answered.
2 CORINTHIANS 1:11

Paul lived in prayer for the churches and had taught them to pray for him and his work, so he felt assured that all would work out well through their prayer and the consequent enablement of the Spirit of Jesus Christ.

He had such a vision of the spiritual unity of the body of Christ through all its members that he felt himself actually dependent upon the prayer of the churches. Where he stood alone he knew God as a God of prayer and had power with Him. But where he had believers to whom he was linked, he felt their prayer to be indispensable for his experience of God's power. It is only when this sense of unity binds minister and people—binds all believers together—that the full power of the Holy Spirit can be expected to work.

We have a lesson here that, if the missionary would train converts in the art of fervent prayer, that missionary would have in them a mighty power to wield against the forces of darkness. On God Paul set his hope that He would continue to deliver him, as they helped him by their prayers.

May we be bound together in the bonds of Jesus Christ in faithfulness to this kind of praying that will bring down the blessing on which the apostle counted so confidently when he wrote these words.

To Proclaim God's Message

Christ lives in you, and this is your assurance
that you will share in his glory.
COLOSSIANS 1:27

"Christ lives in you. . .assurance that you will share in his glory."
The new life itself is nothing else than to have Christ living in
us. This is what Paul regarded as the great mystery he had to
preach to those who did not know Christ (Colossians 1:25–27).

The temptation was ever near to meet the wisdom of man in
those to whom he spoke. We must remember that the Gentiles—
heathen—were not, as so many in our days are, savages in utter
darkness. Egyptian and Babylonian, Grecian and Roman phi-
losophy had trained men to think about unseen things. The
whole spirit of the world tempted Christians to be content with
the first elements of salvation and not to press on to the life in
which the world, with its wisdom and its pleasure, had to be
entirely sacrificed before Jesus Christ could take possession of
the heart and rule the whole life. Paul had been preaching for
twenty years, but he still felt the need of the help of continued
intercession that his dependence might be on God alone to
speak as he ought to speak.

In 1 Corinthians and 1 Thessalonians he tells how his speak-
ing had been in demonstration of the Spirit and of power, and
how his gospel came not in word only, but also in power and the
Holy Spirit and in much assurance. Paul asked for help by their
prayer that he would never preach otherwise!

Praying for Fearless Boldness

And God has given us the task of
reconciling people to him.
2 CORINTHIANS 5:18

Words from God: "All this newness of life is from God, who brought us back to himself through what Christ did. And God has given us the task of reconciling people to him. For God was in Christ, reconciling the world to himself, no longer counting people's sins against them. This is the wonderful message he has given us to tell others. . . . 'Be reconciled to God!' For God made Christ, who never sinned, to be the offering for our sin, so that we could be made right with God through Christ" (2 Corinthians 5:18–21).

The home and the life are to be built on this foundation: "Christ lives in you, and this is your assurance that you will share in his glory" (Colossians 1:27). Christ is our life.

Until the believers were brought to understand and experience what it meant to have Christ dwelling in their hearts and revealed in their lives, Paul could not be satisfied. The very center truth of his preaching to the Gentiles is to have the Spirit of Christ every day dwelling within them, controlling their whole being, and living out His life in them.

The Christian life is a life in which Jesus Christ Himself absolutely and increasingly lives. Following His example is nothing but the natural outcome of His presence within. This high and holy calling—surrender to Christ and fellowship with Him—needs to be total and habitual.

Intercession

Pray for each other.
JAMES 5:16

There is a mystery of glory in prayer. On the one hand we see God in His holiness, love, and power—waiting, longing to bless us. On the other hand is a sinful, unworthy human being—asking God in prayer for the very life and love of heaven to dwell in our hearts.

Intercession gives us a lot of joy when we are bold enough to ask God for what we desire for others. Through intercession we seek to bring to others the power of eternal life. This is one of the holiest exercises as God's children, the highest privilege connected with knowing God—the power of being used by God as instruments for His great work.

The Church should seek above everything to cultivate the power of an unceasing prayerfulness on behalf of those without Christ. There is strength in the unity of believers. God will certainly avenge His own who cry day and night to Him. It is when Christians cease looking for help apart from God and aim at being bound together to the throne of God, that the Church will put on her strength to overcome the world. This comes by continuously asking for the power of God's Spirit.

Open Their Eyes

Elisha prayed, "O Lord, open his eyes and let him see!". . .
Elisha prayed, "O Lord, now open their eyes
and let them see."
2 KINGS 6:17, 20

The prayer of Elisha for his servant was answered in a wonderful way. The young man saw the mountain full of chariots of fire and horsemen surrounding Elisha. The heavenly host had been sent by God to protect His servant.

Elisha prayed a second time. The Syrian army was struck with blindness and was led into Samaria. There Elisha prayed for God to open their eyes, and they found themselves hopeless prisoners in the hand of the enemy.

All the powers of the heaven are at our disposal in the service of His kingdom. How little the children of God live in the faith of the heavenly vision—the power of the Holy Spirit, on them, with them, and in them.

The church is unconscious of its weakness to do the work of bringing others to Christ and building up believers for a life of holiness and fruitfulness. Pray that God may open eyes to see the great and fundamental need of the Church: the need for intercession to bring down His blessing.

Man's Place in God's Plan

The heavens belong to the LORD,
but he has given the earth to all humanity.
PSALM 115:16

God created heaven as a dwelling for Himself—perfect, glorious, and most holy. He created the earth for mankind—everything good, but only as a beginning. The work God had done, man was to continue and perfect. What the earth is today, with its cities and habitations, with its cornfields and orchards, it owes to man. The work God had begun and prepared was to be carried out in fulfillment of God's purpose. So nature teaches us the wonderful partnership to which God calls man for the carrying out of the work of creation to its destined end.

This is equally true in the kingdom of grace. In this great redemption God has revealed the power of the heavenly life and the spiritual blessings. But He has entrusted to His people the work of making these blessings known.

People are diligent in seeking for the treasures of the earth for their use. Shouldn't the children of God be equally faithful in seeking for the treasures of heaven? It is by the unceasing intercession of God's people that His kingdom will come and His will be done on earth as it is in heaven (Matthew 6:10).

Intercession in the Plan of Redemption

For you answer our prayers, and to you
all people will come.
PSALM 65:2

When God gave the world into the power of man, it was His plan that Adam should do nothing except with and through God. God Himself would do all His work in the world through Adam. Adam was to be the owner, master, and ruler of the earth. When sin entered the world Adam's power proved to be a terrible reality. Through him the earth, with the whole race of man, was brought under the curse of sin.

When God made the plan of redemption, His object was to restore man to the place from which he had fallen. God determined that His servants, through the power of intercession, could ask and it would be given them. When Christ became man it was so He might intercede for man. When He left the world, He gave this right of intercession to His children (John 15:16) that whatever they would ask He would do for them. God's intense longing to bless seems to be graciously limited by His dependence on the intercession that rises from the earth.

Christians need to realize they have the right to expect that God will hear prayer. God waits for each individual believer to take his part in the power of intercession to fulfill the petition: "As in heaven, so on earth" (Matthew 6:10).

God Seeks Intercessors

He was amazed to see that no one
intervened to help the oppressed.
ISAIAH 59:16

God had among His people intercessors to whom He listened. In Isaiah we read of a time of trouble when He sought for an intercessor in vain. There was none who loved the people enough or who had sufficient faith to intercede. If there had been an intercessor, He would have given deliverance; without an intercessor His judgments came down (see Isaiah 64:7; Ezekiel 22:30–31).

The place the intercessor holds in the kingdom of God is of infinite importance. God gives us such power, and yet there are so few who know what it is to take hold of His strength and pray for His blessing.

When Christ had taken His place on the throne, the work of His kingdom was given into the hands of men. Prayer is the highest exercise of Christ's royal prerogative as Priest-King upon the throne. All that He was to do in heaven was to be in fellowship with His people on earth. God waits for His people's intercession.

God rules the world and His Church through the prayers of His people. That God should have made the extension of His kingdom to such a large extent dependent on the faithfulness of His people in prayer is a stupendous mystery and yet an absolute certainty. God calls for intercessors; in His grace He has made His work dependent on them.

Christ As Intercessor

He is able, once and forever,
to save everyone who comes to God through him.
He lives forever to plead with God on their behalf.
HEBREWS 7:25

In His life on earth Christ began His work as Intercessor. Think of the high priestly prayer on behalf of His disciples and of all who would believe in His name through them. Think of His words to Peter, "I have pleaded in prayer for you, Simon, that your faith should not fail" (Luke 22:32)—a proof of how intensely personal His intercession is. And on the cross He spoke as intercessor: "Father, forgive these people" (Luke 23:34).

Now that He is seated at God's right hand, He continues, as our great High Priest, the work of intercession without ceasing. Yet He gives His people power to take part in it. Seven times in His farewell discourse He repeated the assurance that He would do what they asked.

The power of heaven was to be at the disciples' disposal. God waited for the disciples to ask for His grace and power. Through the leading of the Holy Spirit they would know what the will of God was. They would learn in faith to pray in His name. He would present their requests to the Father, and through united intercession the Church would be clothed with the power of the Spirit.

The Intercessor God Seeks

O Jerusalem, I have posted watchmen on your walls;
they will pray to the Lord day and night
for the fulfillment of his promises.
ISAIAH 62:6

Watchmen were ordinarily placed on the walls of a city to give notice to the rulers of coming danger. God appoints watchmen not only to warn men but also to summon His help. The great mark of the intercessors is that they do not rest until God gives an answer. They count upon the assurance that God will answer their prayer.

"Don't you think God will surely give justice to his chosen people who plead with him day and night?" (Luke 18:7). The Church of Christ, under the influence of the power of the world, is losing its influence over its members. There is little proof of God's presence in the conversion of sinners or in the holiness of His people. There is an utter neglect of Christ's call to extend His kingdom.

What can be done to interest young and old in the study of God's Word or to encourage corporate worship? It is because of a lack of prayer that the working of the Spirit is so weak. Only united fervent prayer can change this. If ever there was a time when God's children should cry day and night to Him, it is now. Offer yourself to God for this wonderful work of intercession. Learn to count it the highest privilege of your life to be a channel through whose prayers God's blessing can be brought down to earth.

The School of Intercession

While Jesus was here on earth, he offered prayers. . .
with a loud cry and tears,
to the one who could deliver him out of death.
And God heard his prayers.
HEBREWS 5:7

Christ, as Head, is Intercessor in heaven; we, as the members of His body are partners with Him on earth. It cost Christ to become an intercessor. "Yet when his life is made an offering for sin, he will have a multitude of children, many heirs. . . . When he sees all that is accomplished by his anguish, he will be satisfied. . . . I will give him the honors of one who is mighty and great, because he exposed himself [poured out his soul] to death" (Isaiah 53:10–12). "Pouring out the soul" is the divine meaning of intercession and was needed if His sacrifice and prayer were to have power with God. Giving Himself over to live and die that He might save the perishing was a revelation of the spirit that has power to prevail with God.

If we are to share His power of intercession, there will need to be the same intensity and sacrifice that there was with Him. Intercession must not be a passing interest; it must become an ever-growing object of intense desire. It is the life of consecration and self-sacrifice that will indeed give power for intercession (Acts 15:26; 20:24; Philippians 2:17; Revelation 7:11).

The longer we study and think about what it means to exercise this power of intercession, the deeper will be our conviction that it is worth giving up everything to take part with Christ in His work of intercession.

Name of Jesus—
Power of Intercession

You haven't done this before.
Ask, using my name, and you will receive,
and you will have abundant joy.
JOHN 16:24

During Christ's life upon earth the disciples knew little of the power of prayer. In Gethsemane they utterly failed. They had no concept of what it was to ask in the name of Jesus and to receive. The Lord promised them that in the future they would be able to pray with such a power that they may ask what they would, and it would be given.

"You haven't done this before. Ask, using my name, and you will receive." These two conditions are still found in the church. We lack knowledge of our oneness with Christ and of the Holy Spirit as the Spirit of prayer so that we make no attempt to claim the promises Christ gives. But when God's children know what it is to abide in Christ and to yield to the Holy Spirit, we begin to learn that God will give His power in answer to prayer.

Faith in the power of Jesus' name and our right to use it gives us courage to be intercessors. Jesus sent the disciples out into the world with this awareness: He who sits upon the throne, and who lives in my heart, has promised that what I ask in His name I will receive.

Intense and unceasing prayerfulness is the essential mark of the healthy spiritual life. The power of all-prevailing intercession will indeed be the portion of those who live only for their Lord.

The Perfect Work of the Spirit

God has sent the Spirit of his Son into your hearts,
and now you can call God your dear Father [Abba, Father].
GALATIANS 4:6

When Christ prayed "Abba, Father" in Gethsemane, He surrendered to death so that the will of God in redemption of sinners might be accomplished. He was ready for any sacrifice. Jesus would have us yield ourselves as completely to God as He did and pray like He did, that God's will be done on earth at any cost.

God's love was revealed in His desire for the salvation of souls; Jesus' love was revealed when He gave Himself for them. He asks for that same love to fill us so that we give ourselves completely to the work of intercession—at any cost, praying for God's love for those who do not know Christ.

This is not beyond our reach, for the Holy Spirit is actually in our hearts that we may pray in His name and in His power. Now we can understand how Christ could give such unlimited promises of answer to prayer to His disciples; they were first going to be filled with the Holy Spirit. God can give such a high place to intercession in the fulfillment of His purpose of redemption because it is the Holy Spirit who breathes God's own desire into us and enables us to intercede for those without Christ.

Christ Our Example in Intercession

*I will give him the honors of
one who is mighty and great,
because. . .
he bore the sins of many
and interceded for sinners.*

ISAIAH 53:12

"He interceded for sinners." Think of what it cost Him to pray that prayer in Gethsemane: "Father, I want your will, not mine." He had to give Himself as an offering for sin.

It was His love to the Father that moved Him to sacrifice Himself. As Conqueror of every enemy, He is seated at the right hand of God with the power of unlimited intercession. His seed would be a generation of those whom He could train to a share in His great work of intercession.

When we intercede for others, it means that we yield ourselves completely to the holiness and the love of the Father. It means that we, too, say "Your will be done"—cost what it may.

Jesus has taken us into a partnership with Himself to carry out the great work of intercession. He in heaven and we on earth must have one mind—to consecrate our lives to intercession for God's blessing. The burning desire of Father and Son for the salvation of souls must be the burning desire of our heart, too.

God's Will and Ours

Your will be done.
MATTHEW 26:42

When God created man with the power to will and choose what he should be, He limited Himself in the exercise of His will. And when man had fallen and yielded himself to the will of God's enemy, God in His love set about the great work of winning man back. As in God, so in man, desire is the great moving power. Just as man had yielded himself to a life of desire after the things of the earth and the flesh, God desired to redeem him and to educate him into a life of harmony with Himself.

When Christ came into this world, He reproduced the divine desires in His human nature. He yielded Himself up to the perfect fulfillment of all that God wanted. When He prayed "Your will be done," He surrendered to being forsaken by God so that the Satan might be conquered and deliverance obtained. It was in complete harmony between the Father and the Son when the Son said, "Your will of love be done" and redemption was accomplished.

As believers we appropriate that great work of redemption when we pray, "Your will be done in heaven as on earth."

The Blessedness of a Life of Intercession

*Take no rest, all you who pray. Give the LORD
no rest until he makes Jerusalem the object
of praise throughout the earth.*

ISAIAH 62:6–7

What a gift of grace to be allowed to work with God in intercession for the needs of others! What a blessing to mingle my prayers with His! What an honor to have power with God in heaven for those who do not know Christ. What a privilege to bring to Him the Church, individuals, ministers, or missionaries, and plead on their behalf until He entrusts me with the answer! As God's children we are blessed to pray together until victory is gained over difficulties here on earth or over the powers of darkness!

For a long time we may have thought of prayer simply as a means of supplying our needs in life. May God help us to see the place intercession takes in His divine counsel and in His work for the kingdom. May our hearts really feel that there is no honor or joy on earth at all equal to the unspeakable privilege of waiting upon God and interceding for the blessing He delights to give!

The Place of Prayer

They all met together continually for prayer.
ACTS 1:14

Christ spoke these words before He left the world: "Do not leave Jerusalem until the Father sends you what he promised." "When the Holy Spirit has come upon you, you will receive power." "You will tell people about me everywhere. . .in Jerusalem, throughout Judea, in Samaria, and to the ends of the earth" (Acts 1:4, 8).

Such are the marks of the church of the New Testament. The Church that went out to conquer the world was a Church of united and unceasing prayerfulness, a ministry filled with the Holy Spirit, members serving as witnesses to a living Christ, with a message to every creature on earth.

When Christ had ascended to heaven the disciples knew what their work was to be: continuing with one accord in prayer and supplication. This gave them power in heaven with God and on earth with men. Their duty was to wait united in prayer for the power of the Holy Spirit for their witness to Christ to the ends of the earth. The Church of Jesus Christ should be a praying, Spirit-filled church and a witnessing church to all the world.

As long as the Church maintained this character, it had power to conquer. Unfortunately, as it came under the influence of the world, it lost much of its supernatural strength and became unfaithful to its worldwide mission.

Paul as an Intercessor

I fall to my knees and pray to the Father. . .
that from his glorious,
unlimited resources he will give you mighty inner
strength through his Holy Spirit.

EPHESIANS 3:14, 16

We think of Paul as the great missionary, writer, apostle. We usually do not think of him as the intercessor who, through prayer, obtained the power that rested on all his activities.

We see above what he wrote to the Ephesians. He told the Thessalonians (1 Thessalonians 3:10): "Night and day we pray earnestly for you, asking God to let us see you again to fill up anything that may still be missing in your faith." To the Romans (1:9): "Day and night I bring you and your needs in prayer to God." To the Philippians (1:4): "I always pray for you." And to the Colossians (1:9): "So we have continued praying for you."

Paul believed in the power of his intercession for others. He also believed in the blessing that others would bring him. "I urge you in the name of our Lord Jesus Christ to join me in my struggle by praying to God for me" (Romans 15:30). "He will rescue us because you are helping by praying for us" (2 Corinthians 1:11). "Pray for me, too" (Ephesians 6:18–19; Colossians 4:3; 2 Thessalonians 3:1). "For I know that as you pray for me and as the Spirit of Jesus Christ helps me, this will all turn out for my deliverance" (Philippians 1:19).

The whole relationship between pastor and people depends on united, continual prayerfulness. When ministers and people become conscious of the power and blessing of the Holy Spirit that comes from their prayer, then the church will begin to know what pentecostal, apostolic Christianity is.

Intercession for Laborers

The harvest is so great,
but the workers are so few.
So pray to the Lord who is in charge of the harvest;
ask him to send out more workers for his fields.
MATTHEW 9:37–38

The disciples understood little of what these words in Matthew meant. Christ gave them as a seed thought for later use. At Pentecost they must have felt that the ten days of united prayer had brought a special blessing as the fruit of the Spirit's power—workers in the harvest.

Christ was teaching us that however large the field and however few the workers, prayer is the best and the only means for supplying the need. We must not only pray in time of need but all our activity for God is to be carried on in the spirit of prayer. Prayer for workers for God's harvest must be part of our whole life and effort.

When the China Inland Mission had two hundred missionaries, they felt the urgent need of more workers for unreached districts. After much prayer they felt the freedom to ask God to give them one hundred additional workers within a year. They continued praying throughout the year. At the end of the time one hundred men and women and the needed funds had been found.

Churches complain about the lack of workers and of funds to meet the needs of reaching out to the world. Christ calls us to united, unceasing prayer. God is faithful, by the power of His Spirit, to supply every need. God hears the prayer of the Church.

Intercession for Individual Souls

Yet the time will come when the LORD will gather them together one by one like handpicked grain.

ISAIAH 27:12

Many individual believers do not understand that it is necessary for them to testify to others in order to strengthen their own spiritual lives as well as to bring others to Christ. Intercession for those around us, and for the church and its mission, needs restoration to its right place in the Christian life!

Prayer is indispensable to what God in heaven desires to do on earth. Intercession is the main element in the conversion of souls. All our efforts are in vain without the power of the Holy Spirit given in answer to prayer. When ministers and people unite in a covenant of prayer and testimony, the Church will flourish.

What can we do to stir up the spirit of intercession? Begin to get an insight into the need and the power of intercession. Intercede on behalf of single individuals. Pray for your children, your relatives, friends, and for all with whom you come into contact. If you feel you don't have power to intercede, ask the Holy Spirit for that power. God wants every redeemed child of His to intercede for those who do not know Him.

Pray fervently that God will give you the power of His Holy Spirit for this ministry of intercession.

Intercession for Ministers

Finally, dear brothers and sisters,
I ask you to pray for us.
2 THESSALONIANS 3:1

The verse above suggests the strength of Paul's conviction that Christians had power with God. Their prayer would bring new strength to him in his work. He urged them to pray because he realized the interdependence of the Body of Christ, both for their own sakes and for his sake. "Devote yourselves to prayer with an alert mind and a thankful heart. Don't forget to pray for us, too" (Colossians 4:2–3).

The church depends upon its ministers more than we realize. The minister is God's ambassador to bring men and women to reconciliation with Him. Unfaithfulness in prayer must bring a terrible blight on the Church. If Paul, after having preached for twenty years in the power of God, still needed the prayer of the Church, how much more does the minister in our day need it?

The minister needs the prayer of his people. He has a right to it. He is dependent on it. Let us all intercede more faithfully for ministers, whether of our own church or of other churches.

Continue in prayer that ministers may be servants of power and of prayer, full of the Holy Spirit.

Prayer for All Saints

Pray at all times and on every occasion
in the power of the Holy Spirit.
Stay alert and be persistent in your prayers
for all Christians everywhere.

EPHESIANS 6:18

Notice how Paul's words show the intensity of his desire to reach the hearts of his readers. "Pray at all times. . .on every occasion. . . stay alert. . .be persistent."

Paul felt deeply the unity of the Body of Christ, and he was sure that unity could only be realized in the exercise of love and prayer. He pleaded with the believers at Ephesus to pray for all saints unceasingly and fervently, not only the saints in their immediate circle, but in all the Church of Christ everywhere. "In unity is strength."

Often we pray more for ourselves and for what God must do for us. May we realize that we have a call to give ourselves without ceasing to the exercise of love and prayer. The whole Church will be enabled to do its work as we forget ourselves and yield ourselves to intercession for others. There is no greater blessing than abiding communion with God, and intercession for others leads the way to that blessing.

Missionary Intercession

So after more fasting and prayer,
the men laid their hands on them
and sent them on their way.
ACTS 13:3

How do we multiply the number of Christians who will intercede for those without Christ?—that is the supreme question of foreign missions. Those who love this work will pray unceasingly for its triumph.

Missions has its root in the love of Christ. God's children should be wholehearted in seeking to bring Christ's love to all mankind. Intercession is the chief means appointed by God to bring the great redemption within the reach of all.

Pray for the missionaries that their witness may be clear and strong. Pray that they may be men and women of prayer, filled with love, in whom the power of the spiritual life is made manifest.

Pray for national Christians that they may know the glory of the mystery among unbelievers—"Christ lives in you, and this is your assurance that you will share in his glory" (Colossians 1:27). Pray for students in the schools, that the teaching of God's Word may be in power. Pray especially for the national pastors and evangelists that the Holy Spirit may fill them to be witnesses for Christ in their country.

Pray, above all, for the Church of Christ that it may be lifted out of its indifference. Pray that every believer may understand that the one object of life is to help make Christ King on the earth.

The Grace of Intercession

Devote yourselves to prayer with
an alert mind and a thankful heart.
Don't forget to pray for us, too.
COLOSSIANS 4:2–3

There is nothing that can bring us nearer to God and lead us deeper into His love than the work of intercession. Nothing gives us a higher experience of God than pouring out our hearts to Him in prayer for men and women. Nothing can so closely connect us to Jesus Christ and give us the experience of His power and Spirit as yielding our lives to the work of bringing redemption into the lives of others. There is nothing in which we will know more of the working of the Holy Spirit than the prayer breathed by Him into our hearts, "Abba, Father."

As we become a living sacrifice before God with the persistent prayer for His abundant blessing, God will be glorified. In intercession, our souls will reach their highest destiny and God's kingdom will come.

As God's children daily pray together that God will make His Church a light to those who are sitting in darkness, we will experience unity and power in the Body of Christ. How little we realize what we are losing in not living in fervent intercession!

Christ lives in heaven to pray—asking the fullness of the Spirit for His people. God delights in nothing as much as in prayer. Believe that the highest blessings of heaven will be given to us as we pray more.

United Intercession

We are all one body, we have the same Spirit,
and we have all been called to the same glorious future.
EPHESIANS 4:4

There are many who look upon salvation only in connection with their own happiness. There also are those who, through prayer, seek to bring others to share in their happiness. We have a calling to take the whole Body of Christ Jesus into our love and intercession.

It is only when intercession for the whole Church, by the whole Church, ascends to God's throne that the Spirit of unity can have its full sway. Closer union between the different branches of the Church of Christ is cause for thanksgiving. Yet the difficulties are so great that the thought of a united Church on earth appears beyond reach.

Let us bless God that there is a unity available in Christ Jesus, deeper and stronger than any visible manifestation could make it. Unity can be practically exemplified in the work of the kingdom. Intercession in the Spirit can bring true unity. When we as believers learn the meaning of our calling as a royal priesthood, we will see that God is not confined to our limited spheres. He invites us to pray for all who believe or can yet believe. By intercession, the Church of Christ will be bound to the throne of heaven as never before.

Unceasing Intercession

Keep on praying.
1 THESSALONIANS 5:17

The average Christian has a very different standard regarding a life of service to God than that which Scripture gives us. We think about our personal safety—grace to pardon our sin and to secure our entrance into heaven. The Bible's standard is that we surrender ourselves, our time, our thoughts, and our love to God.

To the average Christian the command "keep on praying" is a needless and impossible life of perfection. Who can do it? We can get to heaven without it.

However, to the true believer that command holds the promise of the highest happiness and of a life crowned by all the blessings that come through intercession. Through perseverance it becomes the highest aim and joy upon earth.

"Keep on praying." Take that word in faith as a promise of what God's Spirit will work in us. Let it become our heavenly calling. Christ said, "I in them and you in me." Let us believe that just as the Father worked in Him, Christ will work and pray in us. As the faith of our calling fills our hearts we literally will begin to feel there is nothing on earth to be compared with the privilege of walking without interruption in His holy presence, bringing others around us to the footstool of His throne and receiving His power.

Link Between Heaven and Earth

May your will be done here on earth,
just as it is in heaven.
MATTHEW 6:10

When God created heaven and earth, He meant heaven to be the divine pattern to which earth was to be conformed. "As in heaven, so on earth" was to be the law of its existence.

What constitutes the glory of heaven? God is there. Everything lives for His glory. When we think of what this earth has become, with all its sin and misery, with the great majority without any knowledge of the true God, we feel that a miracle is needed if the Word is to be fulfilled: "May your will be done here on earth, just as it is in heaven."

This can become true through the prayers of God's children. Intercession is to be the great link between heaven and earth. The intercession of the Son, begun upon earth, continued in heaven, and carried on by His people, will bring about the change. As Christ prayed "May your will be done," so His redeemed ones make His prayer their own and unceasingly ask, "May your will be done here on earth, just as it is in heaven."

When we, God's children, learn to pray not only for our immediate interests but enlarge our hearts to take in the whole Church and the whole world that our united supplication will have power with God. Intercession will hasten the day when it will indeed be "on earth, just as it is in heaven"—the whole earth filled with the glory of God.

The Fulfillment of God's Desires

> *For the LORD has chosen Jerusalem;*
> *he has desired it as his home.*
> PSALM 132:13

The one great desire of God that moved Him in the work of redemption was that His heart longed for us to dwell with Him and in Him. He said to Moses: "I want the people of Israel to build me a sacred residence where I can live among them" (Exodus 25:8). As His children we are called to yield ourselves to God to dwell in us and to bring others to become His habitation.

What an honor to find our lives and our joy in bringing others to Christ in whom God may find His heart's delight: "I will live here, for this is the place I desired."

This is what we can do. We can ask God to give those around us His Holy Spirit. It is God's great plan that we will build Him a habitation. God will give His power and blessing in answer to the unceasing intercession of His children. As this desire of God fills us, we will give ourselves totally to work for its fulfillment.

Let us begin, as never before, to pray for our children, for those around us, and for all the world. Pray not only because we love them but also because God longs for them. He gives us the honor of being the channels through whom His blessing is brought down.

The Fulfillment of Our Desire

Take delight in the LORD,
and he will give you your heart's desires.
PSALM 37:4

God is love—an ever-flowing fountain out of which streams the unceasing desire to make His creatures the partakers of all the holiness and the blessedness there is in Him. This desire for the salvation of souls is God's perfect will, His highest glory.

He gives this desire to all His children who are willing to yield themselves completely to Him. The likeness and image of God consists in a heart in which His love takes complete possession.

"Take delight in the Lord" and in His life of love, "and he will give you your heart's desires." The intercession of love will be met with the fulfillment of the desire of our heart.

In fellowship with Him we get the courage to pray with our whole will and strength for those in whom we are interested, in confidence that our prayer will be heard. As we reach out in love, we will take hold of the will of God to bless and to believe that God will work out His own will in giving us the desire of our hearts. The fulfillment of His desire is our delight.

We become God's co-laborers. Our prayer becomes part of God's divine work of reaching and saving the lost.

My Great Desire

The thing I seek most—
is to live in the house of the LORD all the days of my life
. . .meditating in his Temple.

PSALM 27:4

Psalm 27:4 is our response to God's desire to dwell in us. When the desire of God begins to rule our life, our desire is to live in the house of the Lord all the days of our life, to delight in the Lord's perfections, to meditate in His temple, and to learn what God means when He speaks.

The more we realize that God's desire is to give His rest, and the more our desire is to dwell in His temple and behold His beauty, the more the Spirit of prayer will be ours. Whether we think of our church and country, of our home and school, of the saved and their needs, or the unsaved and their danger, the thought that God is longing to find His home and His rest in the hearts of men will urge us to pray. All the thoughts of our weakness and unworth-iness will be swallowed up in the wonderful assurance that He has said of human hearts: "This is my home where I will live forever. . .I will live here, for this is the place I desired" (Psalm 132:14).

God has made fervent, persistent prayer indispensable to His purpose being fulfilled. Thank God for this divine partnership in which God commits the fulfillment of His desires to our keeping.

Intercession Day and Night

Don't you think God will surely give justice to his chosen
people who plead with him day and night?
Will he keep putting them off?
LUKE 18:7

When Nehemiah heard of the destruction of Jerusalem, he cried to God, "Listen to my prayer! Look down and see me praying night and day for your people Israel" (Nehemiah 1:6). God said of the watchmen on the walls of Jerusalem: "They will pray to the LORD day and night for the fulfillment of his promises" (Isaiah 62:6). Paul writes: "Night and day we pray earnestly for you. . .[that] Christ will make your hearts strong, blameless, and holy when you stand before God our Father on that day when our Lord Jesus comes with all those who belong to him" (1 Thessalonians 3:10, 13).

Is such prayer, night and day, really needed and really possible? Most assuredly it is, when our life has been so blessed that nothing can keep us from sacrificing all to intercede.

When we as children of God begin to get a real vision into the need of the church and of the world, a vision of the out-pouring of God's love, a vision of the power of true intercession, a vision of the honor of being allowed to take part in that work, it comes as a matter of course that we regard this work as the most divine thing upon earth.

There is nothing more worth living for than this—how to satisfy God in His longing for human fellowship and love, and how to win hearts to be His dwelling-place. Let's not rest until we have found a place for the Mighty One in our hearts and have yielded ourselves to the work of intercession!

The High Priest and His Intercession

He [Jesus, our High Priest] is able,
once and forever,
to save everyone who comes to God through him.
He lives forever to plead with God on their behalf.
HEBREWS 7:25

There was a difference in Israel between the high priest and the priests. The high priest alone had access to the Holiest of All. He bore the golden crown of "Holiness to the Lord." By his intercession on the Day of Atonement, he bore the sins of the people. The priests brought the daily sacrifices and came out to bless the people. The difference between high priest and priest was great, but greater still was the unity. The priests formed one body with the high priest, sharing the power to receive and dispense God's blessing to His people.

It is the same with Jesus, our great High Priest. He alone has power with God to obtain from the Father what His people need. Yet, though the distance between Him and the royal priesthood is infinite, the unity which His people have with Him is no less infinite than the diversity. The blessing He obtains from His Father for us, His people receive from Him through their fervent supplication to be dispensed to humanity as His representatives.

When once Christians realize that salvation means a vital union with Jesus Christ—an actual sharing of His life working in us and the consecration of our whole being as a royal priesthood—the Church will prove how truly the likeness and the power of Christ dwell in her.

NOVEMBER 22

A Royal Priesthood

*Ask me and I will tell you some remarkable secrets
about what is going to happen here.*
JEREMIAH 33:3

As you pray for God's great mercies to be granted, take with you
these thoughts:

(1) The infinite willingness of God to bless. His very nature
is a pledge of it. He delights in mercy. He waits to be gracious.
His promises and the experience of His saints assure us of it.

(2) Why then is the blessing delayed? In creating man with a
free will and making him a partner in the rule of the earth, God
limited Himself. He made Himself dependent on what man
would do. Man by his prayer would hold the measure of what
God could do in blessing.

(3) Think of how God is hindered and disappointed when
His children seldom pray. The weak Church, the lack of the
power of the Holy Spirit, is all because of the lack of prayer.
How different would be the state of the Church and of the
world if God's people were to unceasingly call on Him!

(4) Yet God has blessed—just up to the measure of the faith
and the zeal of His people. If He has thus blessed our weak
prayers, what will He do if we yield ourselves wholly to a life of
intercession?

(5) This is a call to repentance and confession! Our lack of
consecration has held back God's blessing from the world. He
was ready to save, but we were not willing for the sacrifice of a
whole-hearted devotion to Christ and His service.

A Call for Decision

*Ask me and I will tell you some remarkable secrets
about what is going to happen here.*
JEREMIAH 33:3

Are you willing to give yourself totally to the power of Jesus Christ to make intercession for God's Church and for a dying world? Will you make this the main object of your life? Is it too much to yield your life to the Lord who gave Himself for you?

Intercession should not take a subordinate place in the teaching and practice of the Church with its ministers and members. It is of such supreme importance as to make it an essential, altogether indispensable element in the true Christian life. There can be no doubt about this to those who take God's Word in its full meaning.

Child of God, God counts upon you to take your place before His throne as an intercessor. Renew the consciousness of your holy calling as a royal priesthood. Begin to live life in the assurance that intercession is the highest privilege a man or woman can desire. Accept the Word with great expectation: "Ask me and I will tell you some remarkable secrets about what is going to happen here."

Intercession a Divine Reality

Then another angel. . .came and stood at the altar.
And a great quantity of incense was given to him
to mix with the prayers of God's people.
REVELATION 8:3

Intercession is an essential element in God's redeeming purpose, so much so that without it the failure of God's purpose may lie at our door. Christ's intercession in heaven is essential to His carrying out of the work He began upon earth, but He calls for the intercession of the saints in the accomplishment of His object. Just think of what we read: "All this newness of life is from God, who brought us back to himself through what Christ did. And God has given us the task of reconciling people to him" (2 Corinthians 5:18). As the reconciliation was dependent on Christ's doing His part, He calls on the Church to do her part in the accomplishment of the work.

Intercession is indeed a divine reality. Without it the Church loses the joy and the power of the Spirit life for achieving great things for God. Without it the command to preach the gospel to every creature can never be carried out. Without it there is no power for the Church to conquer the world. In the life of the believer, minister, or member there can be no entrance into the abundant life and joy of daily fellowship with God except as we take our place among God's children who cry to Him day and night.

Church of Christ, awake! Listen to the call: "Keep on praying."

God Will Hear Me

> But the LORD still waits for you to come to him
> so he can show you his love and compassion. . . .
> He will be gracious if you ask for help.
> He will respond instantly to the sound of your cries.
> ISAIAH 30:18–19

The power of prayer rests in the faith that God hears prayer. In more than one sense this is true. This faith gives us courage to pray. This faith gives us power to prevail with God. The moment I am assured that God hears me, too, I feel drawn to pray and to persevere in prayer. I feel strong to claim and to take in faith the answer God gives.

One reason for the lack of prayer is the want of the living, joyous assurance, "God will hear me." If only God's servants would get a vision of the living God waiting to grant their request. If they could see that He longs to bestow all the heavenly gifts of the Spirit they are in need of. Then they would set aside everything and make time and room for this power that can ensure heavenly blessing—the prayer of faith!

When you say in faith "God will hear me!" nothing can keep you from prayer. You know that what you cannot do on earth can and will be done for you from heaven. Let each one of us bow in stillness before God and wait on Him to reveal Himself as the prayer-hearing God. In His presence the wondrous thoughts gathering round the central truth will unfold themselves to us.

A Wonderful Certainty

As for me, I look to the LORD for his help.
I wait confidently for God to save me.
MICAH 7:7

God will hear me. What a wonderful certainty! We have God's Word for it. We have thousands of witnesses that have found it true. We have experienced it ourselves. The Son of God came from heaven with the message that if we ask, the Father will give. Christ prayed on earth; now He is in heaven interceding for us. God hears prayer—God delights in hearing our prayer. He has allowed His people to be tried so that they are compelled to cry to Him and learn to know Him as the Hearer of prayer.

We should confess with shame how little we have believed this truth. We have failed to receive it into our hearts. Accepting a truth is not enough; the living God must be revealed by it so that our whole life is spent in His presence. We must live with an awareness as clear as in a little child toward its earthly parent—I know for certain my Father hears me.

By experience you know how little an intellectual understanding of truth has profited you. Ask God to reveal Himself to you. If you want to live a different prayer life, bow to worship God in silence each time before you pray. Wait there until you have a deep consciousness of His nearness and His readiness to answer. After that you can begin to pray with the words, "God will hear me!"

A Wondrous Grace

The LORD will answer when I call to him.
PSALM 4:3

God will hear me. What a wondrous grace! Think of God in His infinite majesty, His altogether incomprehensible glory, His unapproachable holiness, sitting on a throne of grace, waiting to be gracious, inviting and encouraging you to pray with His promise: "Ask me and I will tell you some remarkable secrets about what is going to happen here" (Jeremiah 33:3).

Think of yourself in your transgressions as a sinner and in your unworthiness as a saint. Praise God for the grace which allows you to say boldly of your prayer for yourself and others, "God will hear me."

Think of what you can accomplish in this wonderful intimacy with God. God has united you with Christ. In Him you have your confidence. On the throne He prays with you and for you. You pray with Him and in Him. His worth and the Father's delight in hearing Him are the measure of your confidence, your assurance of being heard.

There is more. When you don't know what to pray the Holy Spirit is sent into your heart to cry, "Abba, Father," and to be in you a Spirit of prayer. In all your unworthiness, you are as acceptable as Christ Himself. In your ignorance and weakness, the Spirit is making intercession according to God within you.

A Deep Mystery

*I am praying to you because I know
you will answer, O God.*
PSALM 17:6

God will hear me. What a deep mystery! There are difficulties that arise and perplex the heart. There is the question of God's sovereign will. How can our wishes change His perfect will? He knows what is best and loves to give us the very best. How can our prayer change what He has ordained?

What is the need of persevering in prayer? If God is infinite love, delighting to give, why is there need for pleading, for urgency and long delay in answering our prayers?

What of the multitude of apparently unanswered prayers? Many have pleaded for loved ones and they die unsaved. Many cry for physical healing without result. This tries our faith and makes us hesitate when we say, "God will hear me."

Prayer is a deep spiritual mystery. Answers can be given that remove some of the difficulty from our questions but, as little as we can comprehend of God, we can comprehend one of the most wonderful of His attributes—He hears prayer. It is a spiritual mystery.

God hears because we pray in His Son and because the Holy Spirit prays in us. If we have believed in Christ and the Holy Spirit, we should not hesitate to believe in the power of our prayer, too. We can believe and rejoice in it, even where every question is not yet answered. We need to surrender our questions to God's love, trust His faithfulness, and obey His command to pray without ceasing.

A Solemn Responsibility

We always pray for you, and we give thanks to God. . . .
So we have continued praying for you ever since
we first heard about you.

COLOSSIANS 1:3, 9

God will hear me. What a solemn responsibility! Often we complain of failure as if there was no help for it. Yet God has promised an answer to prayer to supply every need and give us His light and strength and peace. We have the responsibility to avail ourselves of these promises. We can feel confident that God's grace will enable us to pray as we should.

Access to a God who hears prayer is meant to make us intercessors for others. If we have truly given ourselves to God for others, we share Christ's right of intercession and are able to obtain the powers of heaven.

The power of life and death is in our hands. In answer to prayer the Spirit is poured out, souls are converted, believers are established. In prayer the kingdom of darkness is conquered, souls brought out of prison into the liberty of Christ, and the glory of God is revealed. Through prayer the sword of the Spirit, which is the Word of God, is used in power.

The Church needs to do the work of intercession. What a responsibility! Every believer must seek to use his or her talent in prayer for others. The more we understand the power in prayer that God has given, the more we will surrender to the work of intercession.

A Blessed Prospect

I fall to my knees and pray to the Father. . .
that from his glorious, unlimited resources
he will give you mighty inner strength
through his Holy Spirit.
EPHESIANS 3:14–16

God will hear me—what a blessed prospect! The failures of my past life have been due to lack of this faith. Especially in the work of intercession, I did not live in the full faith of the assurance that "God will hear me!" I begin to see it and believe it. All can be different.

Commonplace and insignificant though I am, I have access to this infinite God with the confidence that He hears me. I will pray for others for I am sure my God will listen to me; my God will hear me.

What a prospect before me—every anxiety exchanged for the peace of God. We can know that even when the answer is long delayed and there is a call for patient, persevering prayer, the truth remains infallibly sure—God will hear me.

If only we could all give prayer its place, give faith in God its place, or, rather, give the prayer-hearing God His place! This is the one great thing that those who begin to awaken to the urgent need for prayer ought to pray for.

When God first poured out the Spirit on His praying people, He formulated the law for all time: In the degree that you pray you will receive the Spirit.

Great Worship

Worship God.
REVELATION 22:9

Why is it that prayer and intercession with God are not a greater joy and delight? One answer to this question undoubtedly is: We know God too little. In our prayer, His presence is not the chief thing our heart is seeking. And yet it should be. Often when we pray, we think mostly of ourselves, our needs, our desires. But we forget that in every prayer, God must be first, must be all.

So how is one to attain this nearness to God and fellowship with Him? The answer is simple: We must give God time to make Himself known to us. Believe with your whole heart, that just as you present yourself to God as a supplicant, so God presents Himself to you as the hearer of prayer. But you cannot realize this unless you give Him time and quiet. It is not in the multitude or the earnestness of your words in which prayer has its power. Your prayer has its power in the living faith that God Himself is taking you and your prayer into His loving heart. He Himself will give the assurance that in His time your prayer will be heard.

Begin your day with these words: "To you, O LORD, I lift up my soul" (Psalm 25:1). "I thirst for God, the living God" (Psalm 42:2).

God Is a Spirit

For God is Spirit,
so those who worship him must
worship in spirit and in truth.
JOHN 4:24

When God created man and breathed into him of His own spirit, man became a living soul. The soul stood midway between the spirit and the body. It either had to yield to the spirit to be lifted up to God or to the flesh and its lusts. In the Fall humanity chose the latter. Consequently, the human spirit became utterly darkened.

In regeneration it is this spirit that is given life and is born again from above. In the regenerate life it is the human spirit that has ever to yield itself to the Spirit of God. The spirit is the deepest, inward part of the human being. As we read in Psalm 51:6: "You desire honesty from the heart, so you can teach me to be wise in my inmost being." Isaiah says: "All night long I search for you; earnestly I seek for God" (Isaiah 26:9). The soul must sink down into the depths of the hidden spirit and call upon that to stir itself to seek God.

God is a Spirit; and He gave us a spirit with the one object of having fellowship with Himself. Deeper than our thoughts and feelings, God will, in our inmost being, in our spirits within us, teach us to worship Him in spirit and in truth.

Intercession and Adoration

Worship the LORD in all his holy splendor.
PSALM 96:9

The better we know God, the more wonderful our insight into the power of intercession becomes. We begin to understand that it is the greatest means by which man can take part in carrying out God's purpose. God has entrusted the whole of His redemption in Christ to His people to make known and to communicate to men. In all this, intercession is the chief and essential element. Through it, His servants receive the power of the Spirit as their power for service.

The clearer the insight into this great purpose of God, the more we will sense the need to enter into God's presence in the spirit of humble worship and holy adoration. The more we take time to abide in God's presence—to enter fully into His mind and will, to get our whole soul possessed by the thought of His glorious purpose—the stronger our faith will become that God Himself will work out all the good pleasure of His will through our prayers.

Thus, the secret of true adoration can only be known by the soul that gives time to tarry in God's presence and that yields itself to God for Him to reveal Himself. Adoration will indeed fit us for the great work of making God's glory known.

The Desire for God

All night long I search for you.
ISAIAH 26:9

What is the best and most glorious thing that a man needs every day and can do every day? Nothing less than to seek, to know, to love, and to praise God Himself. As glorious as God is, so is the glory which begins to work in the hearts and lives of people who give themselves to live for God.

Have you learned to seek this God, to meet Him, to worship Him, to live for Him and for His glory? It is a great step forward in the life of a Christian when we truly see this and consider fellowship with God every day as the chief end of our lives.

Take the time to ask yourself whether knowing your God and loving Him with your whole heart is the utmost desire of your heart. You can be certain that God greatly desires that you should live in this intimate fellowship with Him. He will, in answer to your prayer, enable you to do so.

Begin today by speaking these words to God in the stillness of your soul: "O God, you are my God; I earnestly search for you. My soul thirsts for you; my whole body longs for you. . . . I follow close behind you" (Psalm 63:1, 8). "[I] search for him with all [my] heart" (Psalm 119:2).

Silent Adoration

I wait quietly before God. . . .
I wait quietly before God,
for my hope is in him.
PSALM 62:1, 5

When we in our littleness and God in His glory meet, we all understand that what God says has infinitely more worth than what a person says. And yet our prayer so often consists of what we need that we give God no time to speak to us.

It is a great lesson to learn that to be silent before God is the secret of true adoration. It is only as the soul bows itself before Him in honor and reverence that the heart will be opened to receive the divine impression of the nearness of God and of the working of His power.

Such worship of God is the surest way to give Him the glory that is due Him. It will lead to a blessedness that can only be found in quiet prayer. Do not think that it is time lost. Do not abandon it if at first it appears difficult or fruitless. Be assured that it brings you into the right relationship with God. It opens the way to fellowship with Him. It leads to the blessed assurance that He is looking on you in tender love and working in you with a divine power. As you become more accustomed to it, you will experience His presence abiding with you all day long, and people will begin to sense that you have been with God.

The Light of His Countenance

God is light.
1 JOHN 1:5

The LORD is my light.
PSALM 27:1

Every morning the sun rises, and we walk in its light and per-form our daily duties. Whether we think about it or not, the light of the sun shines on us all day. Likewise, the light of God shines on His children every morning. But in order to enjoy the light of God's countenance, the soul must turn to God and trust Him to let His light shine in upon it.

Just as you need the light of the sun each hour, so, too, is the heavenly light of the Father's countenance indispensable. If we expect the sun to rise each day and receive its light, we can also confidently count on God to let His light shine on us. Make sure that the light of God shines on you as you commune with Him in the morning. Then expect His light to remain with you all day long.

Remember, it is the ardent longing of your heavenly Father that you should dwell and rejoice in His light. So do not rest until you know that the light of His countenance and His blessing is resting on you. Then you will experience the truth of the words: "They will walk in the light of your presence, LORD. They rejoice all day long in your wonderful reputation" (Psalm 89:15–16).

Faith in God

*Jesus said to the disciples,
"Have faith in God."*
MARK 11:22

As the eye is the organ by which we see, so faith is the power by which we see the light of God and walk in it.

We were made for God, to seek Him, to find Him, to grow up into His likeness and show forth His glory—in the fullest sense to be His dwelling. And faith is the eye which, turning away from the world and self, looks up to God and sees God reveal Himself.

Without faith it is impossible to please God or to know Him. "Abraham never wavered in believing God's promise. . . . He was absolutely convinced that God was able to do anything he promised" (Romans 4:20–21).

Let our one desire be to take time and be still before God, believing with an unbounded faith in His longing to make Himself known to us. Let us feed on God's Word to make us strong in faith. Let that faith have large thoughts of what God's glory is and of what His power is.

Such faith, exercised and strengthened day by day in secret fellowship with God, will become the habit of our life. It will keep us ever in the enjoyment of His presence and in the experience of His saving power.

Alone with God

One day as Jesus was alone, praying. . .
LUKE 9:18

He went higher into the hills alone.
JOHN 6:15

Human beings need to be alone with God. Our fall consisted in our being brought, through the lust of the flesh and the world, under the power of things visible and temporal. Our restoration through salvation is meant to bring us back to the Father's love and fellowship.

We need to be alone with God, to yield ourselves to the presence and the power of His holiness. Christ on earth needed it. He could not live the life of a Son here in the flesh without at times separating Himself entirely from His surroundings and being alone with God. How much more must this be indispensable to us!

Alone with God—that is the secret of true power in prayer. There is no true holiness, no clothing with the Holy Spirit and with power, without being alone daily with God.

When our Lord Jesus gave us the command to pray to our Father in secret, He gave us the promise that the Father would hear such prayers and mightily answer them in our life before others. What a privilege it is to begin every morning with intimate prayer. Let it be the one thing our hearts are set on—seeing, finding, and meeting God alone. The time will come when you will be amazed at the thought that one could suggest five minutes was enough.

Wholly for God

Whom have I in heaven but you?
I desire you more than anything on earth.
PSALM 73:25

As we discover that it is not easy to persevere in being "alone with God," we begin to realize that it is because we are not "wholly for God." Because God is the only God, He alone has the right to demand that He should have us wholly for Himself. Without this surrender, He cannot make His power known. We read in the Old Testament that His servants, Abraham, Moses, and David, gave themselves wholly and unreservedly to God so that He could work out His plans through them. It is only the fully surrendered heart that can fully trust God for all he has promised.

Nature teaches us that if we desire to do a great work, we must give ourselves wholly to it. This law is especially true of the love of a mother for her child. She gives herself wholly to the little one whom she loves. Is it unreasonable then for us to think that the great God of love should have us wholly for Himself? And should we not take the watchword, "wholly for God," as the keynote for our devotions every morning? As God gives Himself wholly to us, so He desires that we give ourselves wholly to Him.

Wholly for God! What blessedness as the soul learns what it means and what God gives with it.

The Knowledge of God

This is the way to have eternal life—
to know you, the only true God,
and Jesus Christ, the one you sent to earth.
JOHN 17:3

The knowledge of God is absolutely necessary for the spiritual life. It is life eternal. Not the intellectual knowledge we receive from others or through our own power of thought, but the living, experiential knowledge in which God makes Himself known to the soul.

Why is it that we so seldom experience this life-giving power of the true knowledge of God? Because we do not give God time enough to reveal Himself to us. When we pray, we think we know exactly how to speak to God. Yet we forget that one of the very first things in prayer is to be silent before God. It is then that He will reveal Himself. To know God in the personal experience of His presence and love is life indeed.

Just as the sun rising each morning is the pledge of light throughout the day, so the quiet time of waiting upon God will be the pledge of His presence and His power resting on us all day.

Learn this great lesson that the sun proclaims each day: As the sun on a cold day shines on us and imparts its warmth, believe that the living God will work in you with His love and His almighty power. God will reveal Himself as life and light and joy and strength to the soul that waits upon Him.

God the Father

*Baptizing them in the name of the Father
and the Son and the Holy Spirit.*
MATTHEW 28:19

It is important to realize that the doctrine of the Holy Trinity has a deep devotional aspect. As we think of God, we remember the inconceivable distance that separates Him in His holiness from sinful humans, and we bow in deep contrition and holy fear. As we think of Christ the Son, we remember the inconceivable nearness in which He came to be born of a woman and to die the accursed death and so to be inseparably joined to us for all eternity. And as we think of the Holy Spirit, we remember the inconceivable blessedness of God dwelling in us and making us His home and His temple throughout eternity.

When Christ taught us to say "Our Father in heaven," He immediately added, "may your name be honored" (Matthew 6:9). As God is holy, so also are we to be holy. And there is no way of becoming holy without considering that name to be most holy and drawing near to Him in prayer.

How often we speak that name without any sense of the unspeakable privilege of our relationship to God. If we would just take time to come into contact with God and to worship Him in His Fatherly love, that intimate place of communion would become to us the gate of heaven.

God the Son

*May grace and peace be yours from God our Father
and the Lord Jesus Christ.*
ROMANS 1:7

It is remarkable that the Apostle Paul in each of his thirteen Epistles writes: "May grace and peace be yours from God our Father and the Lord Jesus Christ." He had such a deep sense of the inseparable oneness of the Father and the Son in the work of grace that in each opening benediction he refers to both.

This is a lesson of the utmost importance. There may be times in the Christian life when one thinks chiefly of God the Father and prays to Him. But later on we realize that it may cause spiritual loss if we do not grasp this truth: It is only through faith in Christ and in living with Him that we can enjoy a full and abiding fellowship with God.

If you desire to know and worship God, seek Him and worship Him in Christ. And if you seek Christ, seek Him and worship Him in God. Then you will understand what it is to have "your life hidden with Christ in God." You will also discover that the fellowship and adoration of Christ is indispensable to the full knowledge of the love and holiness of God.

Take time to meditate, to pray, to expect all from God the Father who sits upon the throne and from the Lord Jesus Christ, the Lamb in the midst of the throne. Then you will learn truly to worship God.

God the Holy Spirit

Now all of us. . .
may come to the Father through
the same Holy Spirit
because of what Christ has done for us.
EPHESIANS 2:18

In our communion with God, we must guard against the danger of seeking to know God and Christ in the power of our intellect or emotions. The Holy Spirit has been given for the express purpose that we "may come to the Father through the same Holy Spirit because of what Christ has done for us." We will find that our prayer is in vain if we do not wait for the guidance of the Spirit.

Remember that one of the Holy Spirit's objectives is to teach us to pray. He makes fellowship with the Father and the Son a wonderful reality. As you pray, give yourself wholly to His guidance as your Teacher in all your intercession and adoration.

When Christ said, "Receive the Holy Spirit" (John 20:22), it was, in part, to strengthen and prepare the disciples for the ten days of prayer and for their receiving the fullness of the Spirit. This suggests three things we ought to remember when we draw near to God in prayer:

First—pray in the confidence that the Holy Spirit lives in us, and yield ourselves to His leading.

Second—believe that the "greater works" of the Spirit for the enlightening and strengthening of the spiritual life will be given in answer to prayer.

Third—believe that through the Spirit, in unity with all God's children, we may ask and expect the mighty workings of that Spirit on His Church and people.

DECEMBER 14

The Secret of the Lord

When you pray, go away by yourself,
shut the door behind you,
and pray to your Father secretly. Then your Father,
who knows all secrets, will reward you.
MATTHEW 6:6

Christ greatly desired that His disciples would know God as their Father and that they would have secret fellowship with Him. In His own life He found it not only indispensable but the highest happiness to meet the Father in secret. We must realize that it is impossible to be a true wholehearted disciple without daily fellowship with our heavenly Father, who waits for us in secret.

God is a God who hides Himself from the world and all that is of the world. God draws us away from the world and from ourselves. He offers us, instead, the pleasure of close, intimate communion with Himself.

Believers in the Old Testament enjoyed this experience. How much more should Christians in the new covenant value this secret fellowship with God. We read: "For you died when Christ died, and your real life is hidden with Christ in God" (Colossians 3:3). If we really believe this, we will have the joyful assurance that our life is safe and beyond the reach of every enemy.

We should day by day confidently seek the renewal of our spiritual life in prayer to our Father who is in secret. As the roots of a tree are hidden under the earth, so the roots of our daily life are hidden deep in God. Our first thought in prayer should be: I must know that I am alone with God and that God is with me.

Half an Hour Silence in Heaven

There was silence throughout heaven
for about half an hour.
Then. . .incense was given to him
to mix with the prayers of God's people.
REVELATION 8:1, 3

There was silence in heaven for about half an hour—to bring the prayers of the saints before God. Many of God's children have also felt the absolute need of silence and withdrawal from the things of earth for half an hour—to present their prayers before God. In so doing, they have been strengthened for their daily work.

How often the complaint is heard that there is no time for prayer. Yet often the confession is made that, even if time could be found, one feels unable to spend the time in real communion with God. Don't think, "I will not know how to spend the time." Just believe that, if you bow in silence before God, He will reveal Himself to you.

If you need help, read some passages of Scripture and let God's Word speak to you. Then bow in deepest humility before God and wait on Him. He will begin to work within you as you intercede for those whom He has laid on your heart. Keep praying, though the time may seem long. God will surely meet you.

Is it not worth the trouble to take half an hour alone with God? In heaven itself there was need for half an hour's silence to present the prayers of the saints before God. If you persevere, you may find the half-hour that seems the most difficult may become the most blessed in your whole life.

God Is Great

For you are great and perform great miracles.
You alone are God.
PSALM 86:10

Men and women of science, in studying nature, require years of labor to grasp the magnitude of the universe. Isn't God more glorious and worthy? And shouldn't we take the time to know and adore His greatness?

Our knowledge of God's greatness is so superficial. We do not allow ourselves time to bow before Him. Therefore we do not come under the deep impression of His incomprehensible majesty and glory.

Meditate on the following text until you are filled with some sense of what a glorious Being God is: "Great is the LORD! He is most worthy of praise! His greatness is beyond discovery!" (Psalm 145:3).

Take time for the meaning of these words to master your heart. Then bow in speechless adoration before God and say, "O Sovereign LORD! . . .Nothing is too hard for you! . . .You are the great and powerful God, the LORD Almighty. You have all wisdom and do great and mighty miracles" (Jeremiah 32:17–19). And hear God's answer: "I am the LORD, the God of all the peoples of the world. Is anything too hard for me?" (v. 27).

The true comprehension of God's greatness will take time. But if our faith grows strong in the knowledge of what a great and powerful God we have, we will be compelled to worship before this great and mighty God.

Fully Committed Heart

*The eyes of the LORD search the whole earth in order
to strengthen those whose hearts are
fully committed to him.*

2 CHRONICLES 16:9

In worldly matters we know how important it is that work should be done with the whole heart. In the spiritual realm, this rule should also hold true. God has promised in Jeremiah 29:13 that "if you look for me in earnest, you will find me when you seek me."

It is amazing that earnest Christians, who attend to their daily work with all their hearts, are so content to take things easy in the service of God. They do not realize that, if anywhere, they should give themselves to God's service with all the power of their will. In the words of our text we get an insight into the absolute necessity of seeking God with a fully committed heart.

What an encouragement this should be to us to humbly wait on God with an upright heart. We can be assured that His eye will be upon us, and He will show forth His mighty power in us and in our work.

O Christian, have you learned this lesson in your worship of God—to yield yourself each morning with your whole heart to do God's will? Pray each prayer in true wholehearted devotion to Him. In faith expect the power of God to work in you and through you.

The Omnipotence of God

I am God Almighty.
GENESIS 17:1

When Abraham heard these words he fell on his face and God spoke to him. God filled his heart with faith in what He would do for him. O Christian, have you bowed in deep humility before God until you felt that you were in living contact with the Almighty?

Read in the Psalms how the saints of old gloried in God and in His strength.

"The LORD protects me from danger" (Psalm 27:1).

"God remains the strength of my heart" (Psalm 73:26).

Take time to appropriate these words and to adore God as the Almighty One, your strength.

Christ taught us that salvation is the work of God and quite impossible to humans. When the disciples asked: "Then who in the world can be saved?" His answer was: "Humanly speaking, it is impossible. But not with God. Everything is possible with God" (Mark 10:26–27). If we firmly believe this, we will have courage to believe that God is working in us all that is well-pleasing in His sight.

Think how Paul prays for the Ephesians, that through the enlightening of the Spirit, they might "begin to understand the incredible greatness of his power for us who believe him" (Ephesians 1:19). When we fully believe that the mighty power of God is working within us, we can joyfully say, "God is the strength of my life."

The Fear of God

Happy are those who fear the LORD.
Yes, happy are those who
delight in doing what he commands.

PSALM 112:1

The fear of God—these words characterize the religion of the Old Testament and the foundation which it laid for the more abundant life of the New Testament. The gift of holy fear should still be the great desire of the child of God today.

Paul more than once gives fear a high place in the Christian life: "put into action God's saving work in your lives, obeying God with deep reverence and fear" (Philippians 2:12). "Let us work toward complete purity because we fear God" (2 Corinthians 7:1).

It has often been said that the lack of the fear of God is one of the things which most characterizes us today. It is no wonder then that we lack the passion for the reading of God's Word and the worship in His house. We feel the absence of that spirit of continuous prayer which marked the early church. We need texts like the one at the beginning of this reading to impress upon us the need for a deep fear of God, leading to an unceasing prayerfulness.

As we pray, let us earnestly cultivate the fear of God. Then take the words "Happy are those who fear the LORD" into our hearts. Believe that it is one of the essential elements of the life of faith.

God Is Incomprehensible

We cannot imagine the power of the Almighty,
yet he is so just and merciful that he does not oppress us.
JOB 37:23

This attribute of God as a Spirit whose being and glory are entirely beyond our comprehension is one we ponder all too little. And yet in the spiritual life it is of the utmost importance to know that, as the heavens are high above the earth, so God's thoughts and ways are infinitely beyond all our thoughts.

With deep humility and holy reverence, we must look up to God. Then with childlike simplicity we must yield ourselves to the teaching of His Holy Spirit. "Oh, what a wonderful God we have! How great are his riches and wisdom and knowledge! How impossible it is for us to understand his decisions and his methods" (Romans 11:33).

Let our hearts respond, "O Lord, O God of gods, how wonderful you are in all your thoughts, and your purposes how deep." The study of what God is ought to fill us with holy awe and the longing to know and honor Him. Just think of these attributes— His greatness; His might; His omnipresence; His wisdom; His holiness; His mercy; His love. How incomprehensible!

As you worship and pray, begin to grasp the inconceivable glory of this Great Being who is your God and Father. By faith, trust that, in a way passing all understanding, this incomprehensible God will work in your heart and life to know Him more fully.

The Holiness of God

You must be holy because I am holy.
I am the LORD, who makes you holy.
LEVITICUS 11:45; 20:8

In Leviticus Israel had to learn that holiness is the highest and most glorious attribute of God. It also must be the marked characteristic of His people today. Those who desire to truly know God and approach Him in prayer, must desire to be holy as He is holy. The priests who were to have access to God had to be set apart for a life of holiness.

The prophet Isaiah, who was to speak for God, was also set apart for a life of holiness. Listen to Isaiah 6: "I saw the Lord. He was sitting on a lofty throne. . . . In a great chorus [the seraphim] sang, 'Holy, holy, holy is the LORD Almighty!'" (verses 1–3)—the voice of adoration and reverence. "Then I said, 'My destruction is sealed, for I am a sinful man and a member of a sinful race. Yet I have seen the King, the LORD Almighty!'" (verse 5)—the voice of a broken, contrite heart. "Then one of the seraphim flew over to the altar, and he picked up a burning coal. . . . He touched my lips with it and said, 'See, this coal has touched your lips. Now your guilt is removed, and your sins are forgiven'" (verses 6–7)—the voice of grace and full redemption. Then follows the voice of God: "Whom should I send as a messenger to my people?" And the willing answer is: "Lord, I'll go! Send me" (verse 8).

Child of God, meet with your Father in prayer. In deep condescension, bow low and ask God to reveal Himself as the Holy One.

The Holiness of God

Holy Father, keep them and care for them. . . .
Make them pure and holy
by teaching them your words of truth.
JOHN 17:11, 17

Christ ever lives to pray this great prayer found in the gospel of John. Expect and appropriate God's answer. Hear the words of the Apostle Paul: "Christ will make your hearts strong, blameless, and holy when you stand before God" (1 Thessalonians 3:13). "Now may the God of peace make you holy in every way, and may your whole spirit and soul and body be kept blameless" (1 Thessalonians 5:23).

God's holiness has been revealed in the Old Testament. In the New, we find the holiness of God's people in Christ, through the cleansing of the Spirit. "We are writing to the church of God in Corinth, you who have been called by God to be his own holy people. He made you holy by means of Christ Jesus" (1 Corinthians 1:2).

Oh, that we understood the blessedness of saying: "Be holy because I am holy." For this purpose the triune God has revealed Himself to us, through the Son and the Holy Spirit. Let us use the word "holy" with great reverence of God, and then with holy desire, for ourselves.

Bow before God in holy fear, and then in complete faith, pray this prayer of promise: "The God of peace make you holy in every way. . .God, who calls you, is faithful; he will do this" (1 Thessalonians 5:23–24). What a privilege to speak these words to God. Wait upon Him until, through the working of the Spirit, these words live in your heart. Then you will begin to know something of the holiness of God.

Sin

> *I was the worst of them all [sinners].*
> *Oh, how kind and gracious*
> *the Lord was! He filled me completely with faith*
> *and the love of Christ Jesus.*
>
> 1 TIMOTHY 1:14–15

Never forget for a moment that your whole relationship to God depends on what you think of sin and of yourself as a redeemed sinner. It is sin that makes God's holiness so awful. It is sin that makes God's holiness so glorious, because He has said: "So set yourselves apart to be holy, for I, the LORD, am your God. . . .I am the LORD, who makes you holy" (Leviticus 20:7–8).

It is sin that called forth the wonderful love of God in not sparing His Son.

It was sin that nailed Jesus to the cross and revealed the depth and the power of the love with which He loved.

It is the thought of sin, ever surrounding you and seeking to tempt you, that will give fervency to your prayer and urgency to the faith that hides itself in Christ.

It is the thought of sin that makes Christ so unspeakably precious. It keeps you every moment dependent on His grace and gives you the claim to be more than conqueror through Him that loved us.

It is the thought of sin that calls to us to thank God with the broken and contrite heart, which God will not despise.

As you fellowship with God in prayer, His one aim is to deliver and keep you fully from sin's power and to lift you up into His likeness and His infinite love.

The Mercy of God

O give thanks unto the LORD;
for he is good:
for his mercy endureth for ever.
PSALM 136:1 KJV

This psalm is wholly devoted to the praise of God's mercy. In each of the twenty-six verses we have the expression: "His mercy endures forever." The psalmist was full of this glad thought. The everlasting, unchangeable mercy of God is cause for unceasing praise and thanksgiving.

Let us read what is said about God's mercy in the well-known Psalm 103. "Praise the LORD, I tell myself, and never forget the good things he does for me. . . . He. . .surrounds me with love and tender mercies" (verses 2, 4). Of all God's other attributes, mercy is the crown. "The LORD is merciful and gracious; . . .full of unfailing love" (verse 8). As wonderful as God's greatness is, so infinite is His mercy. "For his unfailing love toward those who fear him is as great as the height of the heavens above the earth" (verse 11). What a thought! As high as the heaven is above the earth, so immeasurably and inconceivably great is the mercy of God. "The love of the LORD remains forever with those who fear him" (verse 17). Here again the psalmist speaks of God's faithful love and mercy.

How frequently we have read these familiar words without the least thought of their immeasurable greatness! Take time to thank God with great joy for the wonderful mercy with which He crowns your life and say: "Your unfailing love is better to than life itself" (Psalm 63:3).

The Love of God

God is love, and all who live in love live in God,
and God lives in them.

1 JOHN 4:16

The most wonderful word in heaven is love—for God is love. And the most wonderful word in the inner chamber must be love—for the God who meets us there is love.

What is love? It is the deep desire to give itself for the beloved. Love finds its joy in imparting all that it has to make the loved one happy. And the heavenly Father, who offers to meet us in the inner chamber, has no other object than to fill our hearts with His love.

All the other attributes of God find in His love their highest glory. The full blessing of the inner chamber is nothing less than a life in the abundant love of God. Because of this we should approach God with faith in His love. As you set yourself to pray, seek to exercise great and unbounded faith in the love of God.

Take time in silence to meditate on the wonderful revelation of God's love in Christ until you are filled with the spirit of worship and wonder. Take time to believe the precious truth: "He has given us the Holy Spirit to fill our hearts with his love" (Romans 5:5).

As you pray, be assured of this: Your heavenly Father longs to manifest His love to you. Be deeply convinced that He can and will do it.

DECEMBER 26

The Psalms

How sweet are your words to my taste;
they are sweeter than honey.
PSALM 119:103

This book seeks to help us to worship God. Of the sixty-six books in the Bible, the Book of Psalms is given to us especially for this purpose. The other books are historical, doctrinal, or practical. But the Psalms take us into the inner sanctuary of God's holy presence to enjoy the blessedness of fellowship with Him. It's a book of devotions inspired by the Holy Spirit.

If you truly desire to meet God each morning and worship Him in spirit and in truth, then let your heart be filled with the Word of God in the Psalms.

As you read the Psalms, underline the word "Lord" or "God" wherever it occurs, and also the pronouns referring to God. This will help to connect the contents of the Psalms with God, who is the object of all prayer. These underlined words will make God the central thought and lead you to a new worship of Him.

The Psalms, by the power of the Spirit, will teach us to abide in God's presence. Read Psalm 119. Meditate on the thought that the God who is found throughout the whole psalm is the same God who gives us His law and enables us to keep it. This psalm will soon become one of the most beloved, and you will find its prayers and its teaching concerning God's Word drawing you continually up to Him.

The Glory of God

*May he be given glory in the church and in
Christ Jesus forever and ever through endless ages.*

EPHESIANS 3:21

There is no more wonderful image in nature of the glory of God
than we find in the starry heavens. Telescopes have long discov-
ered the wonders of God's universe. By means of photography,
new wonders of that glory have been revealed. A photographic
plate fixed below the telescope will reveal millions of stars which
otherwise could never have been seen by the eye. Man must step
to one side and allow the glory of the heavens to reveal itself. The
stars, at first wholly invisible, will leave their image on the plate.

What a lesson for the soul that longs to see the glory of God
in His Word. Let your heart be as a photographic plate that
waits for God's glory to be revealed. The plate must be prepared
and clean; let your heart be prepared and purified by God's
Spirit. "God blesses those whose hearts are pure, for they will see
God" (Matthew 5:8). The plate must be immovable; let your
heart be still before God in prayer. The plate must be exposed
for several hours to receive the full impression of the farthest
stars; let your heart take time in silent waiting upon God and
He will reveal His glory.

If you keep silent before God and give Him time, He will
leave within you impressions that will be as the rays of His glory
shining in you.

DECEMBER 28

The Holy Trinity

God the Father chose you long ago,
and the Spirit has made you holy.
As a result, you have obeyed Jesus Christ.
1 PETER 1:2

Here we have one of the texts in which the great truth of the Trinity is seen to lie at the very root of our spiritual life. We have been speaking especially of the adoration of God the Father and the need for sufficient time each day to worship Him in some of His glorious attributes. But we must remind ourselves that, in all our communion with the Father, the presence and the power of the Son and the Spirit are absolutely necessary.

We must understand how our communion with the Father is conditioned by the active and personal presence and working of the Lord Jesus. It takes time to become fully conscious of the need we have of Him in every approach to God. But we can have confidence in the work that He is doing in us and assurance of His intimate love and presence as we make intercession.

So, too, the Holy Spirit, working in the depth of our heart, is the One who is able to reveal the Son within us. Through Him alone we have the power to know what and how to pray. Through Him we have the assurance that our prayer has been accepted.

Dear Christian, it is in tarrying in the secret of God's presence that you receive grace to abide in Christ and to be led by His Spirit. What food for thought—and worship!

The Word of God

For the word of God is full of living power.
HEBREWS 4:12

When communing with God, His Word and prayer are both indispensable and should not be separated. In His Word, God speaks to me; in prayer, I speak to God.

The Word teaches me to know the God to whom I pray; it teaches me how He would have me pray. It gives me precious promises to encourage me in prayer. It often gives me wonderful answers to prayer.

The more I pray, the more I feel my need of the Word and rejoice in it. The more I read God's Word, the more I have to pray about and the more power I have in prayer. One great cause of prayerlessness is that we read God's Word too little or only superficially or in the light of human wisdom.

It is the Holy Spirit through whom the Word has been spoken, who is also the Spirit of prayer. He will teach me how to receive the Word and how to approach God.

What power and inspiration would be ours if we only took God's Word as from Himself, turning it into prayer and definitely expecting an answer. It is in the intimacy of God's presence and by the Holy Spirit that God's Word will become our delight and our strength.

Waiting upon God

On thee do I wait all the day.
PSALM 25:5 KJV

Waiting upon God—in this expression we find one of the deepest truths of God's Word in regard to the attitude of the soul in its communion with God. We should begin each day with this attitude of the soul.

When waking in the morning, in quiet meditation, in the expression of our ardent longings and desires, in the course of our daily work, in all our striving after obedience and holiness, in all our struggles against sin and self-will—in everything there should be a waiting on God to receive His blessing. See what He will do, allow Him to be the almighty God.

Meditate on these things and they will help you to value the precious promises of God's Word: "Those who wait on the LORD will find new strength. They will fly high on wings like eagles" (Isaiah 40:31). "Wait patiently for the LORD. Be brave and courageous. Yes, wait patiently for the LORD" (Psalm 27:14). In these words we have the secret of heavenly power and joy.

As we exercise absolute dependence upon God, it will become more natural to say: "On you do I wait all the day."

Wait on God—that He may reveal Himself in us; that He may teach us all His will; that He may do to us what He has promised; that in all things He may be the infinite God.

The Praise of God

*Let the godly sing with joy to the LORD,
for it is fitting to praise him.*

PSALM 33:1

Praise will ever be a part of adoration. Adoration, when it has entered God's presence and has had fellowship with Him, will lead to the praise of His name.

It was when the children of Israel had been delivered from the power of Egypt that, in the song of Moses, the joy of redemption burst forth in the song of praise: "Who else among the gods is like you, O LORD? Who is glorious in holiness like you—so awesome in splendor, performing such wonders?" (Exodus 15:11).

In the Psalms we see what a large place praise ought to have in the spiritual life. Let us take time to study this until our whole heart and life be one continual song of praise: "I will praise the LORD at all times. I will constantly speak his praises" (Psalm 34:1).

With the coming of Christ into the world, there was a new outburst of praise in the song of the angels, the song of Mary, the song of Zechariah, and the song of Simeon.

And then we find in the song of Moses and the Lamb (Revelation 15:3) the praise of God filling creation. Later in Revelation 19:1–6, a great multitude praises God saying: "Hallelujah! For the Lord our God, the Almighty, reigns."

O child of God, let your prayer and quiet time with God lead your heart to unceasing praise.

INDEX